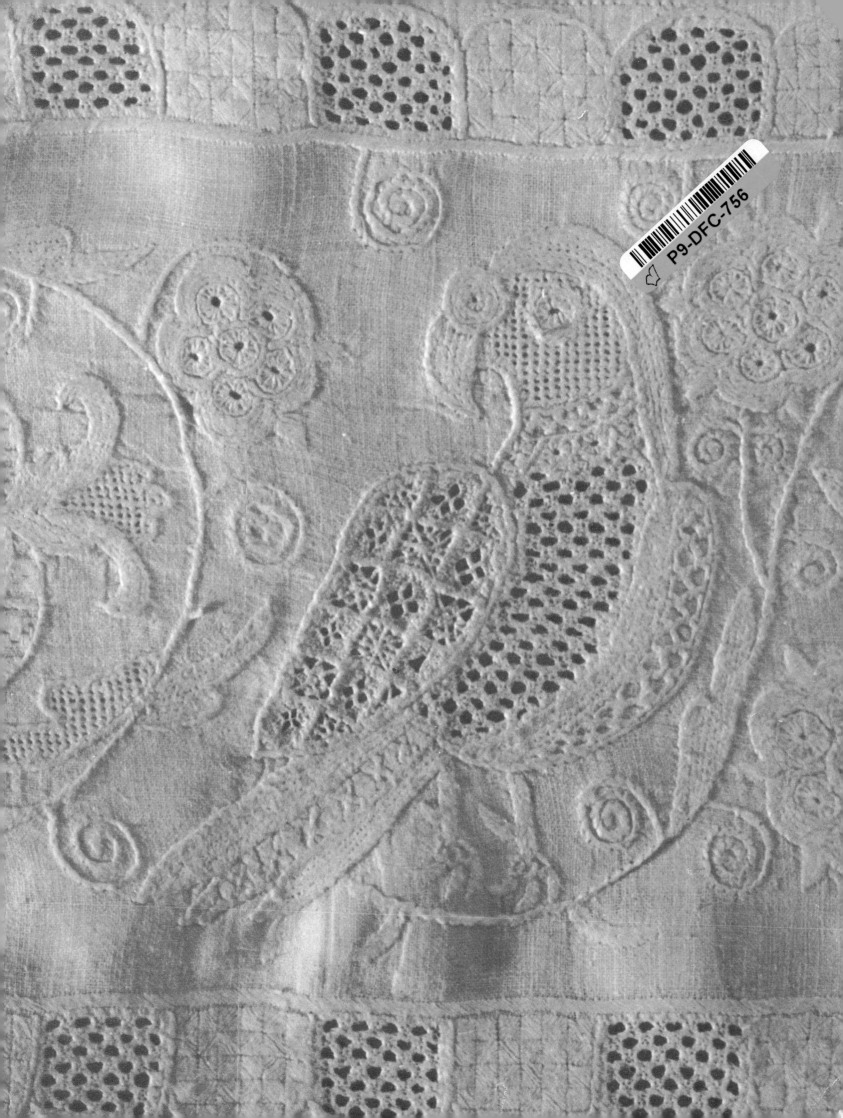

ARCO

FOLK ART OF CZECHOSLOVAKIA

VĚRA HASALOVÁ · JAROSLAV VAJDIŠ

FOLK ART OF CZECHOSLOVAKIA

ARCO PUBLISHING COMPANY, INC.

NEW YORK

Contents

I. Background and Development	7
II. Art in the Life of the People	12
III. Settlements and Village Homes	33
IV. Form and Ornament	88
V. Drawing, Graphics, and Painting	141
VI. Sculptural Works in Folk Culture	201
A. Relief	201
B. Free-standing Sculpture	223
VII. The Specific Character of Czech and Slovak Folk Art in a European Context	277
List of Illustrations	281
Bibliography of Books in the Czech Language	291
Bibliography of Books in the English Language	293
Map of Ethnographical Regions	294
Acknowledgements	296
Photographic Credits	296

Translated by Ivo Dvořák
Graphic design by Jiří Blažek
Chapters I, II, IV—VII © Copyright Věra Hasalová 1974
Chapter III © Copyright Jaroslav Vajdiš 1974
Illustrations © Copyright Artia, Prague 1974

Designed and produced by Artia for
Arco Publishing Company, Inc.
219 Park Avenue South, New York, N.Y. 10003
Library of Congress Catalog Card Number 74—81680
ISBN 0-668-03510-2
Printed in Czechoslovakia by Svoboda, Prague
2/99/43/51

I. Background and Development

2 EASTER EGG WITH BATIK DECORATION,
about 1950, south Moravia.

There is no doubt that each of the two nations that constitute Czechoslovakia makes its own contribution to the development of the forms and, to some extent, the content of its folk art. We shall nevertheless discuss the folk art of the Czech and the Slovak people in conjunction with each other, since there are many fundamental common features. As two closely related Slavonic nations in Central Europe the Czechs and the Slovaks shared, at least partly, identical conditions, and in several important epochs they shared a common history. There is no basic difference between their main types of housing and dress, their ceremonies or the products of their popular arts and crafts. Most of the types and branches of folk art created on Czechoslovak territory exist in both nations.

Nevertheless, even a simple look at a map will show obvious geographical differences between the Czech-speaking lands — Bohemia and Moravia — and Slovakia. Bohemia, located in the westernmost part of the country, is a country ringed by mountain ranges which form its natural frontier. The Elbe and the Vltava along with their tributaries are its main rivers. The land has been populated since prehistoric times, especially along the rivers, and in the period of the greatest flowering of folk art was characterized by a relatively dense farming population and by an intensive, almost garden-like, cultivation of the soil. Markets and guild handicrafts developed from the Middle Ages on. Prague, the seat of the Kings of Bohemia, which still retains its position as the political and cultural centre of the Czech people, is the heart of the country, although the surrounding regions have their own centres as well. More regionally distinct artistic traditions originated in central Bohemia, along the Elbe and in the Sázava River valley, in the north along the Jizera River, in the foothills of the Krkonoše (Giant) Mountains and in the Orlické Mountains, and in the west in the Chodsko district of the Šumava foothills, a region which to this day has preserved remnants of its highly original folklore. Another area with a very specific folk culture was the Pilsen region in the south-west. In south Bohemia the same can be said of the Blata marshlands between the towns of Soběslav and České Budějovice, and of the area around Prácheň and Doudleby. In the east a typical area was that of the Bohemian-Moravian Highlands. Conditions, therefore, differ from one area to another. Rich farmland alternates with much less fertile highlands, the inhabitants of which had to supplement farming with work in the forests and cottage industry, and with jobs in early industrial production. From time immemorial all roads from these regions have converged on Prague, concentrating the life of the country on that city.

Between Bohemia in the west and Slovakia in the east lies Moravia and a part of Silesia. The river Morava, which gave the land its name, runs through it from north to south. Moravia's border is formed in the west by the Bohemian-Moravian Highlands, and in the east by the broad, westernmost ranges of the Carpathians — the Beskydy, Javorníky and White Carpathian mountains — until recently settled by herdsmen, shepherds and mountain farmers, as were the Slovak slopes of these mountains. However, Moravian culture was not determined only by its geographical relationship to Bohemia and Slovakia. On the contrary, it is characterized by a strong 'Moravian' consciousness. This ancient land could, in fact, have been the source of two branches of a once single ethnic group of Slavs, for it was the heart of the first Slavonic state in this part of Europe. Historically it was profoundly affected by the Renaissance, under the impact of occupation by the Hungarian king Matthias Hunyadi, and, later on, the Baroque style did not develop as strongly in Moravia as it did in Bohemia. With the proximity of Vienna the country showed Austrian leanings, causing a temporary weakening of ties with Prague. Thus, in the nineteenth century, there was a slower process of integration. When folk art was at its peak, journeymen from Moravia used to go to Vienna and so did waggoners carrying merchandise to and from the Austrian capital.

The folk art of Moravia was affected by the considerable differences in land use. The people of the fertile Haná region along the middle reaches of the Morava River produced a sedate folk art quite different from the gayer style characteristic of Dolňácko (or Lower Slovácko) and of Podluží in the south. In the central part of Moravia, around the city of Brno, the southern style meets the style of the Haná region. In the west the Brno area touches on the Horácko (Highlands) region along the border with Bohemia. On the Carpathian slopes, later settled by herdsmen, known as Walachians, considerable differentiation developed between folk art from the Valašsko district, the Kopanice area near Starý Hrozenkov and the Horňácko (or Upper Slovácko) district. The northern part of Moravia was affected by German influences from Silesia, and some forms of folk art were also very close to the forms prevalent in the adjacent areas of Bohemia.

Slovakia, on the other hand, is characterized by marked contrasts both in its landscape and its settlement. From the east its backbone is formed by the Carpathian arch which reaches its apex in the geologically young Tatra Range, but then the mountains gradually recede, turn south and dissolve in the vast plains along the Danube and Tisa rivers, most of which lie beyond Slovakia's southern frontier. As he descended down the Carpathian slopes, the mountaineer, with his traditional dress made of wool, hemp, flax and leather, came upon the prosperous farmer and vintner from the southern plains. In central Slovakia lie the ethnographically interesting Upper Hron valley and the Detva district on the slopes of Mt. Polana, which has a remarkable folk art. Original styles of folk art were also to be found in the Hont, Novohradsko and Gemer districts where the last ranges of the Carpathians disappear at Slovakia's southern frontier. Eastern Slovakia has two faces: the Spiš and Šariš districts in the north are mountainous, while the Zemplín area in the south slopes down into the East Slovak Plain. These contrasts were reflected in different architecture and traditional dress, and in the difference between the colourful painted folk art of the southern lowlands and the tradition of wood-carving from the Carpathians. Nevertheless, we may speak of the typically Slovak character of the people and their artistic creation.

The differences in the development of Czech and Slovak village life were prominently marked by the far from peaceful course of history. Nor was the development of village life identical in the different parts of present-day Czechoslovakia. The very consolidation of the two ethnic groups took place in a struggle for cultural supremacy. From its beginning, conversion to Christianity was linked with Western influences (Irish and German missions). But in the ninth century a successful attempt was made in the Great Moravian Empire, which also included the lands adjacent to Moravia, to establish Old Slavonic liturgy, script and culture, oriented towards Byzantium. This was not forgotten, even when the centre of historical development shifted to Bohemia and when Western influence together with Latin liturgy once again prevailed. The

history of the Czechs was shaped by the endeavour to preserve Czech nationhood and independence, while accepting the products of West European culture, transmitted mostly by the Germans. The Hussite Revolution, sparked off by the burning at the stake of John Huss by the Council of Constance in 1415 and influenced by the English theologian and reformer John Wycliffe, anticipated in religious form the ideas of the bourgeois French Revolution and introduced the beginnings of democracy. Subsequent developments were forcibly reversed by the defeat of the uprising of the Czech Estates against Habsburg and Catholic power in the Battle of the White Mountain in 1620, the Thirty Years War which followed and the institution of the Restored Provincial Order. The country was depopulated, deprived of its non-Catholic intelligentsia, who formed the most valuable moral segment of Czech society at that time, and of its native nobility. The burghers were denied their former participation in the administration of the state. The country folk abandoned their devastated villages and, when they returned, took a long time to recuperate from the horrors of the war. Nevertheless, after peace had been restored, new villages began to be built and documents dating from as early as the second half of the seventeenth century confirm a growth of folk culture which, in spite of the period of the so-called second serfdom with its peasant rebellions and uprisings (the greatest of them in 1680 and 1775), and in spite of the Counter-Reformation, successfully continued into the eighteenth century and reached its peak approximately between the abolition of serfdom in 1781 and the abolishment of the *corvée* in 1848.

It is quite obvious that this development of folk culture in many of its aspects, primarily the social ones, was a part of the struggle of the feudal serfs, and that it lost its importance and receded when the focus of social development shifted to the emerging class of industrial workers. However, the character and quality of village life and culture were vitally important in the preservation and rebirth of the nation, which would not have been possible without the basic values preserved and renewed by the people: the language and the national art treasures. Folk art has, therefore, found a deserving place in the Czech history of art, especially at the end of the eighteenth and the beginning of the nineteenth centuries when its social and artistic roles combined to reach a climax.

THE SLOVAKS

In Slovakia, after the fall of the Great Moravian Empire, the people became part of the multinational Hungarian state and were subjected to serfdom by the Hungarian feudal lords, who were alien to them both ethnically and linguistically. This weakened the people's ties with the Czech Lands, although in some periods of history the Czechs and the Slovaks had a common ruler. For a long time, educated Slovaks, who had often studied at the Prague University, did not consider the Czech language to be a foreign one. In the Slovak economy, the promising development of the towns in the Middle Ages and the Renaissance, influenced by German colonization and mining in the Slovak Ore Mountains, did not affect the villages, which were exposed to the arbitrary rule of Hungarian magnates engaged in a constant struggle with the crown for their privileges. There were only occasional attempts to consolidate royal power, as, for example, during the reign of Matthias Hunyady in the second half of the fifteenth century. The brutal oppression sparked off a number of peasant rebellions. The military suppression of the popular uprising in 1514, led by Gyorgy Dozsa, was followed by the period of the second serfdom which was much more drastic in Slovakia than in the Czech Lands and which lasted until the eighteenth century. A special form of resistance against the feudal rule and excesses in Slovakia was brigandry in the seventeenth and eighteenth centuries. In contrast to the Czech Lands, Slovak villages greatly suffered from Tartar and Turkish invasions in the thirteenth and the sixteenth and seventeenth centuries, and their poverty was further increased by the aftermath of the anti-Habsburg uprisings of the Hungarian nobility. Industrialization, initiated by the emergence of factories at the end of the eighteenth century, did not materialize because of the nobility's opposition to the centralism and absolutism of Emperor Joseph II. Thus the course of the nineteenth and twentieth centuries was marked by a growth of the village poor, accompanied by excessive emigration to America, to the French mining areas and elsewhere, especially after 1850. In that period, too, local rebellions and armed uprisings against the landlords were taking place, paralleled by the struggle of the industrial workers. Due to this delayed industrialization, Slovak folk art continued to maintain its vitality until the twentieth century. In many rural areas, especially in the mountainous regions of Slovakia, cottage industry expanded after the abolition of serfdom, and was frequently dominated by the capital of the middlemen. The products of this cottage industry, often designed for house-to-house peddling, included, along with linenware, many articles of folk art. It was only after the Second World War that Slovakia was transformed into an industrial country. The present upsurge of Slovak national life and culture actually represents the culmination of the Slovak national rebirth. In the course of this process, an important and positive factor in forging the close ties between the Czechs and the Slovaks was the Ethnographical Exhibition in Prague in 1895.

OTHER ETHNIC INFLUENCES

Accords and discords are to be found not only in the history of the two nations living in the three lands but also in the permeation of the originally Slavonic settlement from the fourth to the sixth centuries by alien ethnic groups. (It should be noted at the same time that contacts and confrontations between different ethnic groups can be culturally fruitful.) In Bohemia practically the only foreign influence, although relatively strong, was German colonization. The contact between the Czech and German cultures was basically limited to the frontier areas and towns. In Moravia we must add to the German influence the impact of the related Slovak element, and perhaps also the Ukrainian and Romanian elements, introduced during the Walachian colonization of the Carpathian slopes, as well as the Polish element in the north and the existence of a few Croatian villages in the Podluží area, founded by refugees fleeing before the Turks late in the sixteenth century and bohemianized only in the nineteenth century. The situation in Slovakia is still more complex. Besides their long co-existence with Hungarians in the south of their country and their constant relationship with the Czechs and their culture, the Slovaks also experienced German colonization. This had a positive influence on the development of handicrafts in the Spiš area, mining in the Slovak Ore Mountains and the early development of the towns. More so than Moravia, Slovakia was affected by the Walachian settlement of the Carpathian range, and in the Danubian lowlands Croatian villages were founded under the same circumstances as in Moravia. In addition, a close relationship with Poland developed in the north, while Eastern Slovakia has a Carpatho-Ukrainian minority with some notable cultural differences.

Some articles, which by their technique and the nature of their decoration belong to Slovak or Czech folk art, were also used by Jews both in their homes and especially in their religious services. This is true, in particular, of faience jugs showing the ceremonies of Jewish funeral fraternities (the works of Slovak Haban and post-Haban potters) or swathes used to enwrap the Torah, decorated with Moravian folk embroidery. Temple curtains were also decorated with folk ornaments, while painted furniture was frequently found in Jewish homes.

Gypsies, on the other hand, with their nomadic way of life and distinct culture did not make a notable contribution, except in the musical sphere, to the culture of Slovakia and south-eastern Moravia. Lacking permanent settlements and a longer period of consolidation, they could not produce any substantial works of art.

Under these conditions some features of folk art were shared by two ethnic groups or two different communities, while others were exclusively the domain of an alien minority. This is true, for example, of the east Slovak Orthodox and Greek churches and their interior decoration, which are naturally limited to areas settled by Carpathian Ukrainians whose Church differs from that of their Slovak neighbours. The Šumava custom of decorating and displaying boards on which the dead were laid was limited to the German-speaking population, although there was no difference in religion between them and the Czechs. In some instances the influence of the Czech and the Slovak people on the culture of the ethnic minorities can be seen, such as the Slovak impact on the Ukrainian population or the earlier Chod influence on the neighbouring Cheb district with its formerly large German population (but we can also trace reverse influences). There are also known cases of temporary complete isolation of two ethnically different, neighbouring folk cultures. Nevertheless, in the course of time the process of integration usually won through and the consequence was the perpetuation of those elements which belonged to the culture prevailing in the country.

II. Art
in the Life of the People

3 WEDDING BANNER, *detail of embroidery, dated 1850, Bohemian-Moravian Highlands.*

The role of art in the folk culture of villages and country towns grew only slowly from the Middle Ages to the Renaissance. In the seventeenth and eighteenth centuries, however, it gained momentum. Even before the Thirty Years War, the remarkable foundations were laid of that broadly based folk art which would deeply influence everyday life. Its development was certainly affected by the national heritage and also by contemporary movements in art. However, folk art was tied from the very beginning to the everyday life of the people and especially to those important events which occur in the life of every man and give his life a certain rhythm. The Czech and Slovak people had a highly developed sense of form; they liked to use ceremonies to accentuate the rhythm of their life: weddings, baptisms, the end of the harvest, the completion of a house. Scholars often point out that every work of folk art, however small, has an important non-aesthetic purpose, and sometimes more than one, so that its artistic nature is merely a by-product, unappreciated even by its creator. But is it not precisely this fact — that so many types of articles serving different purposes are shaped artistically — which clearly demonstrates the need for what is called 'the aesthetic function', that is, the inherent need of ordinary people to satisfy their desire for beauty under the guise of producing 'utilitarian' things?

THE CONCEPT
OF 'FOLK ART'

The term 'folk art', therefore, does not describe something homogeneous and consequently it is very hard to define. It covers a vast range of objects which may be distinguished by the date of their origin, by the historical situation in which they were made, and by the social status and level of training of their creators; they differ, too, in their purpose and the technical skill required to accomplish them. 'Folk art' can perhaps be defined negatively, as that which does not belong to the great period styles of a nation, the Gothic, Renaissance, Baroque, Empire style, etc.

There is also a layer between folk art and the best of this stylistic art, which could be called provincial art, or even 'semi-folk' art. In addition there are amateur, 'Sunday', paintings, sculpture, various articles of applied art, and primitive art which also, to a greater or lesser degree, differ from folk art.

The most exact, although a somewhat unstable, definition of folk art involves its ethnographic aspect, the fact already mentioned that it is a part of a folk culture, that it somehow belongs to the 'traditional' way of housing, dressing, farming, thinking and feeling of ordinary people. The term 'traditional' has a special meaning here. For if we want to present a somewhat comprehensive picture of folk art in Czechoslovakia, we must look at the period since the sixteenth century and in particular since the Thirty Years War. Undoubtedly the foundations of Czech folk art were very old but in its basic fields (architecture, clothing, pottery, furniture, tools and implements) it was very strongly influenced by the Renaissance and the Baroque styles. In the western part of present-day Czechoslovakia the finest works were made at the turn of the eighteenth and nineteenth century, while in the eastern part the finest works were created later and have also survived longer. These facts must serve as a yardstick, enabling us to determine what was an earlier product of folk art, or which of the older works of art (preserved from the Middle Ages or mentioned in historical sources) belong within our sphere of interest, and to evaluate what has survived from this classic era of Czech folk culture.

Man's own body and clothing, as well as the environment in which he works and lives, his house and the landscape surrounding him offer him the primary opportunity for artistic expression. The villager, whose basic form of livelihood was agriculture, had particular needs. These needs are represented by implements used for tilling the soil and harvesting, for processing the crops and the straw, for hunting and bee-keeping, for animal breeding and production related to it. Here belong several groups of tools, implements and vessels, some of which were used mostly by men, others exclusively by women. The most frequently used articles were given an optimum shape, tested over centuries, a shape which was often artistic in itself. And these implements were often tastefully and simply decorated. Originally these articles were made by the farmer and his wife for themselves. Later their manufacture was taken over by village and town craftsmen, and in many instances they were produced in various branches of cottage industry.

This category includes not only the implements, tools and vessels used by the farmers, but also the vessels used by herdsmen for making cheese, which were made in several ideal shapes with numerous variations, especially by the Carpathian herdsmen. The farmer and the herdsman chiefly provided the shapes, using decoration only where it harmonized with the structure of the article and where it would not hinder its purpose. It was only in the period when Carpathian sheep-breeding was in decline that the herdsman also became a sculptor and carved illustrations of his work and entertainment, and images of his imagination, on jug handles. The bee-keeper originally used only a small cross or magic symbol to mark a natural hive, a hollow tree-trunk or stump, which he brought to his house. But by the end of the seventeenth century there were many cases when he had turned painter and sculptor in order to decorate his hives. The hunter used beautifully ornamented horns in which

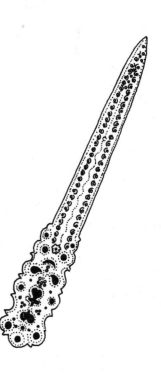

4 HAIRPIN,
19th century,
Western Bohemia.

to keep his powder, while in the wine-producing areas we know of many differently shaped jugs and small casks, as well as wine presses, often made by craftsmen, which are augmented by painted ornaments or sculptured caryatids.

THE WOMAN
AS AN ARTIST

In keeping house and creating the articles and things that traditionally concerned her, the woman did not restrict herself to functional shapes. She never lacked a sense of the hidden beauty in materials and techniques. On feast days even simple pastry was colourfully decorated according to traditional and new ideas of beauty and incorporated magical ornaments, symbols and pictorial charms. Thus there developed the traditional decorated wedding cakes, the braided figures and wreaths baked on St. Nicholas's Day, the Easter 'Judas' cakes, and in north-eastern Moravia and Silesia the tiny pastry Madonnas, mermaids, animals and birds' nests. Dressmaking offered a still greater opportunity for creating beauty and charm in shape and ornamentation. Most women themselves grew flax and hemp and also included among their duties spinning, weaving and bleaching linen or preparing woollen cloth for further treatment. They combined different fibres and designed the patterns of calico or a special, colourful fabric for pillows and covers, and made patterns for the shirts and the simple outer garments for all members of the family. Hems were strengthened with embroidery and seams softened with a kind of simple lace. These original methods were later replaced by more fashionable and complex ones. The pattern-makers and embroiderers frequently learned exacting, imported needlework and lace-making techniques, on the basis of which they created countless variations of floral and bird motifs.

CEREMONIAL
OBJECTS

Closely related to magic, and later to the poetic language of symbols, is the field of ceremonial objects. The language of spells and bewitching symbols, a part of ancient witchcraft, was applied in both most important cycles of customs — the one based on the calendar, the other on the life of the family — as well as in common law and folk medicine. It also left traces in the motifs and compositions of folk ornaments. The folk artists also made use of the symbolic language of nature; variously braided and decorated switches, twigs, branches and trees all played their role in different calendar ceremonies, along with bouquets of plants with magic healing powers and harvest festival wreaths of different shapes, as well as tiny figures made of dried fruit. Here we find ourselves on the dividing line between a magic object and a toy.

Folk customs reflect some concepts of life and death which have existed since time immemorial and so this particular field of folk culture is considered to be the oldest. However, the ancient artistic form of ceremonial objects was influenced by general changes in culture, by the developing traditions of individual regions, and by the ideas of individual artists. This is especially true of the masks, sometimes artistically quite attractive in their natural and highly significant form, which accompanied the course of winter from the beginning of Advent to the end of Shrovetide. Masks were also used on other occasions, such as weddings, the slaughter of a pig, or during the vintage celebrations. Effigies used for symbolic destruction or representing life-giving forces were similarly shaped, as well as articles symbolizing various wishes, expressed at feasts or family celebrations.

MULTIPURPOSE
OBJECTS

Many objects belonging to this category have more than one use. Either they were originally designed to serve several purposes, or their use changed during the course of the life of their users. Thus the embroidered bridal linen square successively becomes the square worn by the mother to church at the end of her confinement, a blanket in which the godmother carries the baby to baptism, a mourning garment and eventually an accessory to the shroud. Equally the decorated laundering or mangling bat, acquired as a gift from a suitor, becomes a cherished souvenir and a room decoration. Even such fine art objects as paintings and sculpture have the additional functions of a charm and a souvenir from a church festival or a fair.

Besides these many uses in the life of the people, however, numerous categories of folk objects in the nineteenth and twentieth centuries acquired an additional use which eventually became their main function. They became the objects of a cottage industry which was widespread in many regions and extensive in its output, in the number of workers involved and in the types of articles so produced.

Originally this industry must have developed in two directions. In order to alleviate the poverty of their families, talented embroiderers and lace-makers, wood-carvers and turners became specialists who, after the farming season was over, worked for remuneration. In the first place they worked for their neighbours, later they sold their products at a church festival or a fair, and still later they worked for a middle-man. This gave rise to lace-making, embroidery, curtain-making, cap-knitting, the making of wooden utensils and toys, carved and modelled figures for Nativity scenes etc. From the Kysúca, Trenčín and Spiš districts many tinkers roamed throughout present-day Czechoslovakia and other countries, selling various articles made of wire, such as decorative plates, trays and coat hangers, which today are displayed in the Museum of the Váh River Valley in Budatín Chateau near Žilina. To this day Easter egg painters in south-eastern Moravia and Slovakia, embroiderers at Zubří, in north-eastern Moravia, figural pastry bakers at Vizovice, and other craftsmen work at home for the Centre for Folk Arts and Crafts, for different co-operatives operating in the same field, or for seasonal sale in the cities. Cottage industries also came into being by a reverse process, when some highly complex crafts — such as those of the cooper, the lathe operator or even the blacksmith — became folk crafts. Both merged into a single cottage industry during the period of early industrialization when in many villages there were insufficient opportunities to make a livelihood.

Many of the individuals involved in cottage industries were true artists. Their varied and complex styles incorporated tradition as well as changing fashion; styles were adapted to prevailing circumstances and the demands of the market, and yet reflected the inner life of the creators. This was only one category of folk artists. Their number was constantly increasing as new creative opportunities or new markets developed. If we return to the initial premise that in its functional element, folk art is defined by its natural place in folk culture, we can see that this basically affects the concept of folk artist. In the past century it was linked with the romantic image of the people as a collective creator. Today we have learned that the great variety of folk culture is a product of the complexity of the social composition of the 'people' and the variety of situations and influences under which folk art was created.

The difference between art in which the creator and the user are one and the same person and 'received' art, created for the user by an artist in a town or a village, is a secondary problem. The relationship between folk production and the professional crafts is a complex one; it changes in the course of development and varies from one region to another. The tailors, seamstresses and furriers, making individual parts of the folk costume, the cabinet makers producing painted furniture, carpenters, blacksmiths, masons and stonemasons, or painters on glass were, in spite of their different social status, linked with village folk culture by their respect for its use, its development, and sometimes also for its regional character. Today, in the category of folk art, we include all typical, artistically shaped objects which the inhabitants of villages and small rural towns used from roughly the middle of the seventeenth century to the middle of the nineteenth century; this period may differ according to the specific character of individual regions and individual genres. Exceptions are the dress and home furnishings of those members of privileged classes who had direct links with the achievements of Central European or the development of national cultural styles.

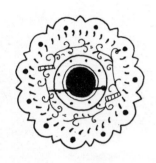

5 WALACHIAN MOTHER-OF-PEARL BROOCHES FOR MEN'S SHIRTS, *19th century, Moravia.*

6 BYŠIČKY, DISTRICT OF NYMBURK, FARMSTEAD IN THE BASIN OF THE RIVER ELBE.

7 SÁDEK, DISTRICT OF SVITAVY. HOUSE IN THE BOHEMIAN-MORAVIAN HIGHLANDS.

8 PŘÍŠOVICE, DISTRICT OF LIBEREC. TWO-STOREY FARMSTEAD IN NORTH-EASTERN BOHEMIA.

9 TCHOŘOVICE, DISTRICT OF STRAKONICE. FARMSTEAD IN SOUTH-WESTERN BOHEMIA.

10 PODZÁMČÍ, DISTRICT OF DOMAŽLICE. CORNER JOINTS BELOW THE EAVES OF A HOUSE IN THE CHODSKO DISTRICT. ▶

11 BŘESTEK, DISTRICT OF UHERSKÉ HRADIŠTĚ. TIMBER-FRAMED BARN IN SOUTH MORAVIA.

12 JEŠETICE, DISTRICT OF BENEŠOV. POLYGONAL BARN.

13 LYSOVICE. DISTRICT OF VYŠKOV. ROW
OF FARMSTEADS WITH PROJECTING *ŽUDR*
PORCHES IN THE HANÁ AREA
OF CENTRAL MORAVIA.

14 LECHOTICE, DISTRICT OF KROMĚŘÍŽ.
HOUSE WITH A TWO-STOREY GRANARY,
CENTRAL MORAVIA.
◄

15 DOUBRAVY, DISTRICT OF GOTTWAL-
DOV. TWO-STOREY GRANARY NEAR
LUHAČOVSKÉ ZÁLESÍ. ►

16 SVINKY, DISTRICT OF TÁBOR. SOUTH BOHEMIAN FARMSTEAD WITH HOUSE, GATE AND GRANARY.

17 KOMÁROV, DISTRICT OF TÁBOR. TWO-STOREY GRANARY WITH ARCHITECTURAL DECORATION OF THE FAÇADE. ▶

18 UNHOŠŤ, DISTRICT OF KLADNO. BAROQUE ARCHITECTURAL ELEMENTS IN THE FAÇADE OF A VILLAGE HOUSE.

19 PALUDZA, DISTRICT OF LIPTOVSKÝ MIKULÁŠ. ARCHITECTURAL DECORATION OF THE FAÇADE OF A VILLAGE HOUSE. ▶

20　VALAŠSKÁ POLANKA, DISTRICT OF VSETÍN. COTTAGE IN THE WALACHIAN AREA OF EASTERN MORAVIA.

21 ŽÍTKOVÁ, DISTRICT OF UHERSKÉ HRA-DIŠTĚ. HEATING SYSTEM IN THE LIVING AREA OF A RURAL HOUSE IN THE KOPA-NICE REGION OF EASTERN MORAVIA.

22 VALAŠSKÁ BYSTŘICE, DISTRICT OF VSETÍN. TABLE IN A LIVING ROOM.

23 VELKÉ KARLOVICE, DISTRICT OF VSETÍN. WALACHIAN COTTAGE.

III. Settlements
and
Village Homes

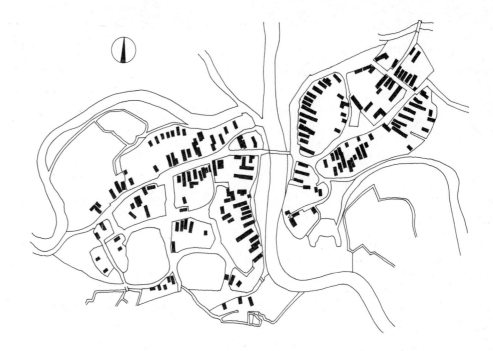

24 MARTOVCE, DISTRICT OF KOMÁRNO. PLAN OF BUILT-UP AREA.

CONDITIONS OF THE
FORMATION OF
SETTLEMENTS

A network of permanent settlements had already grown up on what is now Czecho-slovak territory before the beginning of the historical era, though the density and the forms of settlement were continually changing. The shape of the villages was influenced by a number of ethnic, economic, and geographical factors as well as by historical events. Today's village, therefore, is not a homogeneous unit but combines modern buildings with the remains of older buildings, the origins of which sometimes date from far into the past.

FACTORS DETERMINING
THE LAY-OUT OF THE
DWELLINGS

The house did more than simply protect its inhabitants from the whims of nature. It was also the scene of important events which determined the physical survival and the continuation of the family or clan. The organization of the clan and the family went through a long and complex development. This development naturally also determined the spatial lay-out and the furnishing of the dwellings. Knowledge of the development of the typical Central European dwelling in the prehistoric period therefore helps us to trace the changing human relationships which produced the traditional monogamous family unit. The origin of this type of family served as the impulse for the creation of a dwelling space isolated from communal facilities which served the entire clan. There are still some houses which have been preserved in Czechoslovakia, in which the lay-out indicates the likely arrangement of human dwellings during different stages of the complex development of society.

DIFFERENTIATION OF
SETTLEMENTS IN THE
FEUDAL PERIOD

Archaeological finds from the prehistoric period contain articles which clearly show the existence of a social structure. The same may be said of buildings. With the coming of feudalism, distinctions between buildings belonging to different social groups within the population began to emerge. This can be seen in settlements from the period of the Great Moravian Empire uncovered in southern Moravia and Slovakia.

For the first time there appeared a pronounced difference in the size and lay-out of the houses of ordinary people compared with those of their rulers and those which were for religious use. In that period, too, we see the beginning of the forthcoming

33

development of urban and rural cultures, in which the art of the urban and the rural worlds was sometimes widely separated and at other times almost merged.

The growth of the feudal system had important social consequences for the serfs. Land became the main source of income for the feudal lords and the state, and provided the livelihood of the rural population. In all fertile areas the three crop rotation of fields replaced more primitive forms of agriculture. This represented a major change both in farm production and in the life of society, and the formation and consolidation of rural settlements was completed.

COLONIZATION

In the thirteenth and fourteenth centuries the feudal lords increased their income by colonizing vast, previously unsettled or thinly inhabited areas. (In some parts of the country this process continued until the end of the Middle Ages.) In areas with older settlements the introduction of new and firmer organization strengthened administration and increased agricultural production. Thus, in the period of colonization, not only did new settlements come into being, but the structure of pre-colonization settlements changed as well. In the protracted course of the colonization most of the typical features of the previous settlements disappeared. That period was also a time of large-scale reconstruction throughout the entire state. A network of new towns emerged and the structure of villages was markedly transformed. This process was related to the growth of trade and political activity. All these events were also reflected in the life and the organization of the small settlements which were separated from the large newly-formed centres. The relationship of the serfs to the landlords changed as a result of the so-called *emphyteutic law*, just as their rights and duties and their relationship to the land changed. The fields belonging to many villages were newly distributed. This, too, brought about a gradual reconstruction of the villages according to a new order. In areas with older settlement most villages with a street-type ground-plan or with a central village green came into being at this period. In the previously unsettled areas new villages were built on a circular ground-plan with individual houses placed in a group at the centre of radially extending fields.

Many of the villages founded at that time are arranged in a fairly regular geometrical pattern. The common land was demarcated by the more or less regularly ranged fronts of the individual dwellings. The siting of these settlements was usually determined by a road or brook passing through them, or by the shape of the terrain. The regular order of their construction is the result of the deliberate policy of the

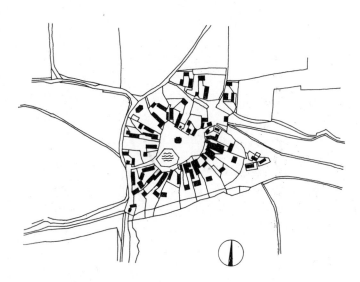

25 NYNICE, DISTRICT OF PILSEN-NORTH. CADASTRAL PLAN OF THE VILLAGE, 1839.

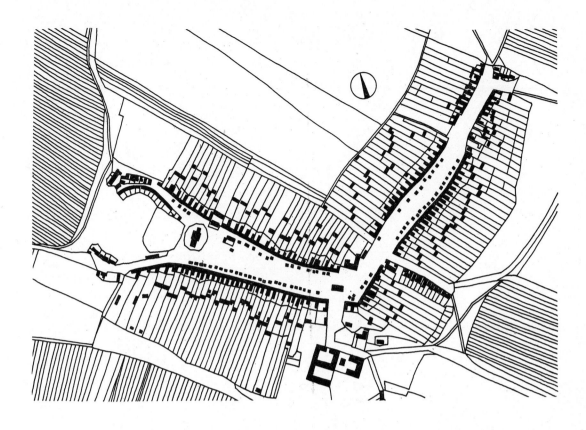

26 BÁNOV, DISTRICT OF UHERSKÉ HRADIŠTĚ. VILLAGE PLAN, 1827.

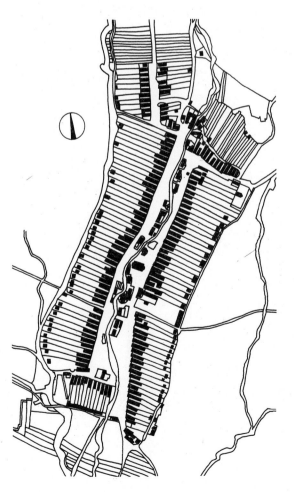

◄ 27 DETVA, DISTRICT OF ZVOLEN. PLAN OF BUILT-UP AREA.

28 VLKOŠ, DISTRICT OF HODONÍN. VILLAGE PLAN, 1832.

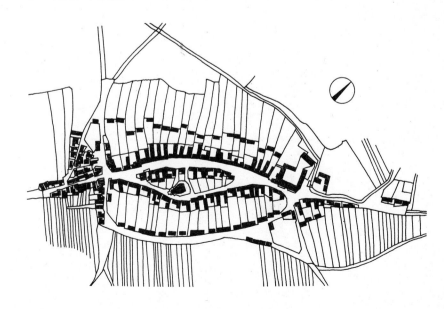

feudal administration in the period of medieval colonization. The basic features introduced in this period include the compactness of the village ground-plans, the regular arrangement of the dwellings and the plots of land belonging to them, and the categorization of communities and individual farmsteads in the newly formed social hierarchy. As in the towns, important villages, too, were provided with religious buildings and, in some cases, with the seat of an administrative official. Some villages also included the home of a minor landlord, a more or less stately, fortified house.

This extensive village reconstruction also provided the opportunity for designing individual houses and for stabilizing construction methods.

Villages without a definite ground-plan continued to exist only in areas which lacked the necessary conditions for any other kind of lay-out. New villages of this type came into being through the random expansion of already existing settlements.

THIRTY YEARS WAR — ITS SIGNIFICANCE IN THE DEVELOPMENT OF THE VILLAGES

The seventeenth century, marked by endless wars in Central Europe, was another significant period in the development of the villages. Postwar reconstruction offered an opportunity of revising their ground-plans. It was then that the face of many villages took on a new shape; their lay-out began to take human needs into account and was made attractive by the gentle curves marking the house fronts. The types of village ground-plans known already in the Middle Ages were used and respected, though in some cases the postwar reconstruction of abandoned settlements may have slightly altered their original design. It was then that the chainlike villages were established in the valleys of the Valašsko district and in the Giant Mountains, as well as in other mountainous areas, but in most cases their roots reach back into the preceding period. As families grew, clusters of newer dwellings gradually surrounded the original, old buildings. The valleys and the slopes became dotted with houses scattered across the countryside. Even in that period the colonization process continued in the hilly regions.

'RAABIZATION'

After the Thirty Years War the oppression of the rural population increased and the serfs were burdened beyond endurance by *corvée* and taxation. Nevertheless, all through the Baroque period and in the age of Neo-Classicism, the development of rural settlements persisted. Naturally, the feudal landlords and the state intervened in this development. These efforts culminated in the third quarter of the eighteenth

29   OSTRÝ KÁMEN, DISTRICT OF SVITAVY. VILLAGE PLAN, 1835.

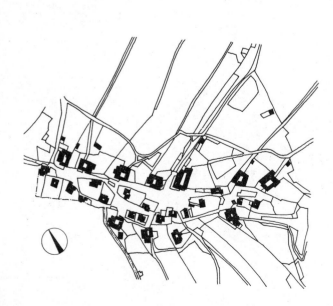

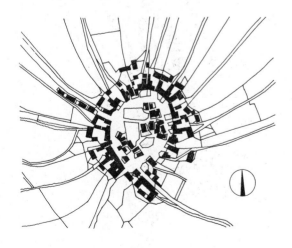

30   JÍVOVÍ, DISTRICT OF ŽĎÁR NAD SÁZAVOU. VILLAGE PLAN, 1835.

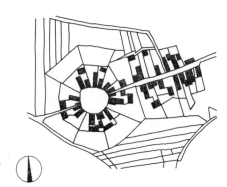

31 BYŠIČKY, DISTRICT OF NYMBURK.
VILLAGE PLAN.

century with the reforms instituted by the Austrian Court Chancellor Raab known as
'Raabization'. New villages were founded or new 'colonies' were added to old settlements. The form of the new settlements was marked by a strict order of ground
plans, either street-type or featuring a green, all in keeping with the rationalism
of that period.

In the eighteenth century and especially in the first three quarters of the nineteenth
century building activity in the villages intensified, and it is precisely then that most
of the outstanding examples of folk architecture that we can still see today originated.

Just as the structure of rural settlements changed over the centuries, so, too, did
the structure of individual dwellings change. From the simple type of pre-feudal
dwelling, usually consisting of a single room with an open fire, it was a short step
to a two-room house. Soon, an entrance room — an ante-chamber — was divided off
from the heated living room. This antechamber not only protected the entrance to
the living room, but was also used as something of a workshop and as shelter for the
smaller farm animals. Such two-room houses could still be found in the middle of
the twentieth century in remote mountain areas where the old ways of life persisted
much longer than in the fertile regions. From the two-room house developed a house
with a still more complex ground-plan which, in addition to the living room and the
ante-chamber, also included a larder. This change was due to the consolidation of
rural life in the Middle Ages and was connected with the reconstruction of villages
in the period of colonization, although the time of expansion of this type of dwelling
varies in different regions.

The three-room ground-plans proved to be the best. At the beginning they were
also used in the oldest town structures. The main room of the house was the living
room with an open fire from which smoke was drawn off in a most primitive and
ineffective fashion. The central part of the house was occupied by the hall — the
ante-chamber — which was not heated. At the other end was the third room which
in the economically more advanced areas was used as a larder for storing food and
other necessities. However, in regions with a large grain production this larder could
not hold the entire harvest and therefore special facilities were built for that purpose.
The storing of grain in holes dug in the ground persisted for a long time and was used
as late as the seventeenth century during wars. More common were one- and two-
storey granaries built of timber, and occasionally of masonry. They were separated
from the house. In some localities, especially in some Moravian and Slovak districts,
the two-room dwellings persisted for a long time and in place of a larder there was

DEVELOPMENT OF
DWELLINGS

THREE-ROOM GROUND-
PLANS

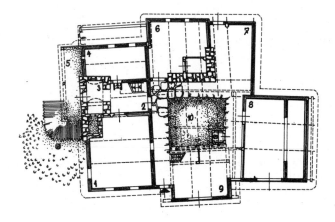

1 Living room
2 Hall
3 Black kitchen
4 Larder
5 Tool shed
6 Cowshed
7 Waggon shed
8 Barn
9 Two-storey granary
10 Yard with manure heap

32 PASEKY, DISTRICT OF CHRUDIM. PLAN OF THE GROUND-FLOOR OF A FARMSTEAD.

a two-storey granary which soon came to be joined to the dwelling house, with which it formed a single unit.

GRANARIES

The living conditions of the population improved slowly as changes were being made in the spatial relations within the framework of these basic ground-plans. The general pattern of homesteads was also affected by the existence of granaries and their location with respect to the dwelling house, which in most cases determines the character of homesteads in individual regions. However, there was one simple rule which was observed in all regions without exception. The granary, as the structure containing the most precious property of the family, had to be constantly within sight. Therefore it was situated so that it could be seen from the windows of the living room, with its entrance facing the house.

In regions where farming was less developed, cowsheds were built instead of larders and were accessible from the yard as well as directly from the hall. However, the traditional, three-room pattern with a larder prevailed and was most advantageous for a rural home.

METHODS OF HEATING

The character of the interior for a long time corresponded to the few requirements of the rural population. Under conditions prevailing in Central Europe, the key factor in the habitability of a house was the method of heating which for a long time remained quite primitive. In a corner of the living room stood an oven for baking bread and next to it an open fire from which the smoke rose freely up to the roof. The introduction of wicker chimney hoods, eliminating the smoke from the living room, was a basic step forward in the habitability of the interior. This development culminated in the construction of masonry chimneys gradually introduced along urban patterns.

BLACK KITCHENS

The construction of chimneys made possible the establishment of what were known as 'black kitchens' where all the dirty work connected with the tending of the fire was concentrated. This system was also used in village houses in the economically and culturally more advanced regions from the end of the Middle Ages onwards. In three-room houses the black kitchen was located in the back part of the hall. To a lesser extent, especially in some of the more remote areas, we find other arrangements. However, in most of the remote areas, which had little access to the achievements of civilization, the old system of heating with chimney hoods persisted and in a few isolated cases it has survived even to the present century in the Valašsko and Kopanice districts, around Jablunkov and in the mountain districts of Slovakia. On the other hand, in some areas the more progressive system of heating rooms with tiled stoves, originally built only for urban houses and country manors, was soon introduced.

Fire was an almost constant danger threatening both property and human life, and thus protection against fire was another factor influencing the construction of dwellings. 'Fire Patents' issued by the authorities from the seventeenth century onwards affected the construction of both urban and village homes. Thus, the Fire Patent issued under the reign of Empress Maria Theresa in 1751 directly banned the building of wooden houses. (Because it did not have universal validity, it was subsequently revised.) This measure, particularly in southern and central Moravia and in the adjacent parts of Slovakia, encouraged the transition to clay and elsewhere to brick as building materials.

Central Europe offered excellent natural materials for the construction of human dwellings, which had outstanding insulation properties, protecting man against cold and other adversities of weather. There was wood from the vast forests covering this part of Europe, and clay from large deposits of loess. Wood was used as building material in most parts of what is today Czechoslovakia. Logs which formed the walls were joined by means of tenons at the corners where they crossed each other. This method, known already in prehistoric times, was improved over the centuries. In the western part of the country much use was made of what is known as half-timbered construction. The logs were joined to form a timber framework and the spaces between the frames were filled either with clay on a wicker base, or with bricks. In the southern parts of the country unbaked clay was chiefly used. The walls were made either by packing finely ground clay between boards, which were removed when the clay had

33 KACEŘOV, DISTRICT OF PILSEN-NORTH.
CADASTRAL PLAN, 1839.

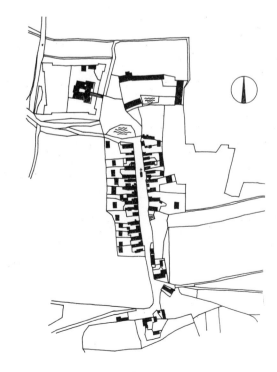

dried and hardened, or from sun-dried bricks. In addition, stone was used in some places for building both dwellings and other structures. In the second half of the nineteenth century all these materials were replaced by bricks.

DIFFERENCES IN TYPES
OF HOMESTEADS
BETWEEN REGIONS

In spite of many features that are common to folk architecture throughout the territory of Czechoslovakia, the types of homestead in the individual regions differ both in their ground-plans and in the relations between their individual parts, in the materials used and in the application of decorative elements.

These differences were also due in part to the conditions prevailing within the feudal society. The division of the country into a large number of feudal estates with a minimum of opportunity for material and cultural interchange created a situation whereby, in architecture, some features determined by the natural environment or by tradition dating as far back as the pre-feudal era were preserved. A major contribution of the seventeenth and eighteenth centuries in this respect was the endeavour to introduce more artistry into building. In the Baroque period, which represents something of a culmination of the traditional forms of building, all the features which distinguish folk architecture also reached a peak in their development.

The appearance of the buildings was influenced by natural and climatic conditions which vary considerably in diverse parts of the country. Thus buildings had different tasks in different regions. The result was the division of folk architecture into many regions, each with a highly specific character of its own. In Czechoslovakia the regional types of rural homesteads attained almost as great a diversity as the traditional folk costumes. In most cases, however, several regions constitute a larger unit in which one finds architectural masses and dispositions of basically similar types. And now, let us look at the face of folk architecture in these individual regions.

CENTRAL BOHEMIA

Central Bohemia has one of the longest histories of settlement in the Czech State. The character of rural homesteads in central Bohemia along the middle reaches of the Vltava, Berounka and Sázava rivers is documented by a few extant structures with thatched saddleback roofs. Facing the village greens are trapezoidal gables articulated with lathwork of differing forms. The top of the gable ends with a small cone-shaped projection — a tiny hipped roof. Profiled wooden frames and parapet window cornices are used in the façades and the windows are frequently paired. The dwelling houses are almost without exception three-room structures. Opposite the house in a line with the façade stands a one- and sometimes two-storey granary built over a stone cellar. The village carpenters and wood-carvers paid close attention to the structural elements of the galleries and the surfaces of the granaries. Their rich ornamental decoration expresses the importance of these small structures, in which the family's most prized possessions were stored. At the south-eastern limit of central Bohemia, along the Želivka River, there are still some granaries which have a barrel vault of wooden beams roofing the second storey. They represent a very old element of folk architecture. A remarkable feature of farmsteads in central Bohemia, in the southern part in particular, was the polygonal barn with a steep thatched roof resting on low walls made of framed timber beams.

However, in the areas of central Bohemia where timber-framed structures prevailed, stone, too, was frequently used as a building material. It was used for building cellars and even entire farmsteads as early as the Middle Ages. Later on, stone gradually

34 BOROVÁ, DISTRICT OF SVITAVY. FARMSTEAD WITH BUILDINGS ENCLOSING A YARD.

36 VELKÁ NAD VELIČKOU, DISTRICT OF HODONÍN. COLOUR DECORATION OF THE STREET FRONT OF A VILLAGE HOUSE.

37 KLEČATY, DISTRICT OF TÁBOR. ARCHITECTURAL ARRANGEMENT OF THE VILLAGE GREEN.

38   PLÁSTOVICE, DISTRICT OF ČESKÉ BUDĚJOVICE. GROUP OF FARMSTEADS IN SOUTH BOHEMIA.

39 KUŽELOV, DISTRICT OF HODONÍN. WINDMILL IN THE BORDERLAND BETWEEN MORAVIA AND SLOVAKIA.

replaced timber until, in the nineteenth century, it was used almost exclusively in some areas. However stone, too, was eventually replaced by brickwork.

As well as structures of traditional form, in some villages near Prague there are farms built of masonry, with façades of Baroque style. Some of them were constructed by architects who took part in the large-scale Baroque construction and re-construction of Prague.

The central Bohemian type of rural structure penetrated deep into eastern Bohemia. There it touched on the hilly region of the Bohemian-Moravian Highlands whose northern border range is characterized by villages laid out on the basis of long strip fields attached to every farmstead. These can be found around the towns of Polička, Chrudim and Litomyšl. Isolated farms have a compact, enclosed shape, with the dwelling and the farm buildings framing a courtyard, thus protecting it against the adversities of the severe climate. The exterior of the timber-framed structures is characterized by white pointing of the joints and the spike-like lathwork of the gables ending at the top with a cone-shaped projection and demarcated at the bottom by projecting eaves. An important part of the overall lay-out is the granary which forms a second storey above a room for waggons and tools. A notable part of the farmsteads are the polygonal barns, usually separated from the other structures, and in rare cases included in the enclosure. Farm cottages with their small outhouses also often form a yard, which on one or even two sides may be enclosed by a high wall with a small shingled roof.

In the neighbouring Orlické Mountains we find a different type of hill-country structure. The framed buildings are designed so that all the living and utility rooms are under one roof. This design is also the product of the harsh mountain climate. The saddleback roof is covered with shingles which also frequently appear on the gables. In modern times shingles have been replaced by transite tiles. In the case of large farmsteads, three or even four wings of the buildings enclose the yard. In the vicinity of Náchod and Dobruška, log-houses with white-pointed joints have thatched roofs with perpendicular or feather-like lathwork gables. A covered porch runs along the entire length of the dwelling house, with the overhanging roof supported by decoratively carved columns and lathwork walls. This space is used for storing firewood for the winter, which is always severe in this region.

In both the Polička district and in the Orlické Mountains log-houses were replaced, in the nineteenth century, by structures built of stone and, still later, of brick. The arrangement of their structure and space changed in some respects. First to be modernized was the system of heating, and the number of rooms was increased. The façades were articulated by Neo-Classical architectural elements. And the gable of the dwelling house and the entrance gate were frequently other important compositional factors.

The Broumov spur in north-eastern Bohemia is remarkable primarily for its large farmsteads built of masonry, with Baroque and Neo-Classical designs on their façades. An important aspect of their composition is the entrance with stone portals, frequently bearing the date of their construction.

In the fertile parts of north-eastern Bohemia farming reached a high standard. The farmsteads have richly decorated gables. Especially in the Jizera River valley we find village houses of fine architectural design. The main structure in these farmsteads is a two-storey building containing the living rooms, a larder and cowsheds on the ground floor and granaries on the second floor. A gallery usually runs along the entire length of the structure. The gable, facing the street or the village green is divided by profiled cornices. A cone-shaped projection (or a hipped roof), lathwork, small columns, miniature blind arcades and galleries are frequent elements of decoration. The structural parts of the galleries are also richly carved. The painted decoration with floral and geometric ornamentation is quite interesting, too. The barn usually stands at the back of the yard. The centre of this region with its two-storey farmsteads is in the vicinity of Turnov, but similar structures may also be found in other parts of north-eastern Bohemia.

Especially prominent decoration is typical of gables in the vicinity of Stará Paka. They are divided into many squares with a great variety of carved decoration. The main building is a one-storey structure but the farmstead includes small two- to three-storey granaries where the decorative carving on the gables and galleries achieves richness without, however, disturbing the compositional order. The ornamental elements underline the logic of the construction and give expression to the shaping of the materials.

In the vicinity of Jaroměř and Josefov we find farmsteads with attic granaries projecting from the main façade and supported by two or three columns. In the higher parts of this region some people made their living from cottage industries such as weaving or making various glass products, or the working of semi-precious stones. Their occupation was reflected in the more modest auxiliary parts of their houses.

In north-eastern Bohemia many small towns were built of wood and survived in this state until the first quarter of the twentieth century. In some of these towns framed houses are still to be found on the outskirts. These urban homes usually had a greater number of living rooms, some of them on the second storey. Their façades are similar to those of village houses, but more frequently we find, under projecting gables, arcades supported by wooden columns. These arcades face the street or the town square.

ELBE RIVER LOWLANDS

In the south this region touches on the fertile Elbe River lowlands where farmsteads are characterized by prominently articulated gables in which the usual motifs are supplemented by the radiating ornament of the rising sun. In the central part of the Elbe lowlands these gables projected from the façade of the house and were supported by carved columns forming an arcade. The farmstead usually consisted of a one-storey dwelling house whose gable faced the street, and a one-storey granary and barn standing at the back of the yard. The cowsheds were located behind the dwelling house, the individual structures forming three sides of the yard. Some barns had a polygonal ground-plan.

CENTRAL BOHEMIAN RANGE

The two-storey design of farmsteads in the Central Bohemian Range is very similar to that of the farmsteads in north-eastern Bohemia. However, their walls were enriched with blind arcades formed by the ornamentally carved posts. This element, known in German as *Umgebinde*, extends in the north to Lusatia, beyond the Czechoslovak frontier, and also to the western frontier areas. The posts support the mass of the upper storey which, in the area of the Central Bohemian Range, is a framed

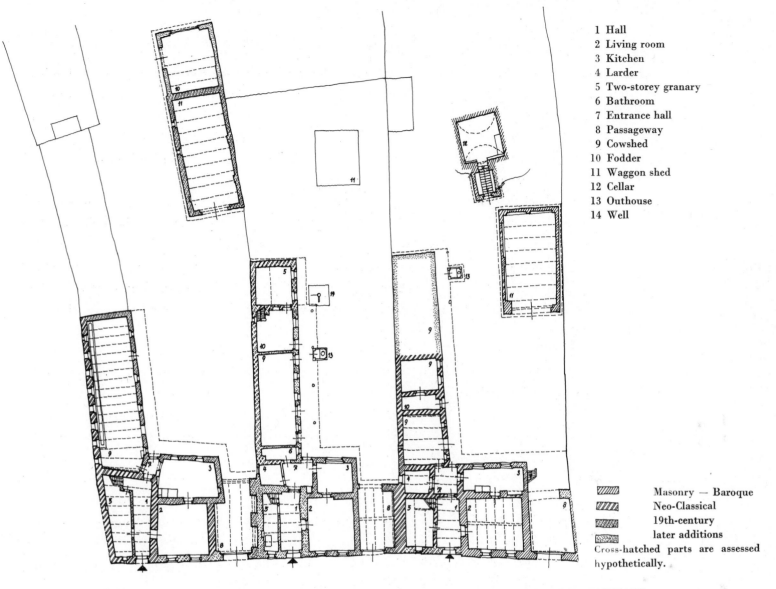

1 Hall
2 Living room
3 Kitchen
4 Larder
5 Two-storey granary
6 Bathroom
7 Entrance hall
8 Passageway
9 Cowshed
10 Fodder
11 Waggon shed
12 Cellar
13 Outhouse
14 Well

///// Masonry — Baroque
///// Neo-Classical
///// 19th-century
///// later additions
Cross-hatched parts are assessed
hypothetically.

40   RYMICE, DISTRICT OF KROMĚŘÍŽ. ANALYSIS OF THE DEVELOPMENT OF A GROUP OF FARMSTEADS.

structure but which, in the western frontier areas and in Lusatia, is frequently half-timbered. With their richly decorated gables, galleries, columns and lathwork, especially in the area between Litoměřice and Nový Bor, these houses rank among the most valuable works of folk architecture. North of Nový Bor single-storey buildings prevail, with decorative posts supporting the roof structures and the surface of the façades being covered with lathwork.

WESTERN BOHEMIA

The western frontier area is a region of half-timbered structures of a type developed in Western Europe in the Middle Ages. It occurs as far east as the area around the towns of Slaný and Mělník. Basically, the use of half-timbered constructions corresponds to the spread of German settlement in past centuries. In the Cheb area outer walls were richly articulated with wooden frame constructions which often have an ornamental character. Two-storey dwelling houses with a framed or stone base and half-timbered upper storey formed three and, more frequently, four sides of the yard. These enclosed farmsteads were ranged along the roads with strip fields extending beyond them. However, in older settlements the houses surrounded a village green. The main part of these farmsteads was a two-storey house with living rooms on the ground floor and, in some cases, on the upper floor as well, which also housed the granaries. These houses had a gallery on the side facing the yard. The cowsheds were close to the living rooms. The waggon shed, opened with two or three arcaded bays, usually with richly carved woodwork, stood on one side of the yard. The half-timbered barn often had half-timbered gables. Framed granaries with several storeys completed the farmsteads. The more recent structures in that area, built of brick by professional masons, display many elements of the traditional construction and articulation of mass but in a simplified form.

In the other parts of western and south-western Bohemia, farmsteads were constructed in a similar manner to those of Central Bohemia. Near Pilsen the gables of framed, whitewashed farms faced the village green. The granary stood by the wall, which had a gate of masonry and of Baroque or Neo-Classical design. The gables of both the dwelling house and the granary, made of feather-shaped or perpendicular lathwork, were topped with a massive pyramid instead of the cone-shaped projection common elsewhere.

North of the west Bohemian town of Manětín, dwelling houses had asymmetrical roofs. Under the elevation on the side facing the yard was a projecting gallery with carvings. The gallery was connected to the granaries located in the attic. In western Bohemia, too, farmsteads had two-storey granaries of architecturally complex patterns. Also to be found there are framed granaries whose upper space was vaulted. In western Bohemia and especially in the vicinity of Kralovice and Plasy polygonal barns were built as well.

Most villages in the vicinity of Pilsen were reconstructed in the nineteenth century. The buildings made of masonry in that period are larger, but the traditional positioning with the façade of the dwelling house projecting beyond the building line was preserved. The richly articulated gables provide evidence of the growing prosperity of the farming population following the abolition of serfdom.

CHODSKO

The ethnographically unique area of Chodsko in south-western Bohemia is a most interesting architectural region. The dwelling parts of the farmsteads are usually only on the ground floor and are situated behind a massive two-storey granary. The original framed structures were later replaced by structures built of masonry. A special feature is the bread oven, located outside the house.

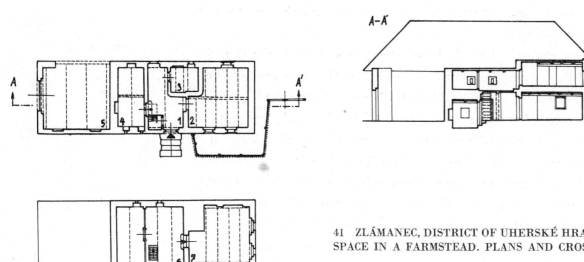

1 Hall
2 Living room
3 Kitchen
4 Larder
5 Passageway
6 Granary
7 Granary

A–A′

41 ZLÁMANEC, DISTRICT OF UHERSKÉ HRADIŠTĚ. ARRANGEMENT OF THE SPACE IN A FARMSTEAD. PLANS AND CROSS-SECTION.

South Bohemia was still separated from the other parts of the Czech Kingdom in the Middle Ages by the great Central Bohemian Forest. This isolation gave rise to the independent development of many cultural elements in this area. Although the farm dwellings were framed structures as elsewhere, the shape of their roofs gave a different character to the outline of their masses. Gambrel roofs ended in trapezoid gables with perpendicular lathwork, projecting prominently from the façade of the house. In the mountain areas the houses also had galleries, but their design was less decorative than in other parts of the country. The roofs of isolated farmsteads in the Šumava Range had little belfries — used as a warning system to signal that an enemy was invading the country. Many of the old houses were solidly built of stone, significantly since it was their inhabitants who guarded the frontiers.

In the low-lying parts of south Bohemia, the construction of ponds reduced the extent of the forests from the sixteenth century onwards. This gradually produced a shortage of timber for building purposes. The fire-prevention measures instituted in the eighteenth century and the permission to produce bricks on land belonging to the serfs, granted at the beginning of the nineteenth century, opened up a wide field of activity for village masons. They began by building granaries and cowsheds, but gradually they were also called upon to build houses, for the prosperity of most of the village population had increased following the reforms instituted by Empress Maria Theresa and Emperor Joseph II, and especially after the abolition of the corvée shortly before the middle of the nineteenth century. The masons introduced architectural elements with which they had become acquainted while working in the towns to the rural environment. Structures dating from the eighteenth and the early nineteenth centuries show forms which approximate to the then prevalent Baroque and Neo-Classical architectural styles. Village construction in south Bohemia boomed after the middle of the nineteenth century. Smaller districts within the larger region of south Bohemia emerged, marked by the creative efforts of individual master masons, especially those of Šoch and Paták in the vicinity of Soběslav, and Burza in the Volyně district. In the vicinity of České Budějovice, Jindřichův Hradec, Týn on the Vltava, Písek and other places, there were other masons, each of whom had his own style and means of expression. They did not know about compositional logic of the structural system, nor about the relationship of form and proportions of the Baroque and Neo-Classical styles. They developed their own method of combining decorative elements which articulated and rimmed the gables and façades. Similar forms of architecture, developed by individual masons, also occurred in other regions but nowhere on such a scale and of such value as in south and south-western Bohemia. Some affinity to this creative endeavour can be found in southern Moravia.

In the area of the Bohemian-Moravian Highlands the oldest village houses are made of timber as in central Bohemia. However, the character of the buildings and the pattern of villages dating from the original period of settlement, centering on a village green, clearly differs from the character of the villages built during the subsequent colonization period, with strip fields extending radially beyond individual farmsteads. In the former type of village, the framed houses had a form similar to those in central Bohemia. However, in the latter type of village the farm buildings were grouped into close formations, in which granaries did not play a major role, their function often being fulfilled by an attic. This is true especially of the high-lying areas which were settled only in the seventeenth and eighteenth centuries. The house plan which prevailed was the type where the hall of the living section was directly joined to the cowshed. Usually, a small barn was also connected with the other rooms under a single roof. Only the larger farms and the mayor's house had more spacious auxiliary farm buildings enclosing the yard on three or on all four sides.

The architectural expression of farm buildings in the Bohemian-Moravian Highlands is characterized by framed walls — either whitewashed or with white pointing — and gables with cone-shaped projections and eaves. The surface of the gables was articulated with feather-like lathwork with decorative carvings on the lattices and wings. A remarkable feature of folk architecture in this hilly area was the ornamental painting of surfaces and the coloured articulation of the gables. In the last century, houses of masonry began to be built throughout this area, which architecturally were not substantially different from structures built elsewhere.

NORTHERN MORAVIA

The type of building in the vicinity of Polička, with the yard enclosed by the dwelling and farm structures, extends to the area around the town of Svitavy in Moravia. There, the villages of the strip-field type mostly consist of masonry farmsteads of considerable size.

A similar type and pattern is also found in other parts of northern Moravia. Around Litovel and Hranice the spatial lay-out of the yard is supplemented by an arcaded walk along the wing containing the cowsheds. In the mountain area of the Jeseníky Range the farmsteads are built mostly of masonry and only a few less valuable half-timbered structures of the former German settlers have been preserved.

North-eastern Moravia is an area of framed buildings. In the Hlučín and Kravaře districts numerous two-storey framed granaries with vaulted upper storeys are still to be found. They are witnesses to now-forgotten building techniques and patterns of designing and furnishing farmsteads.

CENTRAL MORAVIA

An interesting region from the architectural point of view is a strip of territory extending across Moravia roughly from Boskovice to Valašské Klobouky into north-western Slovakia. It covers the ethnographically interesting Haná district, parts of Moravian Slovakia and the Valašsko areas. The building materials used there were unbaked clay and adobe bricks. The remains of framed structures have been found in many places, pointing to a previous relationship to folk architecture in the neighbouring regions, as does the lay-out of the farmsteads, based on the three-room design with a two-storey granary built within the dwelling house. Yet throughout this region there also exist separated granaries, remnants of an older building era.

The exteriors of farmsteads in this region are characterized by hipped thatched roofs, small windows set in a relatively unarticulated mass, and a portal-like accentuation of the entrance. In the latest stage of development, two-storey structures were built with granaries in the attic. The houses were built along the street-line, while the farm buildings were situated at right angles to them. The barns were located at the far end of the lot, but were sometimes grouped together at the end of the village where the road led into the fields. In the central part of this region the barns have gates at both gabled ends and can be driven through from end to end.

42a, b HORNÍ BEČVA, DISTRICT OF VSETÍN. LAY-OUT OF A WALACHIAN FARMSTEAD. GROUND-PLAN AND CROSS-SECTION.

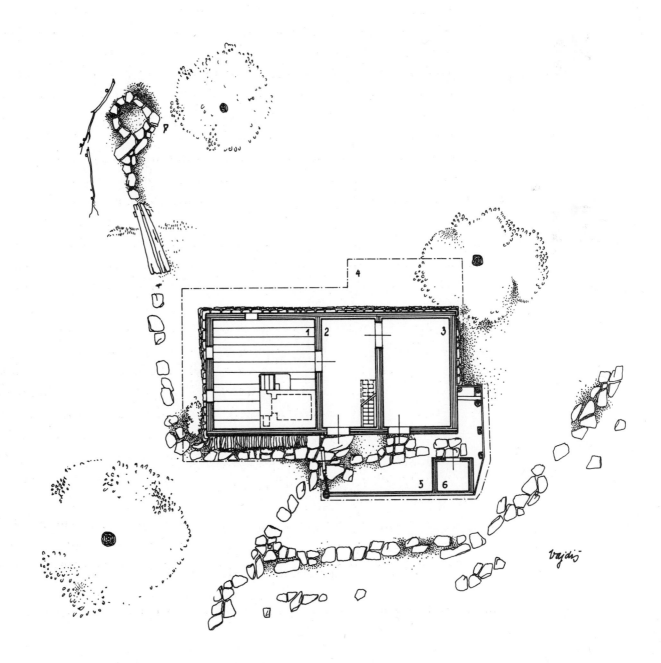

1 Living room
2 Hall
3 Cowshed
4 Waggon shed
5 Entrance hall
6 Pigsty
7 Spring

The farms of the Haná district in the northern part of central Moravia present a special type of the above lay-out. The basic three-part disposition is supplemented by a two-storey structure in front of the main entrance from the street, known as a *žudr*. This differs from the earlier mentioned farm building with its portal-like entrance in that it is a massive wing projecting out from the front of the building with the entrance proper on the ground floor and a granary upstairs. On village greens or streets the sequence of these projections creates an interesting rhythm which is also accentuated by the colour patterns of their walls. Similar formations can be found in the Vyškov district where, however, the granary is situated in the framed and vaulted attic of the *žudr*. In the Boskovice district these projecting wings were constructed of timber.

In the southern part of Moravian Slovakia the construction of village buildings was closely connected to the development of the architecture of the Danubian Lowlands. The houses, built of clay, were situated parallel to the road. The cowsheds and other farm buildings were placed at right angles to the house. In the yards of some farmsteads a row of clay columns supported the overhanging eaves of the roof, covering the approach to the cowsheds. The entrances were enhanced with portal-like structures. The hipped roofs were thatched. The frontal walls and the interiors of houses in Moravian Slovakia in the area around Břeclav, Hodonín, Strážnice and Uherské Hradiště were decorated with coloured surfaces framed by white plaster. Because clay did not permit the use of three-dimensional ornamental designs, mural painting developed in this region. Talented village women, without any patterns or preliminary tracing, were able to create various ornamental motifs — usually scrolls, but also geometric and animal designs in traditional colouring and formal composition. Wall openings, window and door frames, were surrounded by ornaments, which were also used to articulate larger surfaces. Some elements of this decoration also have symbolic meaning.

The character of architecture in eastern Moravia was influenced by its geographical and historical ties to the Carpathian area. From the sixteenth century on, the Walachian settlement changed the way of life of the local population. The mountain slopes and remote valleys were gradually inhabited, though the isolation of individual families and of the entire region helped to preserve the ancient cultural forms and the primitive structural patterns of the Carpathian type of building until quite recently. The two-room house had a hall and a living room, but no larder. The room was heated by an oven next to which was an open fire with a chimney hood. Chimneys were not introduced until the nineteenth century, but even then the open fire remained in frequent use. As living conditions improved, a larder was added to the living room. Harsh climatic conditions made the people build the cowsheds and other auxiliary facilities under the same roof as the dwelling. Only large farmsteads had several buildings.

The buildings were constructed in a remarkable way. The pointing of the framed walls was not emphasized, but was sealed with moss and wooden laths. The walls of some structures were covered with shingles. The framed prism of the structure

43 ŽDIAR, DISTRICT OF POPRAD. FARMSTEAD IN THE EASTERN PART OF THE TATRA MOUNTAINS AREA. ▶

45   ZUBEREC, DISTRICT OF DOLNÝ KUBÍN. TIMBER-FRAMED COTTAGES IN THE ORAVA VALLEY.

◄

44   HUBOVÁ, DISTRICT OF LIPTOVSKÝ MIKULÁŠ. GROUP OF TIMBER-FRAMED, CLAY PLASTERED COTTAGES.

46 VYŠNÉ RUŽBACHY, DISTRICT OF POPRAD. A VILLAGE IN THE FOOTHILLS OF THE BELANSKÉ TATRY MOUNTAINS.

◄

47 VYŠNÉ RUŽBACHY, DISTRICT OF POPRAD. TIMBER-FRAMED FARMSTEAD WITH A SIDE GATEWAY.

49 JAKUBANY, DISTRICT OF POPRAD. GROUP OF HOUSES WITH THEIR GABLES FACING THE STREET.

◄

48 ZÁVADKA NAD HRONOM, DISTRICT OF BANSKÁ BYSTRICA. HOUSE IN CENTRAL SLOVAKIA.

50 DAČOV LOM, DISTRICT OF ZVOLEN. THATCHED CLAY COTTAGE IN THE LOW-LYING PART OF CENTRAL SLOVAKIA.

51 DOBRÁ NIVA, DISTRICT OF ZVOLEN. LIVING ROOM OF A FARMSTEAD. ▶

53   VELKÁ TRŇA, DISTRICT OF TREBIŠOV. CLAY HOUSE WITH HIPPED ROOF IN EASTERN SLOVAKIA.

◄

52   TERŇA, DISTRICT OF PREŠOV. TWO-STOREY GRANARY WITH FRAMED VAULTING OF ITS UPPER STOREY.

54 PRUŠÁNKY, DISTRICT OF HODONÍN. STRUCTURES HOUSING WINE-PRESSES AND WINE-CELLARS IN SOUTH MORAVIA.

55 SUCHÁ HORA, DISTRICT OF DOLNÝ KUBÍN, TIMBER-FRAMED HOUSES IN THE NORTH OF THE ORAVA VALLEY ▶

56 PRUŠÁNKY, DISTRICT OF HODONÍN. GROUP OF STRUCTURES HOUSING WINE-PRESSES IN SOUTH MORAVIA.

58   TASOV, DISTRICT OF HODONÍN. *ŽUDRO* PROJECTION OF A HOUSE IN SOUTH MORAVIA.

◄

57   ČIČMANY, DISTRICT OF ŽILINA. ORNAMENTATION ON TIMBER-FRAMED WALLS.

59 TRAKOVICE, DISTRICT OF TRNAVA. CLAY HOUSE IN THE LOWER PART OF THE VÁH LOWLANDS.

60 KÁTOV, DISTRICT OF SENICA. HOUSE IN THE AREA OF THE RIVER MORAVA. ▶

61 SALAJNA, DISTRICT OF CHEB. A MILL IN AN AREA OF HALF-TIMBERED STRUCTURES.

was covered with a saddleback shingle roof, ending in gables fitted with cone-shaped projections at their peaks and eaves at the bottom. The gable was articulated with vertical or, more rarely, feather-like lathwork. Around the rim of the gable the laths formed a step-like motif and on its surface they created an ornament resembling envelopes. Also to be found are miniature blind arcades and the motif of the rising sun. The gables of village houses were whitewashed and painted with scroll patterns. On some houses biblical quotations were painted at the bottom of the cone-shaped projections of the gables, with the names of the builder and the owner and the date of completion. The walls of the mountain houses were usually enlivened with spots of whitewash around the door and window frames and on the beams below the eaves. Here the decorative function was secondary: the spots were rather 'magic charms' intended to protect the interior of the house against evil powers. In the Valašsko region the folk structures blend well with the surrounding landscape, demonstrating a special skill in achieving a symbiosis with the natural environment.

A quick glance at a map of the Slovak Socialist Republic will show that Slovak territory is made up of two different parts — the mountainous north and the southern lowlands. This difference in terrain also determines the basic division of Slovak folk architecture, its character and forms. The wooded mountains provided a wealth of timber for building, while in the flat south the most frequent building material was clay.

The mountainous area on the border between Moravia and Slovakia, settled relatively late by hill farmers, is the home of primitive forms of dwellings built of hard wood. Clusters of small farmsteads on the slopes of the steep hills are typical of this area. Walls of roughly shaped beams with clay plaster enclosed two rooms. The living room was heated by a bread oven with an open fire and a chimney hood. The hall, frequently without a ceiling, provided shelter for a cow or two, unless there was a separate stable, which was not too common in this poor area. The thatched hipped roofs had steep slopes to withstand the weight of snow during the hard winters. Barns were built of logs.

From Moravia, the Walachian style of building also penetrated into Slovakia. Thus, in the Orava River valley in north-western Slovakia, the village structures were remarkable for their perfect carpentry work and the outstanding decorative elements used to articulate the gables. The wealthier villagers built two-storey houses. These houses had ornamentally carved galleries on the side facing the yard as well as on the front. Shingled roofs overhung the walls on all sides. On the main façade they had a steep slope which supported a small gable ending at the top with a cone-shaped projection. This small gable was articulated with radiating or spike-like lath-work. Conspicuous features were the windows which were often doubled and framed with broad wooden planks. The bread oven in the living room, heated from the black kitchen in the hall, was a prominent feature of the interior. Next to the oven stood a tiled stove which was essential in the harsh mountain climate. In the Orava valley most of these stoves were cylindrical. Until recently the smoke from the fire-place was drawn off through a chimney hood.

The villages of the Orava valley are remarkable for their strict and regimented order. The houses are placed close to each other with their gables facing the street —

SLOVAKIA

KOPANICE

ORAVA VALLEY

the houses in the front, the cowsheds behind them and the barns at the far end. Beyond the villages stand groups of barns for hay and in the yards of the farmsteads or in front of them, on the village green, there are granaries with framed vaulting or with a flat ceiling on the upper floor.

Semi-detached houses with a common roof and sometimes also a common hall and bread oven are a special feature in some villages in the Liptov area at the foot of the Tatra Mountains. They, too, are placed closely together, and the living room of each house looks out onto the street through two windows. The front wall is covered with a gambrel roof with a gable whose surface is articulated with vertical, spike-like, or radiating lathwork. Although the carpentry work on Liptov houses is of a good standard, large parts of the walls are covered with a clay plaster which is whitewashed or blue. These colours enliven the appearance of the villages.

WESTERN SLOVAKIA

The mountainous area near Trenčín in the central part of western Slovakia was rather isolated, and thus some very archaic cultural forms survived there until quite recently. Both the remote farmsteads scattered over the mountain slopes and the villages in this area, built of timber, are quite interesting. The more advanced forms of furnishing did not penetrate there until the beginning of the twentieth century. For example, the medieval system of heating without chimneys was common there for a very long time. Also, the spatial arrangement of the houses was adapted to suit local forms of family life. Čičmany is among the architecturally outstanding villages in this area. Completely isolated, life in this village developed along quite different lines to that in other, more accessible, communities. In Čičmany, young married couples continued to live with their parents in what was called a large family. Thus, the houses were designed so that there would be rooms for the young couples on the upper storey or in the attic. Evidence of the long history of this type of construction is provided by framed vaulting in the upstairs rooms. The Čičmany houses, however, are remarkable above all for the wealth of their exterior decoration. The walls are covered with ornamental paintings consisting of several basic geometric forms. Some of the older houses still preserved show the original sober use of ornamentation, but the structures rebuilt after a great fire in 1923 have an overabundance of *décor*.

CENTRAL SLOVAKIA

Village houses in the upper Hron valley are characterized chiefly by the artistic quality of their gables. Their vertical lathwork is topped with a cone-shaped projection with a small sphere on the apex. Many houses have a high retaining wall with a cellar to compensate for the inclination of the terrain. Their ornamental *décor* is concentrated in the base of the cone-shaped top, the rims and other parts of the gable, and also in the main gate and the smaller, side gate, which usually have a small roof covered with shingles. The entire surface of the saddleback roofs is also shingled.

Folk architecture in central Slovakia reveals the former composition of the local population. Slovak houses have retained the basic characteristic features of framed structures as in other parts of the country. What distinguishes them is their perfect carpentry work and their well-ordered positioning in the villages. Their gables with eaves have the usual cone-shaped projection at the top. German houses, especially in the vicinity of Kremnica, Banská Štiavnica, Banská Bystrica, Brezno and other mining settlements, lie parallel with the street and usually have two storeys. The three-room houses are joined to the cowsheds, the rooms on the upper storey being entered from a balcony. Their hard wood walls are plastered and whitewashed. Besides the wooden houses one may also find some stone structures.

In the Detva district of central Slovakia houses were usually built of masonry. Their saddleback, thatched roofs end in gables, the lathwork of which forms different ornaments and patterns. At the base of the gable there is a hipped roof (the eaves) and at the top, the cone-shaped projection. The houses have the standard three rooms. At the back of each house are, one behind the other, the cowsheds and the other farm buildings, ending with the barn. In front of the house, on the street, is the granary. An especially interesting architectural element is the gate leading into the yard. Some of them are decorated in front, with wheelwright's rosettes engraved with compasses being the most prominent ornament. In this district, too, isolated hill farms, known as *lazy*, are scattered on the mountain slopes. In these farms the buildings enclose the yard. Attached to the three-room house are the barn, the cowshed, the waggon shed, the sheep pen and other out-buildings. However, there also exists a simpler arrangement of buildings in two wings. Hipped roofs are covered with overlapping layers of thatch.

Greatly varied architectural forms characterize the vicinity of Rimavská Sobota in the southern part of central Slovakia. In most cases the longer side of the house faces the street, but there are also houses which do so with their gable end. In villages in the northern part of this district timber was the prevalent building material, while in the south clay was used. However, some structures were built of stone as well. The columns of some gates and wickets are richly carved. The windows are closed with grilles of wrought iron and shutters of sheet-metal. The sober character of the architecture is accentuated by its lack of colour. Most of the houses are simply whitewashed.

In the area of Spiš, structures of a Slovak character mingle with the architecture introduced in the past by German settlers. There are interesting houses there with entrance halls and passageways closed by a large gate in the main façade. An entrance leads from the passageway to a hall which has no ceiling and which contains the heating system. The living room faces the street, while the larder is located on the yard side of the house. This type of dwelling can be found from upper Liptov to the very heart of the Spiš area. In the north-western part of this region a usual type of house is one with a masonry living room, framed hall and a larder under one roof. The plan of this type of house differs in practically every village. One very interesting kind has a passageway with a living room and a larder on one side and a cowshed and other farm facilities on the other. The whole unit has a common roof. A remarkable feature of the exterior structure of the Spiš houses are the gables, which are divided into several parts in steplike form, joined together with hipped roofs. The bottom part of the gable juts out from the line of the façade. The top of the gable is cut off with a small hipped roof. If the older houses had a chimney at all, it was in the shape of a slightly conical prism and was protected at the top with a wide, conical covering. Rainwater was drained off by wooden gutter troughs projecting far into the street.

Besides houses, however, there are also many structures with the usual three-part plan to be found in Spiš. They face the street with their gables topped with a cone-shaped projection and a small sphere at the apex. Located in the streets or village greens, or even in the yards, are framed granaries with vaulted upper stories, plastered with clay and covered with thatched roofs.

The villages included such auxiliary buildings as simple flour mills, sawmills, oil presses and other primitive facilities providing for the needs of the population. The exterior surfaces of the masonry houses are decorated with stucco. Carved decorations appear on the wooden structures. The ornamentation of the façades is augmented by the contrast between the natural material used in the wooden structural parts and the colouring of the decorations, or by their distinction from the whitewashed surfaces of the masonry buildings.

TATRA MOUNTAINS

The mountain style of architecture with its perfect carpentry work and its clearcut architecture penetrated into Slovak territory from the north on both the eastern and the western sides of the Tatra Mountains. Houses of this type were built of thick logs which, more frequently than elsewhere, were left uncut and round on the outside. Their saddleback roofs are covered with shingles cut to a point, their triangular gables are topped with a sphere, and their exteriors are frequently decorated with radiating lathwork or geometric patterns of lattices. The surfaces of the gables project from gambrel roofs, the eaves of which extend far out from the walls of the houses. The main entrance of such a house, leading into the hall, is situated in the centre of the long side of the house. It is protected by a small portico with wooden columns which support a small saddleback roof and a gable. There is often a balcony extending on both sides of the entrance, with an ornamentally carved wooden railing.

SPIŠ

A hall at the side, a kitchen and a living room constitute the living quarters of the typical farmstead at Ždiar on the eastern side of the Tatra Mountains, though similar farmsteads were built with certain variations in other villages as well. Special features of the Ždiar homes were the rich *décor* of their interior — a painted oven in the kitchen and ornamentally carved ceiling beams — and their façades, where geometrical ornamentation was applied to the corners and around the windows and doors. The architectural effect of the structures in Ždiar is also sometimes enhanced by colour articulation. Thus, for example, the surfaces of the beams may be ochre-coloured, whilst the pointing between them is blue. The auxiliary structures of the mountain farmsteads enclose the yard on three or even four sides, their spatial relationship being determined by the division of the cadastres into strips of land. These mountain villages often extend across the entire width of the cadastral area.

EASTERN SLOVAKIA

In the area north-west of Bardejov, in eastern Slovakia, the farming character of the villages is reflected not only in the furnishing of the farmsteads, where high granaries dominate the outline, but also in the straw-covered roofs, bordered with shingles.

A remarkable feature of the villages in the Šariš region is the colourful character of the framed walls of the houses, covered with clay plaster. The houses have hipped straw roofs where the thatch is arranged in steps. Some barns were built on a hexagonal plan and the farmstead included two-storey granaries, many of which were vaulted.

In the easternmost part of Slovakia human settlement is concentrated in narrow valleys. The arrangement of village structures in this region is rather confused. They are usually built of logs plastered with clay. Their walls are a brilliant blue against the background of the surrounding greenery, this blue contrasting with the natural colour of the thatch on the hipped roofs. The houses have two or three rooms. The modest farming facilities did not permit the development of a specific system in arranging the farmstead as a unit. A few of the old houses still do not have a chimney. The long fronts of houses in some villages in the northern part of this area are broken by passageways opening into the yard. Hipped roofs are covered with thatch laid in steps which accentuates the impression of massiveness created by the houses.

Although the needs of the population of the southern parts of Slovakia did not differ from those which determined the way in which houses in the north were built, the different natural environment asserted itself in the prevailing architectural forms. The character of villages in the low-lying, flat or slightly undulating parts of the country differs by their more highly developed lay-out, made possible by the shape of the terrain. The settlements are mostly of the street type but some also feature a large village green. Only the somewhat uneven terrain on the periphery of the lowlands forced the construction of more compact or irregularly grouped villages. Southern Slovakia has a substantially warmer climate than the mountainous areas to the north of it. Therefore, its inhabitants had to protect themselves both against the cold of the winter season and the heat of the summer. This problem was solved by the massive character of the houses, with their hipped, thickly thatched straw roofs. The roofs projected far out from the façade and shaded the windows and the doors. The natural conditions also influenced the character of farming in this region and therefore some types of structures are found only in the south, whilst they are missing elsewhere in Slovakia. This is true, for example, of the different shelters made of straw loosely heaped on a frame of wooden poles held up by slim wooden pillars, of straw shelters for shepherds in the fields, small structures for drying maize, etc. Also seen in this area are ears of maize tied together in pairs and hung below the eaves for drying. This is so typical that one can scarcely imagine a village house in the Danubian Basin without them.

In this ethnically diverse area there are also noticeable differences between the structures built by the separate national groups. Perhaps the greatest single difference between the houses of the Slovak and the Hungarian populations lies in their coloured decoration. In many Slovak villages there is a wealth of ornamental painting in the interiors. This is true of villages in the vicinity of Pezinok north-east of Bratislava and around Trnava. Elsewhere there is a pronounced use of colour to decorate the façades of the houses, as for example in the area extending from Bratislava to Nitra in central Slovakia.

The ground-plan of houses in the Danubian area matured and crystallized on the territory of former Pannonia, the south of Slovakia being only on the periphery of this vast area. The Slovaks living there created a structural system which was closely related to the customs of the neighbouring territories settled by Slavs. However, this style was soon influenced by new elements from the south. One important factor in this respect was the incorporation of Slovakia in the Hungarian state. Thus the elements of several cultures intermingle in southern Slovakia today. However, the three-room plan is preserved even in areas where the style of building common in the adjoining area to the south is used.

The most striking architectural feature of this area is the covered walk along the length of the house, where the overhanging roof is supported by a row of columns. Such covered walks are found in farmsteads from the south of Moravia all the way

62 LADOMÍROVÁ, DISTRICT OF BARDEJOV. WOODEN CHURCH OF THE ARCHANGEL MICHAEL, 1742.

63 KOČÍ, DISTRICT OF CHRUDIM. WOODEN BELFRY AND COVERED BRIDGE OF THE CHURCH OF ST BARTHOLOMEW. ▶

64 BULHARY, DISTRICT OF BŘECLAV. YARD FRONT OF A FARMSTEAD IN THE AREA ALONG THE LOWER DYJE RIVER.

65 TEKOVSKÉ LUŽANY, DISTRICT OF LEVICE. HOUSE WITH A YARD ARCADE IN SOUTHERN SLOVAKIA. ▶

to the Košice region in easternmost Slovakia, but their shapes differ. The eaves jutting far out into the yard are supported by a row of columns or pillars ending with a capital. In older buildings these columns or pillars are quite massive and are connected at the bottom by a low wall. In the second half of the nineteenth century they were built lighter and taller; the low walls either disappeared or were replaced by a lighter balustrade. Elsewhere the eaves are held by variously shaped arched arcades. In the east the eaves are supported by wooden columns joined by a decorative wooden balustrade, ornamentally carved, which also makes smaller the open space between the balustrade and the eaves.

In south-western Slovakia as well as in southern and central Moravia one can find small portals of different forms, shaped from clay or built of adobe bricks in front of the entrances to houses and farm buildings. There are often several such small portals along the length of the house front facing the yard. They are called by different names, of which the most popular is the Moravian *žudro*. Houses built of clay, too, usually face the yard, which means that they stand on one side of the plot. A narrow façade with two windows faces the street. These façades are divided at regular intervals by the open spaces of the yards. Between the houses there are gates leading into the individual yards. In exceptional cases, these gates are made of wooden frames with a wicker filling, but most frequently they are of a more solid construction of wooden beams and planking. In some places they were richly decorated with carved geometrical and scroll patterns. In south-western Slovakia, just as in southern Moravia, the space between the individual houses was filled by a wooden shed — a structure of columns supporting a hipped roof. The shed was actually a passageway into the yard and was closed from the street with a gate.

The clay structures are usually covered with thatched roofs, but occasionally we also find saddleback roofs with frontal gables. In southernmost Slovakia there even exist saddleback roofs with a purlin supported by forked columns. These belong amongst the oldest structural elements in European architecture. Clay houses with gables can also be found on the Morava River. These were the homes of Anabaptists, called *Habans*, and their composition and shape are exceptional in this environment.

In a number of places, near Levice and in the vicinity of Košice in eastern Slovakia, hipped roofs developed into gambrel roofs with gables at the top, the surface of the gables being decoratively carved. Some decorative effect is also obtained from gables made of wickerwork, though sometimes they were covered with clay plaster.

Buildings with walls made of wickerwork are as common in this area as those of clay. However, they were exclusively farm buildings. Amongst the most interesting wickerwork structures are some barns in western Slovakia. They have low walls, plastered on the inside with clay, and gambrel roofs which extend close to the ground.

In this whole area it was possible until recently to find many houses and farm buildings of very primitive forms. Some of these are still standing, though now they are very rare. Most remarkable in this respect are the bread ovens situated in the yard outside the houses. They are built of clay and, less frequently, of stone. The oldest were hemispherical in shape; the more recent ones look like little houses with saddleback roofs and chimneys. The earlier type has to this day retained the shape of prehistoric ovens as we know them from archaeological finds.

Any picture of Czech or Slovak villages would be incomplete without their numerous religious structures. Wooden and stone crosses, wayside chapels of all sizes, large and small belfries, churches and graveyards play no small part in shaping the character of the Czech, Moravian and Slovak landscape. The church buildings are especially interesting. Their design was determined by liturgical needs and their architectural expression was developed to utmost perfection by professional architects. Therefore the appearance of the village church depends basically on the style prevalent in its particular period of building. Nevertheless, even here the elements of folk art occur to a considerable extent.

There exist many examples of these sacred structures of all periods which either approach folk architecture or belong fully to it. They include structures built of stone, brick and wood. Some of them are of high artistic value because of the original articulation of their mass and space, the perfect craftsmanship of their construction, and the wealth and high standard of their ornamental *décor*.

The small wooden churches in Silesia, in the Elbe River Basin, in the Orava Valley and in the northern part of eastern Slovakia are most interesting in this respect. Among these, the Bojkov and Lemkov groups of churches are outstanding in their pronounced, three-part lay-out, for their interiors and for their unique structural and architectural elements. We must add to them the *Hucul* type of small churches built on a cross-shaped ground plan, though some of these structures approach monumental dimensions.

One important question is that of the relationship between urban and rural architecture. Both common and distinguishing elements of the two architectures were already emerging in the period of advancing feudalism, as a more pronounced distinction between the two environments developed. In the early stages of their growth, many towns did not greatly differ from the villages in the character of their buildings. The differences grew with the advancing consolidation of the towns. However, the factors which tied the urban environment to the country never really disappeared, especially since the population of many (especially of the smaller) towns continued to farm. Therefore, too, purely village structural elements and types of buildings persisted in the towns for quite a long time.

On the other hand, some features of urban architecture appeared in the villages. Naturally, the development of village houses was guided by the needs of the rural, farming population, but it was not blind to new stimuli coming from the towns. Of these we should mention primarily the introduction of chimneys, black kitchens and tiled stoves. The same is true of stone and brickwork vaulting, some forms of portals and window jambs, stucco *décor*, etc. Many of these features thus became characteristic not only of urban architecture, but also of the rural areas. The urban elements were usually absorbed by the rural environment, though adapted and frequently transformed. Thus, for example, stylistic decorative elements were often applied in a newly emerging system irrespective of their original meaning and intent. It is in this creative transformation of principles and details that the originality and artistic value of folk architecture lies. It is for this that folk architecture has its place in the life of twentieth-century man as an artistic heritage of the past, which speaks to our soul with its own unique and original language.

IV. Form and Ornament

66 WROUGHT-IRON SEPULCHRAL CROSS,
19th century, south Bohemia.

HARMONY OF
UTILITY AND
AESTHETICS

It is a special feature of folk art that a chapter dealing with architecture cannot be followed — as has become customary in textbooks on the history of art — by chapters on painting, sculpture and, finally, on applied art, for we must remember that all popular artistic creation is 'applied'. Even painting and sculpture have their non-artistic role, as already indicated in the chapter on art in the life of the people. However, we are interested in these objects as carriers of an artistic message, of artistic values, primarily from the viewpoint of their form. Form is the product of the function of the object — its role as a piece of furniture or clothing, a tool or a vessel. But at the same time it is an expression of the author's aesthetic endeavour and is determined by the harmony or conflict between his efforts and ideas on the one hand and his abilities and skill on the other. It may be that ornamentation, which is so profuse in folk art, is sometimes unwittingly assigned the role of concealing this disagreement, to make up, by its perfection and thematic wealth, for the absence of something which is not always given to the folk artist. This seems to be indicated by the overabundant decoration of the interiors of some guest rooms in village homes, and by Sunday and festive finery which in most cases was the product of the final stage of development of folk culture in the period with which we are concerned. The knowledge that the maximum is being attained is already accompanied by a foreboding of the end, a feeling that there is no longer a way ahead in this direction.

However, at the beginning and in the classic age (end of the 18th and the first half of the 19th century) when the development of folk culture had reached its zenith, ornamentation and decoration — which is not always quite the same thing — had a different meaning. And yet even then its significance was not only that of a magic symbol, but lay in the very artistic structure of the object created by the popular artist.

The tension between the form and the ornament, and their resulting harmony, are quite prominent, for instance, in the embroidered 'arrowhead' bodices from the Těšín area or the paintings on glass from Frýdek, to give only two of many possible examples. In the composition and furnishing of a room they are not very striking, and yet they are there. The classic minimum requirements for a room (a table in the corner opposite the oven, benches around) constitute the basic form, which was subsequently supplemented with additional articles. Ornamentation was increasingly applied in their *décor*. Older pieces of furniture — tables and chairs — are all of a single colour and are carved. Whilst the tables have articulated footrests, the backs of chairs are decorated with a heart-shaped cut-out and frequently also with ornamental relief. Their essentially Gothic shape is rusticated and only moderately developed. On the other hand, the younger pieces of furniture (painted chests, corner cabinets, beds with or without a canopy, wardrobes, cupboards, cradles) are more colourful. They are frequently decorated with a rich variety of hues. This decoration supplements the basic structure of the different pieces of furniture, is subordinated to it and always appears in segmented and framed fields. The shape of village furniture was determined and altered by stylistic developments from the Renaissance to the end of the nineteenth century. In some regions rusticated Neo-Gothic and Neo-Renaissance forms were also made use of. Decoration remained in its essence, which was floral, true to its inspiration from Renaissance painted ceilings. However, it reacted sensitively to the Baroque expansion of forms as well as to the example set by Empire landscapes and figurative painting. The peak period of this painted furniture lasted from 1700 to 1870. Painting with glue-based colours was supplemented in northern Bohemia with marbling and in Silesia with engraving. The ornamentation never had the character of a symbol.

67 WROUGHT-IRON SEPULCHRAL CROSS, *early 19th century, Klatovy area, south-western Bohemia.*

Whitewashed interior walls, as they appeared increasingly from the beginning of the nineteenth century onwards, were supplemented in the houses of the wealthier Catholic families with something of a picture gallery above a corner table used for family ceremonies, consisting of a row of engravings, paintings on glass and, later, colour prints. In villages and small towns along the lower reaches of the Morava River women used to decorate certain parts of the interior walls, after these had been freshly painted, with simple finger-drawings in the manner of *graffiti*, which uncovered the old wall paint Later, especially talented women known as *maléréčky* decorated the halls and living rooms around the oven with colourful floral ornaments arranged in clusters or in strips; into these floral motifs they sometimes introduced masterfully drawn birds — for instance, a cock, a peacock or a pelican.

The forms and decorations of folk dress are extremely varied. The dress worn by village people in some European countries from the seventeenth to the nineteenth centuries evolved, mainly under the impact of the Renaissance and the Baroque, into a typical product of popular aesthetic feeling and therefore has become an attractive subject for ethnographers. The folk costumes of the Slav nations in particular are characterized by a great wealth of variety and colourful decoration, and among these nations the Czechs and Slovaks hold a leading place. Whilst the Czech population drew its inspiration mostly from the West, the Slovaks and the inhabitants of the Moravian parts of the Carpathian Range were also influenced from the east and the south.

DRESS

The main part of the traditional women's dress in Czechoslovakia was a straight, narrow chemise made of hemp or linen cloth, still called *rubáč* in the eastern part of the country to this day, and held on the shoulder by a single, diagonal strip of linen.

WOMEN'S DRESS

68 WEATHERCOCK,
19th century, Moravia.

Skirts were tied over the chemise from the back and aprons from the front. This basic model (supplemented by sleeves and bodices) resulted from the Renaissance replacement of the one-piece medieval tunic by a new type of dress divided at the waist. The *rubáč*, which was originally the only piece of clothing worn in the summer, eventually became an undergarment. For a long time it was not considered a garment which should be covered. To this day, for example, the saffron-yellow, finely pleated skirts of the dress worn by the women of Velká in Slovácko provide an effective contrast to the white of the *rubáč*. The other outer parts of the dress — skirts and aprons, bodices, jackets and fur jackets — were subject to changes in fashion and formed geographically limited variations. They were frequently supplemented by a Renaissance ruff or an embroidered, square-cut Baroque collar. However, in almost every case a figure was thus created with a remarkable sense of the style of the particular region, characterized by a conspicuous silhouette. Once it was an archaically wrapped figure in white skirts and linen squares (the village women from the mountainous Jablunkov area, as depicted by Josef Mánes in 1846), at other times it was reminiscent of the Renaissance with its white, embroidered costume made of home-made white linen (the women of Čičmany in western Slovakia). But we also encounter more expensive materials. A Haná bride had an opulent ruff made of many yards of lace. In some localities it was not until the Biedermeier period that Baroque-like, billowing and brilliantly hued brocades and fine embroideries on thin fabrics came to be used (the Blata area of South Bohemia, south-eastern Moravia and Slovakia). In Moravia the Empire period had such a strong impact that it almost eliminated the Baroque. In the Valašsko (Walachian) region a woman would not go to church without a small bouquet of fresh, fragrant flowers in her *décolleté*. In south-western Bohemia, on the other hand, a Chod woman with her red stockings is both serious and colourful in her Sunday dress. There are scores of regional types of traditional costume with pronounced variations in each of the three geographical areas — Bohemia, Moravia and Slovakia.

MEN'S DRESS

The basic garment of the men's dress, too, was the shirt. With the strength of its material — rather coarse in the older types — the simplicity of its cut and decoration, and its length, it also partly replaced the medieval tunic, although the tradition of the ancient, 'Barbarian' breeches in the eastern part of Czechoslovakia is also prominent. Breeches of different types and colours were often richly decorated with embroidery or lacing and were supplemented with waistcoats and different types of coats, fur jackets and fur coats, which in many cases were strikingly embroidered. The Slovak and East Moravian greatcoats made of greyish or white woollen homespun are of great originality and beauty. These coats are truly monumental garments which by their length and volume, rustic material, ingenious cut and great, square-cut collars, give their wearers majestic dignity. There are many different types of coats, ranging from the solemn *šerka* — a long coat from grey homespun — worn by the Chods, to the Walachian *župica* made of green broadcloth with a shaped waist, or the Haná *carrick*. These types, too, adopted from the fashions of different periods, were adapted to fit the wardrobe of the country people.

ACCESSORIES AND
FOLK COSTUMES

The accessories of the country dress reflected original features of folk creation and also adopted or adapted external influences. Thus, primitive footwear (for example,

90

sandals shaped from a single piece of leather or home-made cloth, etc.) was gradually replaced by laced and buckled shoes. In the eastern part of the country, perhaps under the impact of the Turkish wars, women's dress included high boots of many types and colours, sometimes made of soft leather. Similar changes affected hair-styles and headgear, although in many places the traditional, ceremonial forms for both men and women survived.

TEXTILE MATERIALS

The basic materials for garments, originally made usually at home, were linen (hemp or flax) and woollen homespun, which were supplemented by leather and fur. Producing linen was the woman's job — from sowing the flax or hemp seed to spinning the yarn — and frequently she also processed the sheep's fleece. In some places the weaving was done at home; elsewhere the yarn was given to a professional weaver to process, and the cloth was made by drapers. From the seventeenth century on-wards, these basic materials were supplemented and, in Bohemia, soon replaced by fabrics bought in the market. The early simple colours (white or natural beige in the case of linen and off-white or greyish in the case of woollen cloth) were augmented after the Thirty Years War by domestic and imported dyes. Birch bark was used to dye cloth black (black was the colour for formal occasions and its use was stimu-lated by a wave of fashion), woad was used for blue, while the rich yellows of the women's skirts in the Horňácko district of south-eastern Moravia were obtained from saffron, which was also used to tint the lace on the ruffs of the Haná women's dress. There were, of course, professional dyers, too, associated in guilds. In the nine-teenth century small workshops in country towns produced blue-print fabric — made by a batik-like process — and supplied it mainly to the territories of Moravia and Slovakia where, from the second half of the eighteenth century onwards, it had become an essential component of the peasants' dress. In the Haná region, around the towns of Uničov and Přerov, the blue-print fabric was supplemented with addi-tional colours — most frequently yellow and red — in an effort to achieve greater variety. In the south of Moravia blue-print aprons were also embroidered. However, blue-print fabric soon became a material for everyday use because, in addition to its relatively low cost and its beauty, it was also highly practical.

DYEING

BLUE-PRINTS

In the nineteenth century festive dress was enriched with a number of skirts, some of which were made of silk rep, brocade or even satin. The cheaper skirts from linen, fustian or blue-print fabric remained underneath. The flax linen of the shirts and em-broidered squares began to be replaced by finer and thinner cotton material. From the Empire period onwards (in Bohemia roughly from 1820 and in Moravia after 1830) women covered their heads and shoulders with richly decorated and colourful Leipzig or 'Turkish' scarves. Even in the eighteenth century, village women took to wearing the gold-braided bonnets which they saw being worn by burghers' wives.

RARE MATERIALS

Weaving was an ancient and widespread craft in what is today Czechoslovakia. The possibility of dyeing and combining flax and wool fibres produced, in the nine-teenth century, patterned woven fabrics — sometimes made by a professional weaver who was frequently given instructions by the customer as to the pattern and colours which should be used. At other times they were made by the farmer or his wife for their own use. The most common fabric of this kind was striped or checked gingham manufactured in the Czech Lands chiefly between 1840 and 1880. Special mention

PATTERNED FABRICS

should be made of cloth from the Horňácko district of south-eastern Moravia, which did not reach the peak of its production until the last third of the nineteenth century. It has survived with certain modifications almost to this day, and is the western-most example of the Carpathian technological variety of weaving on simple looms. Especially effective, too, are east Slovak fabrics made of flax, hemp and cotton. They are not technologically uniform. We distinguish four principal types frequently used for components of the ordinary dress as well as for accessories of the festive dress (match-maker's towels, tablecloths, ceremonial linen squares) and for interior decoration (bedspreads, pillowcases, etc.). The technical as well as the artistic quality of these east Slovak fabrics, the wealth of their patterns and harmony of colours exceed anything that has been created by the local population in this field on Czecho-slovak territory.

EMBROIDERY

After the Thirty Years War the inhabitants of villages and small towns were swept by a desire to embroider and decorate almost everything, which helped to differ-entiate folk dress geographically and socially, and made embroidery essential for the dress of the village population. However, in the period from 1830 to 1840 em-broidery types diverged in some respects. One line continued to develop the traditional dress, while the other line, represented, for example, by the 'white embroidery' of the Walachian area, pursued the thorny path of exacting and low-paid production for the urban markets, as had been the case with lace-making.

The oldest documents of advanced folk embroidery in the Czech areas are ante-pendium cloths donated to churches by village women, often showing an embroidered date and the name of the donor. They come from the seventeenth and eighteenth centuries. In Slovakia and eastern Moravia no less important documents are broad ceremonial cloths made of two strips of embroidered linen, connected longitudinally by netting, with an embroidered bouquet of flowers, the Tree of Life, heraldic birds, the Lamb of God, Abraham's sacrifice, etc. The themes of these embroideries are reminiscent of the Renaissance pattern-books published at the end of the sixteenth and in the seventeenth century and used as models for embroidering the trousseaux of the nobility. We know today that skilful village women bound by the *corvée* used to be called to work on the trousseaux, and from there — in spite of a ban by the lord of the manor — artistic needlework made its way into folk culture by the usual route through the church, the mayor's house, the mill and the bigger and richer farmsteads. At first this decoration was used on ceremonial articles, linen squares and scarves, but later on it appeared on women's sleeves and men's shirts. In this way the people learned all the popular Renaissance techniques of needlework. This wealth of beauty was a true revelation for the Czech and Slovak villages and small towns. After the horrors and desolation of the Thirty Years War and in spite of the increasing repression of the second serfdom, the people slowly recovered and gradually created in this modest postwar boom — if one may use this term at all — their own concept of culture, which, while based on reasonable economy, was marked by a great sense of social grace, especially in home furnishings and in festive dress.

69   IRON CROSS, *1890, originally from the hill country of south-western Bohemia.*

70   BRASS-PLATE BINDING OF A PRAYER-BOOK, *1839, south-western Bohemia.*   ▶

93

72 PAINTED CUPBOARD,
*folk Baroque, first half of the
19th century, north Bohemia.*

◄

71 DETAIL OF A CUPBOARD
FROM NORTH BOHEMIA,
about 1800.

73 WARDROBE CHEST, *dated 1874, western Slovakia.*

74 PAINTED TOY CRADLE, *north Bohemia.*

75 BACK OF A CHAIR, *1799, north-eastern Bohemia.* ▶

76 WOODEN PEW FROM THE WOODEN CHURCH OF
ST JOHN THE BAPTIST IN SLAVOŇOV. *Detail. 18th century,
north-eastern Bohemia.*

77 WEDDING IN THE CHEB AREA (WESTERN
BOHEMIA). *Detail from an early 19th-century watercolour
painting.*

▶

◄

78 EMBROIDERY FROM THE COLLAR OF A WOMAN'S
CHEMISE, *about 1900, south-eastern Moravia.*

◄

79 DETAIL OF A BLUE-PRINTED APRON WITH
EMBROIDERY, *about 1900, south-eastern Moravia.*

80 WOVEN PILLOWCASE, *early 20th century, eastern Slovakia.*

81, 82 BRIDE AND BRIDEGROOM FROM THE BECHYNĚ AREA, *south Bohemia. Gouache on paper, 1836.*

▶

83 YOUNG GIRL FROM MORAVSKÉ LIESKOVÉ, *western Slovakia, mid-20th century.*

84 DETAIL OF THE DECORATION OF A MAN'S COAT, *southern Slovakia, 20th century.*

85, 86 **EMBROIDERY ON A WEDDING SCARF OF 1706.** *Kostelec nad Vltavou, south Bohemia.*

87 **EMBROIDERY ON A CEREMONIAL LINEN SQUARE,** *19th century, Moravia.* ▶

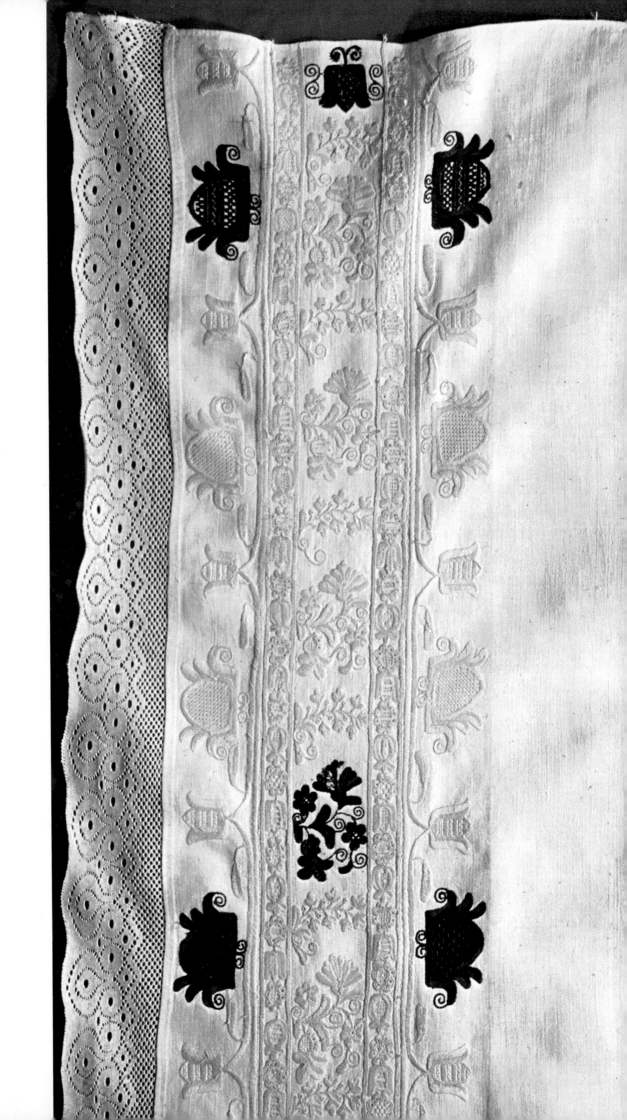

89 NETWORK INSERTION WITH EMBROIDERY ON THE THEME OF ABRAHAM'S SACRIFICE, AND LACE BORDER. *Detail of antependium, 19th century, central Slovakia.*

88 BLUE-PRINTED APRON WITH TWO-COLOURED PATTERN. *Detail. Liptov, central Slovakia, end of 19th century.*

90 INSERTION FROM CORNER HANGINGS. *Detail. About 1800, central Slovakia.*

91 DETAIL OF EMBROIDERED INSERTION FROM 18th-CENTURY CORNER HANGINGS, *central Slovakia.*

92 CORNER EMBROIDERY FROM A WALACHIAN WOMAN'S SCARF, *19th century, Moravia.* ▶

93 SATCHEL KNOWN AS A *CÍGR, dated 1826, south Bohemia.*

Reference is most often made to folk Baroque, but where decoration and ornaments used on traditional dress or in village architecture are concerned, we can speak primarily of folk Renaissance, although a delayed one. In Slovakia we can also trace Turkish influences in folk ornaments and the use of colours.

The Baroque, Rococo and Empire trends in embroidery also affected folk art. While in Slovakia the course of history prolonged the life of the Renaissance style, in Bohemia it was the Baroque which left a profound imprint on folk art. The Counter-Reformation created a means of winning over the people through art which made use of phantasmic effects, picturesqueness, and the mellowing of regular Renaissance forms. To the classic Renaissance combination of red and blue hues a veritable flood of yellows and purple was sometimes added. The scarves of the Blata and Pilsen regions flowered with rich, exuberant and heavy patterns. Home-made linen cloth was replaced by fine cotton batiste which blossomed with floral patterns of many new colours, although the popularity of white persisted. The new colours were further embellished with silver and gold threads and trinkets, in the Blata area even with fish scales. Colourful tailor's and shoemaker's embroidery on breeches, bodices, fur jackets, shoes and boots reached the peak of its excellence, making use of colourful cloths and satins, wools and silks, ribbons and braids. Gold- and silver-braided bonnets alternated with embroidered silk bonnets. Frequently they were embellished with long, wide ribbons, light green or pink, with fine, woven ornamentation.

The refining influence of the Rococo and the Empire styles produced fine white embroidery which gained fame especially in Moravia (in the Štramberk, Telč and particularly the Rožnov areas) where true masterpieces of this type were produced in the 1830's to 1850's. White embroidery was also quite widespread in Bohemia and Slovakia. The subsequent development of embroidery in the period when traditional dress was gradually disappearing on the one hand consisted in enlarging the patterns and adding colour to a more naturalistic floral ornament, and, on the other hand, was influenced by the trend towards cultivating 'national distinctiveness'.

While embroidery decorates the base on which it is developed and which can exist without it, lace is produced, like fabric, in free space. Modern Czech lace stresses this spatial nature in contrast to the flat character of the traditional lace. Its shape is the same as the ornament it creates. In traditional folk lace we rarely meet with abstract patterns, these being genetically older and deriving from simpler techniques. More frequently we find younger floral patterns which draw — as does embroidery — on the heritage of the Renaissance, on Oriental influences and on the native imagination reshaping domestic and exotic forms of vegetation.

Lace became a part of Czech and Slovak folk textiles in the seventeenth century. It softened the hard outlines of scarves and linen squares and later also of *décolletés* and shirt sleeves, of bonnets and aprons, and formed wavy ruffs. The ruff of a Haná bride required several yards of lace. Lace mellowed, lightened and enlivened the material of a dress or a decorative fabric. It was produced by a number of different techniques — netting, drawn thread work, loom- or needle-knitting, crochet, needle-point, and bobbin — of which the last was most frequent. Different materials were used for lace-making — bleached or natural flax yarn, thin white and heavily starched cotton thread, raw silk or nettle fibres. The lace was of a single colour (white, fawn, black, gold, silver) or supplemented the basic colour with a thread of a different hue, which, as the strip of lace grew, followed and emphasized the basic line of the pattern. Sometimes the lace formed the entire object, such as a bonnet, and sometimes two types of lace were combined. Thus in the Walachian region a piece of needlepoint lace, known as *mřežka*, was sewn onto a network bonnet to adorn the forehead.

In the history of the art of lace-making, questions are raised mainly with respect to bobbin lace. Its development in Bohemia was influenced by workshops and schools run by the nobility in the sixteenth and seventeenth centuries, especially in the Ore and Orlické Mountains and in the Chodsko district, where village girls used to learn how to make bobbin laces of the Brussels, Valenciennes and Flanders types. This laid the basis for an extensive production of lace in these areas in workshops and in people's homes, not only for supplying local towns and villages, but also for export to Moravia and Slovakia, as well as to Poland, Romania and even Turkey. Slovakia had its own lace which is remarkable for its originality. Its coarser material, more pronounced striped themes, colour accents and the inventiveness of its own original designs distinguish this lace from Bohemian laces, perhaps with the exception of those made in the Chodsko district. In this respect much can be explained by close contact with the Italian Renaissance, by rustication of the patterns and especially by the unusual and uninhibited way in which the Slovak craftsmen also adapted other imported achievements (e.g. painting on glass).

JEWELLERY

In traditional folk dress a role similar to that of lace was played by jewellery in the form of brooches, buckles, buttons, hairpins, combs, or in pure decoration. There also existed quite primitive jewellery made of beads or even of dried berries and spices strung on a piece of thread. There is an old and well developed tradition of metal jewellery (made of copper, brass, iron, lead or tin) shaped by casting or working and sometimes further embellished by engraving or embossing. This was made by village blacksmiths, locksmiths, tinsmiths, and in Slovakia by older shepherds, who sold their products in the markets or at country fairs. A classic piece of Czech folk jewellery was a heart-shaped pin with two little birds on top in a heraldic composition. Such *bijouterie* was set with Bohemian garnets or polished pieces of coloured glass (in the Chodsko district and Eastern Bohemia). Cast hairpins were decorated with ornamental profiles which were usually embossed. Another type of hairpin, known as *třaslice*, was made more attractive by the glitter of light beads and other trinkets. A remarkably fine piece of jewellery for men was the round *kotula* — a large, decorative button made of mother-of-pearl with a gently waved edge pierced with several tiny holes and engraved with foliated ornamentation. Different types of copper and brass brooches and clasps were quite widespread. The most precious, however, were the jewels which, although of urban origin, were produced and worn in the Těšín area until recently. They were made of silver and its alloys and were sometimes combined — for greater effect and fine colour harmony — with gilded silver. Their surfaces often consisted of several layers of decoration in relief, basically cast and supplemented with chiselling and filigree or with tiny festoons made of miniature ringlets. In this manner beautiful women's belts with rosettes, richly decorated necklaces and clasps were produced in the Těšín area. Their motifs were often taken from animal life and mythology (a mermaid). Filigree silver jewellery was also still made in western and central Slovakia at the beginning of the twentieth century. The filigree technique is frequently linked with the handicraft traditions of Eastern Europe, but the fact is that the techniques of producing this jewellery have been common to European goldsmiths and silversmiths since the Middle Ages and the Renaissance.

The use of alloys of copper and sometimes even of iron, lead and tin for making cheaper jewellery indicates how rare and expensive a material metal used to be for country people. They treasured it so much that even utilitarian objects made of metal were often given a fine form and decoration. The blacksmith's art in what is today Czechoslovakia developed quite early in connection with the primitive smelting of ore and with the subsequently devised water-powered forges known as *hamry*. Profiled and chiselled patterns made up of several tiny, variously arranged motifs were sometimes used to decorate sickles, spades and axes, and were almost always found on the metal parts of waggons, chests, doors and windows. The best examples of this work again demonstrate a rare interplay of form and ornamentation. Decoration is always a subdued affair, subjected to the shape of the object. Since the Middle Ages artistic form was given to candlesticks, kindling wood holders and spit supports. In fruitful contact with professionally trained craftsmen and artisans, village workshops also produced different types of wrought-iron crosses or weather vanes in the symbolical shapes of birds, the Sun and the Moon, etc.

The popularity of brass can be explained by its colour, glitter and resonance, as well as by its relative workability. Slovakia's Jelšava became famous for its cow and sheep bells of different shapes and tones, which used to be exported to Lower Hungary and Transylvania. In the Orava Valley such bells were cast and worked by the shepherds themselves. The most valuable brass products are book bindings decorated with an embossed ornamentation or relief figures of saints or the Pietà, and set with ground and polished pieces of glass or Bohemian garnets. These gems of folk handicraft, for example from western Bohemia, are very close to Czech jewellery both technically and in their conception of form.

However, neither textile, as an already artificially pre-processed material, nor metal, as a raw-material requiring rather exacting extraction and treatment, is the basic and most typical material used in folk culture. That material was wood, which could be worked in countless ways. Wooden articles seem to exude the warmth of organic matter. A variety of colours, shades, structural patterns, a wide choice of hardness and grain are only some of the advantages offered by wood, the classic material used by villagers. It was plentiful when the country was covered with large forests. Much has already been written of the symbiosis of man and the tree from which he built his home, farm, place of worship and the cross for his grave, and from which he shaped his tools and implements, his kitchen utensils and the idols and symbols which he venerated. Each of the techniques of wood-working also offered the villager a means of shaping his material in an aesthetically satisfying way and sometimes of developing his creative thinking, his phantasy and invention.

From wood the ancient tillers of the land in what is today Czechoslovakia shaped some perfect tools and vessels which may rightly be described as masterpieces of folk arts and crafts. They include some old textile and farming machines, woodworking benches, flax-breaking frames, chaff blowers, etc., well-designed sets made of finely shaped parts and lightly decorated with carved or notched ornaments in parts which were not functional. The best known of such items, outstanding for their ornamental decoration, are distaffs. Some spinning-wheels and windles, too, were decorated with carved ornaments and sometimes even with figural designs. Carved butter moulds which are most frequently decorated with relief bouquets of flowers are especially worthy of interest.

CARPATHIAN WOOD-CARVING

Slovakia and to a certain extent Silesia and Moravia are also linked with the Balkans, Transylvania and Trans-Carpathian Ukraine by the decorative wood-carvings of the Carpathian shepherds. These Carpathian carvings form a component part of a specific culture which grew out of the closeness of man to Nature. This is the source of the different types and time-tested forms of cheese-making implements and vessels and the furnishings of shepherds' chalets, of the monumental shapes of Walachian horns and the sensitive modelling of primitive violins, of the inlaid shepherds' *fuyaras*, and the metal ornamentation of knife hafts. A parallel to the butter moulds in this region are two-part moulds for *oštěpek* — a type of smoked sheep's milk cheese — decorated with a large central theme, frequently that of a bird.

SHEPHERDS' JUGS

One vessel which became quite popular was the *črpák*, a wooden jug for sheep's milk whey, shaped from a hollowed piece of wood, secured at the bottom with a metal hoop or withy and fitted with a large, decorative handle. In the nineteenth century these handles were richly carved and this carved decoration developed in several different ways. The simplest type of shepherds' jug is the westernmost variant from the Jablunkov and Těšín districts with an ornamentally decorated horizontal handle. The jugs from Slovakia's Liptov region, which are taller and have a narrower base, are decorated with a snake's head on a protruding neck, recalling medieval miniatures, magic, and fairy tales. Another type of shepherds' jugs is to be found in the Detva region of central Slovakia. They are short and cylindrical and have a wealth of decorative relief showing scenes from the life of the shepherds, such as the milking of sheep, fighting with a bear, a shepherd playing his *fuyara*, etc. These figural carvings often depict surprisingly well and tersely a typical shape or motion. There are also scenes of men and animals interestingly arranged along the curve of the handle. Although this is a relatively late manifestation of period interest in genre scenes, the end product is an original type which incorporates realistic scenes in the ornamental composition of the *črpák*. In a number of other artefacts this basic ornamental system becomes more pronounced and adopts forms of typical Slovak architecture, such as the Renaissance elements of the attic storey, known as swallows' tails, or forms of stylized animal bodies.

CORN BINS

Differing from this normal shepherds' production is a special type of chest which is an important example of the shepherds' culture and which by its sarcophagus-like shape and by the basic features of its construction seems to indicate not only a Balkan origin, but perhaps an origin which dates back to late Antiquity. Its relationship with other cultures has not yet been fully clarified, since we know of similar chests from the Alps and from the north and west of Europe. Some scholars are sure that these chests, called *súsky*, developed from medieval types, while others are convinced that the striking parallels in historical styles have a purely technical origin — that is, they arise from the way the chests were made. This purely technical aspect seems untenable as the sole explanation in view of the expressive and sophisticated form of these chests. This viewpoint, however, might be entertained where the engraved decoration of the fire-blackened surfaces of these chests, usually used as corn bins or for storing flour, is seen as a symbol of the Sun, while the ornaments of six-petalled targets are a natural division of the circle when using carpenter's compasses.

A comparison with similar corn bins from Romania, Poland and Trans-Carpathian Ukraine proves the universality and the antiquity of this type in Carpathian folk culture. In Slovakia some interesting, smaller *súsky* were produced as bridal chests for the safekeeping of the more valuable part of the dowry; they were made with a fine sense of proportion and were painstakingly decorated.

We may say in general that the woodwork done by the shepherds was mostly of an ornamental character. This is well documented by several types of openwork spoon racks from the Tatra area, laundering or mangling bats with heavy ornamental engraving or relief, and by the inlay decoration of shepherds' *fuyaras*. The shepherd used these previously exclusively functional objects as providing an opportunity for demonstrating his skill as a carver, his compositional talent and his wealth of motifs. These objects then became products made for sale, as did the later, figurally decorated shepherds' jugs. They were intended for sale to wealthier households, and eventually became the objects of tourists' and collectors' interest in the special vanishing culture of the Slovak mountain pastures and shepherds' chalets.

Wood is also the material used for many traditional toys, later manufactured by cottage industry in several Czech and Slovak centres. Of course, toys do not actually belong in this chapter in which we are trying to trace the harmony of form and ornamental decoration. They were often made by the children themselves or by their parents from pieces of fabric, clay, maize husks, pieces of wood and various natural products. Most toys were made, however, by semi-professionals. Unless they were sculptured (and thus belong to the sphere of figural carving and modelling) they are related to some of the types already mentioned here. Thus children's wheelbarrows and toy cradles produced in Valašská Bystřice in Moravia and decorated with yellow linear or circular ornamentation engraved in a fire-blackened surface have the same decoration as the *súsky*, the shepherds' corn bins. Other toys are simple musical instruments (usually pipes) with ornamental decoration.

TOYS

Perfectly functional and pleasantly rounded forms — traditional and newly developed — natural lustre and warm colour, and a feeling of lightness and flexibility — these are all qualities offered by vessels, baskets, smaller forms of furniture, implements and household articles plaited from straw, rushes, reeds, maize husks, withies or rootlets. Wickerwork is a part of folk culture not only in areas along large rivers with thick groves of osier along their banks (the Morava, Danube and Váh, for example), but also in Bohemia. In some places, such as in the Šariš region around Bardejov in eastern Slovakia, baskets were even woven from long, narrow roots. Straw was used in southern Slovakia not only for shallow, plate-like baskets, but also for cylindrical vessels with low, conical lids used for storing bread.

BASKET-MAKING AND NATURAL PLAITING MATERIALS

The same method was used to make straw beehives, primarily in southern Slovakia. The basic component in weaving the hive was a strand of straw twisted round and tied with bast or rootlets. Derived from ceramics, hives were made in the form of

STRAW HIVES

pear-shaped vessels and in Slovakia were usually plastered with clay and fitted with colour accessories to look like the devil's head (the Hont, Novohradsko and Malacky districts). In Bohemia, straw hives were occasionally shaped (in the Tachov district) in the form of a maiden's torso with thick braids. The surviving artefacts date from a later period — the nineteenth and twentieth centuries.

Basket-weavers also worked as craftsmen in the larger towns. In the villages, especially along the rivers, this production was spontaneous and traditional and was carried out without any formal training, mostly on a semi-professional basis, as an auxiliary cottage industry. The products included baskets of different types and sizes, vessels for transporting yeast, and, in southern Slovakia, mats and large butcher's meat satchels were woven from rushes. The technique used in their production often approached that of weaving rather than plaiting or braiding. There exist voluminous pattern-books of the different traditional methods of producing wickerwork, combining barked and rough wicker, plaiting wicker round a straw core, etc. Only in a more recent period have curled, wet maize leaves been used to produce bags of different types, handbags, sandals and similar articles.

In this field, too, just as in the case of decorative textiles or lace, patterns are created directly by the composition of the basic and the auxiliary materials used in the production of the respective article. The pattern is identical with the basic technique. By its properties of colour, lustre, and flexibility the material is the principal factor in the forming of a harmonious combination in which there is nothing superfluous.

CERAMICS

Perhaps even before wood, man used clay for making practical articles and for giving shape to his ideas. Earth itself with its unique properties challenged man to mould it. Food stored in clay vessels, whether it was cooked or fermented, did not lose its aroma or taste. The making of pottery is a profession in which, together with advanced products of high technological and stylistic standards, there has existed for thousands of years production of a definitely folk character. Most of the articles which we consider today to be 'folk ceramics' were, in fact, produced in the workshops of professional potters, often concentrated in particular villages. Up to the Second World War, and in some cases even after the war, these potters used to take their products to markets in provincial towns or displayed their wares at a special potters' market on Kampa Island in Prague. The contact between the manufacturer and the consumer was direct and thus the popularity of certain types and decorative patterns always directly influenced future production.

The decoration of utility vessels remained in most cases at the stage of simple structural shaping, underlined by artistic elements. Into this was set an ornament which was thematically close to other central European folk ceramics and technically differentiated (engraved, painted, marbled, set in relief, etc.), standing, out from the shape of the vessel, the colour of its body and its glazing. These three latter elements are also factors contributing to the creation of a particular type of decoration. Thus, for example, not only in Czechoslovakia but also in Poland, Hungary and Romania so-called 'black' (smoke-blackened) pottery used to be made. This not fully baked, inexpensive type of pottery, produced since the Middle Ages, has an unusual beauty. It was traditionally decorated by the most appropriate method — simple, glossy lines, waves, network and, rarely, simple floral patterns drawn with flint on the matte surface of the unbaked body.

In other types of ceramics, too, the ornamentation logically complemented the form, the charm and rhythm of which people could appreciate when assessing the beauty of kitchen utensils. The most popular types of vessels (jugs, milk and butter pots, 'twin' cups, wine flasks), both plain and glazed, were decorated in a way which harmonized with the colour of the clay and the method of baking, the full or partial glazing, and with the vessel's function. A beautifully concave shape and a fine finish were typical of a special kind of pots used for carrying food. They had a lid and a single large holder at the top, and were called 'corner pots' because neighbourhood women used to carry nourishing food in them to a woman in confinement who lay isolated 'in a corner'. Together with the 'corner hangings' this pot belongs to the old, traditional concept of mother and child care which, while based on ancient superstitions, in fact ensured, under the prevailing conditions of that time, maximum hygiene and proper nourishment for the woman in confinement. The ornamentation on the 'corner pots' and 'corner hangings' does not contain any of the magic symbols against evil and danger that one might expect. The usual decoration of such a pot is sometimes replaced by a first name written in white on the glossy, reddish-brown surface which was the most usual type of utility pottery, especially in the Czech Lands. Of the many former production centres the workshops in Koloveč, in the west Bohemian Chodsko district, and in Moravia at Valašské Meziříčí are still operating today. They still produce this type of pottery, usually with a white decoration in the form of dots, half-circles, stripes, simple blossoms and occasionally birds. At Koloveč this white decoration is also supplemented with subdued colour. In Slovakia there are still several pottery production centres in operation. In some of them — such as the Pozdišovce workshops — pottery has been made since the Middle Ages.

Some white-glazed vessels, in particular Moravian and Slovak faïence, hold a special place in Czech and Slovak ceramics. Their advanced painted decoration, often figural, exceeds the scope of the present chapter, and will be dealt with in the next.

Amongst ceremonial articles, ornamentation is fully applied on painted Easter eggs, which are common almost everywhere in Czechoslovakia. Historical documents show that these eggs were called by their traditional name *kraslice* as early as the fourteenth century. This, together with the discovery of medieval coloured egg-shell fragments, some even showing traces of ornamentation, demonstrates the antiquity of the custom of painting and decorating these ancient symbols of life and fertility. The most frequently used colour was red and, of the natural dyes, reddish-brown, obtained by boiling the eggs with onion skins. The ornamentation, and some particular motifs, such as variations of the swastika, is often surprisingly similar in places quite distant from each other and without means of contact. It may be that these symbols are directly related to magic spells. The obviously symbolic meaning of egg decoration, however, was soon made more complex by new decorative techniques and new pictorial genres and inscriptions. The oldest combinations of themes have apparently come down to us on Easter eggs decorated by a process of batik-like wax painting common in most ethnographic areas of Czechoslovakia. This decoration represents the most typical and traditional form of Czechoslovak Easter eggs abounding in

EASTER EGGS

119

a wealth of compositions, motifs and colours. In other types the ornament depends on the technique used. Thus Easter eggs in which the decoration is scratched into the applied colour usually show shaded blossoms and pomegranates or genre scenes with inscriptions. Etched Easter eggs have patterns similar to those which used to be painted on glass with soap, scratched in wet wall plasters, or sprinkled on earthen floors with water. In the area of Haná a highly elaborate and most effective method was used — that of pasting straw on the eggs; the effect created by the contrast between the light and shaded surfaces of the straw and its natural gloss is very striking. The application of fine rushes, pith of the common elder, small pieces of cloth and even tiny pictures of saints was taught at the end of the last century in convent schools and was thus also used in wealthier town families. But simpler methods of decoration are still in use: finely shaped plant leaves are tied to the eggs before they are dipped in colour, or the eggs are painted with coloured wax which hardens into tear-like droplets creating different floral patterns, stars, etc.

THE GENESIS OF FOLK ORNAMENT

It is clear that many articles in popular use were the result of a search for a certain balance between form and decoration. In spite of the growing emphasis on the richness of decoration which came with advancing techniques, the ornamentation in almost every case was subordinated to the structure of the article and frequently ensued from the technique used. Therefore, the ornament was sometimes geometrical or abstract, perhaps with traces of some ancient symbolism. Often what we consider to be an abstract motif is an abbreviated form of a once realistic shape to which we have lost the key. Figural ornaments on floral, animal and human themes draw from the rich sources of the Renaissance, absorbed from the south in the sixteenth century and from the west in the seventeenth century. These Renaissance influences were supplemented by motifs and combinations typical of subsequent periods of style, but first and foremost, they were enriched with a wealth of rusticated variations and original products of native phantasy and compositional talent.

As the patterns were being developed and compositionally expanded, a strong need was felt to give them a certain rhythm. This need produced different forms, ranging from the very simple to the highly complex. Simple symmetry along a central axis, a simple or interrupted sequence of motifs, a central composition, rhythmic arrangement of details in harmony with the structure of the object — all these are represented in folk art and all have their function. Even in such strikingly developed works as, for example, in the decoration of the original fireplaces in south Slovak interiors, the rhythm which guides the movements of the painter's hand is the determining factor of the composition.

There were times — from the 1880's well into our own century — when scholars and the general public considered folk art and folk ornament to be one and the same thing. Today, without underestimating the exciting problems of its original meanings, affiliation and changes, we view ornamentation as only one component of folk art. However, we are now also attracted by other products of folk art which were ignored in the nineteenth century because of aesthetic prejudice against their sometimes irregular and 'deformed' appearance. These are the branches of popular artistic creation in which the ornamentation is subsidiary and in which the creator devotes himself entirely to figural painting or sculpture.

94 SILVER CLASPS FROM WOMAN'S DRESS IN THE JABLUNKOV AREA, *Silesia, mid 19th century.* ▶

95 SILVER BELT FOR WOMAN'S DRESS, *Těšín area, Silesia, 19th century.*

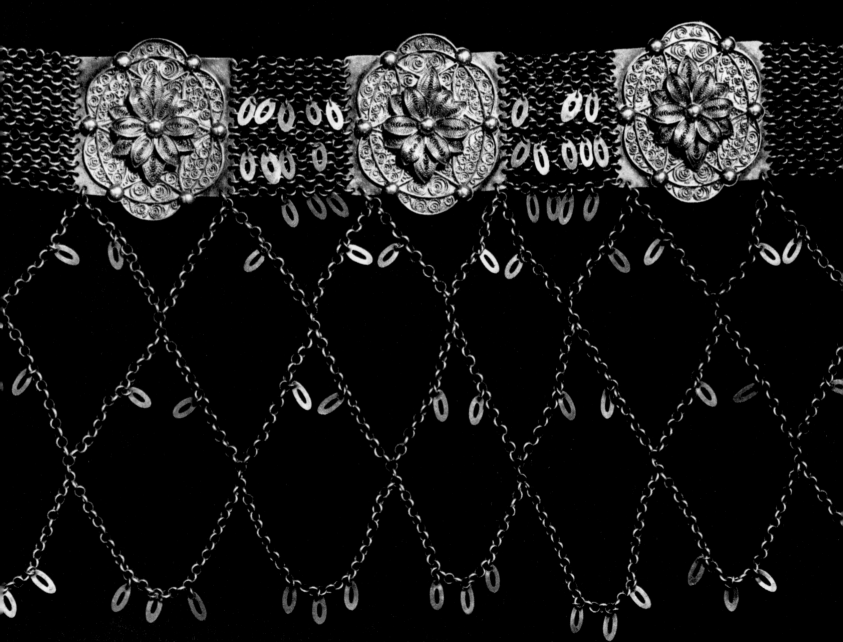

97 WINE-PRESS, *western Slovakia, 1791.*

◄

96 CROSS FROM THE OLD CEMETERY AT DOLANY, *District of Klatovy, south-western Bohemia, late 18th century.*

99 WOODEN SEPULCHRAL CARVING. *Krupina area, central Slovakia, second half of the 19th century.*

100 MANGLING BAT, *courting gift of 1890, Osuské, District of Senica, western Slovakia.*

◄

98 SHEPHERD'S SCULPTURE, *central Slovakia, 20th century.*

101 CORN BIN KNOWN AS A *SÚSEK*, *Luhačovské Zálesí, eastern Moravia.*

OF DETVA TYPE, *central Slovakia, early 20th century.*

102 *SÚSEK CORN BIN, 19th century, Kyjatice, District of Rimavská Sobota, central Slovakia.*

103 SALT BOX FROM ZÁZRIVÁ, *central Slovakia, 19th century.*

104 WOODEN TANKARD, *Železnice, north Bohemia, about 1850.*

107 GLASS JUG AND TUMBLER WITH ENGRAVED DECORATION, *south Bohemia, first half of the 19th century.*

◄

106 *ČRPÁKY* MUGS OF DETVA TYPE (a, b, c), AND LIPTOV TYPE (d), *central Slovakia, 19th and 20th centuries.*

108 CANDLE-MAKER'S VESSEL, *ceramic, dated 1775, eastern Slovakia.*

109 FAÏENCE JUG, *dated 1820, Stupava, western Slovakia.* ▶

112 GINGERBREAD TOYS FROM NORTH BOHEMIA, *18th and 19th centuries.*

◄

110 FAÏENCE JUG, *western Slovakia, second half of the 19th century.*

◄

111 SMOKE-BLACKENED CERAMIC JUG, *Pozdišovce, eastern Slovakia, 19th century.*

113 **SMOKE-BLACKENED CERAMIC STORAGE POT,** *19th century, western Slovakia.*

114 SMOKE-BLACKENED CERAMIC STORAGE POT WITH POLISHED AND RELIEF DECORATION, *first half of the 19th century, south Moravia.*

115 MORAVIAN EASTER EGGS WITH SCRATCHED AND BATIK DECORATION FROM THE WALACHIAN, SLOVÁCKO AND MORAVIAN HIGHLANDS AREAS, *19th and 20th centuries.*

116 POT FROM POZDIŠOVCE AND BATIK-DECORATED EASTER EGGS, *eastern Slovakia, 20th century.* ▶

V. Drawing, Graphics, and Painting

Nowá pjſeň

f Pané Marpi.
Swato-Wamberické.

118 ST ANNE WITH THE VIRGIN MARY AND INFANT JESUS.
Woodcut from the title page of a stall-keepers' print, north Bohemia, 19th century.

DRAWING

The basic form of expression from which both figural painting and sculpture proceed is free drawing. Ornamentation is always created on an already finished form or together with it, so that it is bound to it and always directly influences it in one way or another, strengthening or relaxing it. Figural drawing, on the other hand, has its own objectives. It largely ignores the structure of the object, sometimes even disturbing it (as in coloured drawings on ceramics), and even extending to the frame, as in the case of some relief pictures. At best, it makes use of the space left to it on the object by the ornamentation, filling it with its own content which is closely or loosely related to the purpose and function of that object. In doing so, it most often makes use of the differentiation and effects offered by colour, so that pure drawings are quite rare in folk art.

MEDIEVAL ARTEFACTS
OF POPULAR ORIGIN

Most frequently the drawing is engraved into the surface of an object. Here we must mention rare medieval artefacts whose conspicuously primitive and rustic abbreviations and symbols still do not make them works of folk art. For example, we may point to figures engraved in the harnesses found by archaeologists in tombs from the period of the Great Moravian Empire of the eighth and ninth centuries, to figural and animal drawings on Romanesque capitals and tympana, to some small articles of medieval applied art such as seals and Gothic stove tiles, and to some Renaissance tombstones. We should remember, of course, that because of the nature of stone and stone-cutting techniques, two-dimensional drawing rarely appears on stone, just as it is quite rare in clay. Thus, the most usual form is mostly that of relief. However, if we set aside these relics, we leave open the question as to what extent we can define as being of folk origin those ancient creations which were produced within the framework of the art and handicrafts of the time but which were not included in the mainstream of folk culture.

Perhaps the first major type of product which found its way into folk culture and

141

which made use of rustically simplified drawing were wafer irons — iron pincers for baking and decorating ceremonial wafers. The technique of drawing used is that of iron engraving. The examples we possess of these products of the blacksmith's trade date from 1550—1800. Besides ornamental decoration with geometric and floral themes and heraldic and religious motifs, they show heads and figures of saints, and later even entire scenes from books which were popular among the village people, and frequently other secular themes as well. From the viewpoint of cultural history, for instance, a scene showing work in an iron foundry, depicted on a pair of wafer irons displayed in the Municipal Museum at Železnice, is interesting. The degree to which these artefacts may be considered a form of 'folk art', however, varies and, it may be said, grows as time progresses.

Figural drawings engraved in metal became the principal decoration of the pewter ware designed for festive occasions and weddings. These vessels show pictures of the bride and groom, members of the wedding party and sometimes the musicians, not unlike the embroidery on wedding banners in conception, while on other vessels intended for guild banquets we find scenes from the workshops of various craftsmen. There is no need to stress the importance of these engravings in the study of cultural history, period dress, workshop equipment, etc. The dated pewter plates (1680—1722) from the Ostrava Museum show, moreover, that the process of decorating them, as regards the endeavour to depict human figures and their environment, is not dissimilar to that employed by the village blacksmith, potter or embroiderer. It makes use of the same ingenious reductions which preserve the character of the regional dress and sometimes also of human posture. Simplified engraved drawings were also applied to copper and brass; one of numerous documents from the sphere of bell-founding is, for example, the tongue of the bell from Vranov near Brno with its engraved image of the Holy Virgin of the Corn.

More widespread in the village environment, however, was the engraving of drawings into wood. On the bats used in Slovakia for laundering and mangling, which we have already mentioned, the wealth of decoration, from the beginning of the nineteenth century onwards, in some cases overcame the originally utilitarian purpose of these bats — or rather, short boards with a handle — and turned them into tokens of affection and love or 'art objects' used for interior decoration. It is interesting that in the 1820's some of these bats, for example from the vicinity of Bratislava, depicted not only engraved and carved symbols of life and love (the Sun, hearts, and animal themes) but also Christian themes (Adam and Eve, the Virgin Mary, the Crucifixion, and the Pietà). The engraving on these objects is so fine and inventive that they rank among the most valuable relics of folk figural drawing in Czechoslovakia. They are sometimes said to be close to work inspired by the culture of the Carpathian shepherds. However, as we have already said, in this work the characteristic decoration is not figural drawing inspired by religion, but geometric patterns, abandoned in favour of organic forms only at the end of the nineteenth and the beginning of the twentieth centuries. The bats are reminiscent of the engraved decoration on some wooden beehives. They also bring to mind engravings in the leather of whip handles, as we know them, for example, from a handle depicting the Passion of Christ, bearing the signature of the maker and owner of the whip, Juro Funta.

Figural embroideries executed on a base on which the pattern was first drawn are also a type of drawing. These embroideries developed into remarkable and yet robust and touching forms, especially in eastern Bohemia and in the Bohemian-Moravian Highlands. On 'corner hangings' and especially on wedding banners which in these areas in the nineteenth century used to be the property of the community and under which wedding processions marched to neighbouring villages, various stitches with red and other coloured threads were used to depict the bride, groom and wedding guests, sometimes the entire wedding procession, babies, and humorous scenes. Or a long teamster's belt from south Bohemia is decorated with embroidery showing the teamster with his loaded waggon drawn by six horses. Some of these figural embroideries are said to reflect the influence of German neighbours in ethnically mixed areas. They also occur in a similar environment in Slovakia.

FIGURAL
EMBROIDERIES

In ceramics, engraved drawings are usually limited to patterns, although some stone and roof tiles are exceptions. On the other hand, engraved drawings are plentiful on glass, both of Czech and Slovak origin, which of course can be considered only in part as folk art. Even so, engraved drawings are frequently unequivocally of folk origin. This is especially true of the gift drinking cups and jugs from south Bohemia of the first half of the nineteenth century and bottles from central Slovakia, quadrangular in shape. The engraved decoration of these objects, with ornamental (undulating and spiral lines, scrolls and branches with blossoms) or, more often with figural drawings (for example a drawing of a stylized Madonna and Child, conceived ornamentally and in the style of flat gingerbread moulds) is clearly of 'folk' character.

ENGRAVED DRAWING
ON CERAMICS
AND GLASS

Drawing becomes more precise and some formal features are stabilized in the field of popular woodcuts. Unfortunately no collectors appeared in time to save from destruction what undoubtedly would have been a large number of charming single-sheet woodcuts. Like the woodcuts done by professional artists, which were often coloured by village people, popular woodcuts in many cases depicted themes which the village people considered important, and were executed in a form which was certainly better understood than that used in professional prints. These cheap graphic sheets had roughly the same function as the later paintings on glass. The brilliance achieved by painting on glass was, of course, missing but even so with their hand-coloured light hues, they introduced some colour to a room. They could easily be nailed to the wall or pasted to the inside of a wardrobe door or the lid of a chest without glass or frame, and therefore they were usually destroyed or thrown out when they were no longer required.

WOODCUTS

We somehow feel that only we, in the twentieth century, with our tastes formed by modern art which was inspired by works of the popular imagination, have finally come to understand the artistic value of these woodcuts. Unfortunately very few examples have survived, those which have being found mostly in Moravia and Slovakia. The Slovak woodcuts especially are marked by that charming frankness which some of the greatest artists of the early twentieth century saw as the hope for a revival of simplicity and truth in art. They had undoubtedly undergone considerable development since the sixteenth century — perhaps since even the fifteenth, if we accept as correct the dating on the single-sheet woodcut of the Třeboň Crucifixion with Mary and John, in which tall flowers beside the Cross, large stars in the background and other features are elements which appear in later folk graphics. These graphics are characterized by a considerable degree of formal reduction in the ingenious modelling of the bodies and robes. The scheme often becomes something closely approaching ornamentation and framing the scene with flowers is a favourite device — a feature subsequently taken over by painters on glass. Stress is also laid on features by which certain iconographic and pilgrimage types could easily be identified. All these aspects made the Czech and Slovak woodcuts highly communicative.

To a lesser extent the themes of these single-sheet folk woodcuts are secular, deriving from folklore but also drawing on history and legend. The great majority, however, are religious in theme, related to the engravings of Baroque artists and their provincial imitators working for town publishers. The surviving prints relate to pilgrimage themes from Moravia (the Madonna of Štíp, the Veraicon of Jaroměřice) and Slovakia (the famous Pietà of Šaštín which very frequently occurs in different genres of folk art). Moreover, the woodcuts reproduce many images of saints and religious themes popular in the Czech Lands and Slovakia — St John of Nepomuk, St Florian, St Barbara, the Holy Family and the Holy Trinity, the Passion of Christ, and others. The artists were mostly untrained individuals, who perhaps even made other devotional articles as well to earn their living near places of pilgrimage.

So far only two workshops have definitely been identified. One was operated by the Mašlíks, a family of church fair stall-keepers from Štíp in the Gottwaldov district of Moravia in the eighteenth and nineteenth centuries, the other one by Imrich Spevák of Jastrabá in the Slovak Ore Mountains in the nineteenth century. The surviving blocks and prints give evidence of the purely popular character of these workshops, while older records and documents seem to confirm the probability that Moravian and Slovak woodcuts were exported to the Polish area and to Ukrainian Galicia. The Slovak woodcuts are unique in their use of decoration. As regards the ornamentation on the Moravian prints, it shows a striking similarity to the decoration of the Moravian paintings on glass from the period before and around 1800, which supports the well-founded theory that some of these early paintings were based on woodcuts. In Bohemia, large prints have been preserved only in a few instances and their form indicates a close relationship to works by professionally trained artists. The workshops seem to have been located in Prague, Příbram and Cheb, and there were probably others elsewhere, too.

Surviving in greater numbers are the smaller woodcuts usually used for decorating the title pages and for illustrating the popular stall-keepers' leaflets — religious songs, love songs 'for lads and lasses', ballads reporting on disasters and murders, and sometimes even socially critical songs. These secular pictures, printed from blocks carved with varying degrees of skill, sometimes reveal an Empire sentiment (pairs of lovers, a tombstone with a vase and Cupid); in other instances they are simple although inventive in their eloquence and expression. This is also reflected in numerous pictures of Our Lady of Grace which display a fragility of sentiment and love of ornamentation.

Besides their role as souvenirs with religious, erotic or even sensational and horrifying undertones, the minor woodcuts also had some bizarre uses of a magic nature in the past. This is clear, for example, from sheets of 'swallowing pictures' — tiny engravings or woodcuts depicting the Pietà, the Holy Trinity or the Madonna.

119 WOODCUT FROM THE TITLE PAGE OF A STALL-KEEPERS' PRINT, *Chrudim, eastern Bohemia, 19th century.*

120 WOODCUT ILLUSTRATION, *19th century, south Moravia.*

121 WOODCUT FROM THE TITLE PAGE OF A STALL-KEEPERS' PRINT, *Chrudim, eastern Bohemia, 1864.*

They were supposed to be taken and swallowed as pills during illness or as a protection against the plague in the seventeenth and eighteenth centuries, and the Church administration alternately banned or ignored them. It is interesting that as late as the beginning of the twentieth century the custom was discussed by Central European church authorities. Of a similar magical significance were different folding pictures, such as the Magic of Christ's Length or St Benedict's Cross Against Spells and Magic (preserved among the Štíp woodcuts), which used to be pasted on cowshed doors.

These prints were published in the towns of Vrchlabí, Jindřichův Hradec, Chrudim, Králíky and also Prague in Bohemia, Olomouc and Brno in Moravia, Těšín in Silesia, and Skalica and Banská Bystrica in Slovakia.

BOOK DECORATION

Quite a large category of cultivated, semi-traditional drawing and painting consists of hymn and prayer books written and decorated for village men and women from the end of the seventeenth century to approximately the 1830's. These books were copied by hand and decorated by village teachers and chroniclers. The best known are the illuminated hymn and prayer books from eastern Bohemia and Moravia, but they were common in other regions as well. It seems that their authors, who originally copied them for their own needs and for their friends, later did so on a semi-professional basis. At the same time, they were directly continuing the tradition of the town scribes and illuminators whose workshops had produced the great hymn books of the lay singers' brotherhoods in the sixteenth century. Thus they were also followers of the centuries-old tradition of *scriptoria* and the medieval book illuminators. These village copyists and book decorators first appeared mainly in places where the Counter-Reformation bans and Jesuit censorship prevented the publication of printed

122 LEGEND OF THE HOLY BLOOD IN WALLDÜRN, *woodcut from a printed prayer, Chrudim, eastern Bohemia, about 1850.*

Protestant books. A non-Catholic book could only be produced and distributed in this ancient manner. This example was later followed by Catholic prayer books designed for different occasions.

The decoration of these books is mainly concentrated on the calligraphically ornate title page (which included the year of completion, the author's signature, sometimes a dedication and often a coloured figure drawing), on the framing of the pages, initial letters, and sometimes on a few full-page illustrations. The patterns used were most often woodcuts sold at church fairs. The initials and marginal decorations, usually drawn by pen and lightly coloured, in many instances echoed the medieval drolleries, though with new ideas and themes. The ornamentation drew on simple, universally popular motifs, both abstract and floral, and on the Renaissance heritage, or, to a lesser degree, on the heritage of other period styles with their specific forms and decorative systems. Instead of hand-drawn illustrations, some of these manuscripts contain hand-coloured woodcuts or engravings pasted into them. As regards their calligraphic standard, the formal refinement of their ornament, the invention and degree of skill of the draughtsman, these relics are of greatly varying value.

PAINTING OF WOODEN INTERIORS

Renaissance inspiration found its way into book illumination as a successor to the medieval tradition. However, the main genre which was strongly influenced by Renaissance painting was the painted decoration of timber ceilings and later of wooden furniture. The oldest preserved documents of beam and coffered ceilings in wooden churches and in the attic rooms of parsonages and richer farmsteads reflect the subdued ornamentation of the Renaissance scroll, only rarely supplemented by animal or figural motifs from mythological or religious spheres. After the Thirty Years War, the brilliant craftsmanship of the sixteenth century gave way to a gradual rustication of form. This process can be traced in the interior of the wooden parish church at Slavoňov, built in 1553, which is completely covered with such decoration from the sixteenth and the two following centuries. It can be seen as well on the ceiling and the choir loft of the Church of St Bartholomew at Kočí, which was decorated in 1678, when, after a fire, its Gothic stone nave was supplemented with wooden furnishings. In the eighteenth century some outstanding work was done in decorating attic rooms in the Turnov district, in the Orlické Mountains and elsewhere. Their rich ornamental composition often includes secular scenes, such as ploughing, a doctor visiting his patient, etc. Of exceptional value is the painted decoration of the interior of wooden churches in Slovakia — Protestant and Catholic in the west and Orthodox in the east. The paintings in these churches in the western part of Slovakia, in the Orava Valley in particular, combine a vigorous eloquence with an urgency of expression and emotion. In the east, the village *bogomazi* ('painters of God') soften the severity of the Byzantine heritage of icon-painting with a human interest in facial expression, and with their love of legendary scenes and their interest in the fate of the damned in pictures of the Last Judgement. There, too, the range of expressions is broad and the folk character of the painting manifests itself differently to, for example, the painting of Easter eggs. The picture of folk culture in the Slovak east would not be complete without these paintings because the artists there expressed themselves primarily through painting. Figural sculpture remained almost entirely within the bounds of coloured ornamental relief.

PAINTED FURNITURE

Painted furniture, so typical of nineteenth-century village households in the Czech Lands and most of Slovakia, adopted the decorative techniques used in Renaissance wooden ceilings and was also influenced by the use of the floral motifs — bouquets in vases sometimes supplemented with colourful birds — which predominated in them. But the Empire and the late Rococo styles influenced the decoration of most of this furniture. Among the extant examples we can distinguish the style of a number of workshops, some of which supplemented the floral ornaments with images of saints and locally venerated Madonnas, while other workshops preferred pictures of strolling lovers or married couples in different dress (town, artisan, or rural). The ornamentally framed surfaces of chests were also filled with *vedutas* and pictures of quiet town scenes with stork nests on the roofs, with genre scenes from village life, or with prominently articulated patterns. The painting of furniture survived in the west Moravian town of Mohelno which supplied this furniture until the 1920's.

PAINTINGS ON PAPER

The pictures of saints which appear on furniture in northern and western Bohemia had the same graphic patterns as did the paintings on glass or the gouache and distemper paintings on paper which are preserved in museums in western Bohemia (Pilsen, Domažlice, Cheb). They used to be hung on living-room walls, in chapels, field sanctuaries or the tiny chapels of the Stations of the Cross. Especially ambitious in this respect are the relics from the Cheb area, which in their presentation sometimes extend beyond the bounds of folk art. Today it is difficult to identify or to decide on the social status of their German creators, who perhaps also included nuns as well as teachers and craftsmen.

GODPARENTS' LETTERS

Beginning late in the eighteenth century, a custom developed in the Cheb area by which after a baptism the godfather or the godmother gave the baby not only a present but also a commemorative letter. These letters were usually painted according to engravings but sometimes, to a lesser extent, also had original themes. They were always executed with great skill. The artists who made them were undoubtedly members of the more educated urban classes and had at least some artistic training. In the course of the nineteenth century, the decoration progressed from simple framing of the written text and a picture of a baby in swaddling clothes to pictures of saints and group scenes with, at the top, a scene of the baptismal ceremony.

Commemorative letters folded in a decorative manner and painted letterheads are also known in other parts of Czechoslovakia. Their origin lies somewhere in the sphere of book decoration and they are related to the souvenir albums which, after the peak of their popularity in the Empire and Biedermeier periods, and after an extensive rustication and sentimentalization of Empire themes, spread from the urban environment to the villages and eventually, as do so many manifestations of folk ceremonial, enjoyed their last vestiges of popularity amongst children.

The more complex technique of oil painting is found in folk art as well. Oil paintings on wooden panels, votive pictures and portraits of saints from numerous churches and chapels, sign boards and marksmanship targets, draw on the tradition of painted ceilings and furniture. However, folk artists also used canvas, sheet metal or cardboard for their oil paintings. Since they usually show the date of their presentation, votive pictures are used for dating works from other spheres of folk art, although this method is not always reliable. Votive pictures have been preserved from the Rococo and the following periods. They usually express prayers for protection, but also in a most interesting manner they depict accidents of an unusual nature with a happy ending, for which thanks were given to God or to a saint. These votive pictures display similar compositional types as this kind of painting does elsewhere in central Europe and are also of the same importance for cultural history, showing the donor's family in period costume, animals, household articles, etc. They reflect different degrees of professional training or talent and naïveté of expression.

Baroque and Rococo emotionalism and aesthetics survived in a popularized form for a long time, well into the nineteenth century, in the pictures of provincial painters who by now have become anonymous. In south-eastern Moravia a large number of oil paintings on canvas from the nineteenth century have been preserved, executed with traces of the Rococo sensitivity which pleasantly softens their simplified forms. Their often overworked themes are enlivened by the intimate presentation of people and through the use of vivid colours. They indicate that the paintings served the local cult (the Madonna of Bzenec), and were placed in the tiny painted chapels built at intersections in the long village streets typical of that area, or were used to decorate field sanctuaries. The interiors of the wealthier households in the rural towns of south-eastern Moravia, too, used to be decorated with similar paintings, as did the aisles and chapels of local churches.

These works are not usually marked by what is called 'local colour'. They show only a few features to identify the workshop in which they were produced. They were also produced in quite large numbers in Silesia and in north-eastern and south-western Bohemia, and can be found in other parts of Czechoslovakia as well. The selection of themes was determined to a considerable degree by the popularity of local and more distant places of pilgrimage. A popular theme in Bohemia was the Madonna of Svatá Hora; in south-eastern Moravia the Madonnas of Bzenec and Provodov; in the Brno area the Black Madonna of St Thomas's Church and the enthroned Madonna of Tuřany; in the Haná region the Madonnas of Svatý Kopeček and Hostýn; and in Silesia the Madonna of Czestochowa.

123 WAFER IRON WITH AN ENGRAVING OF JOHN HUSS AT THE STAKE, *Bohemian-Moravian Highlands.*

124 TEAMSTER'S BELT. *Detail. 1803, south Bohemia. Leather with colour embroidery.*

125 THE INFANT JESUS OF PRAGUE. *Wood-engraver's block, western Slovakia, 19th century.* ▶

126 WOOD-ENGRAVER'S BLOCK, *19th century, western Slovakia.*

127 DECORATION OF A HAND-WRITTEN PRAYER BOOK. *1820, Bohemia.*

129   DOCTOR VISITING A PATIENT. *Painting on wood, 1709. Detail of the decoration of a framed attic room in Lab, District of Turnov, north Bohemia.*

128   INTERIOR OF THE WOODEN CHURCH OF ST JOHN THE BAPTIST, *Slavoňov, north-eastern Bohemia, 16th—18th centuries.*

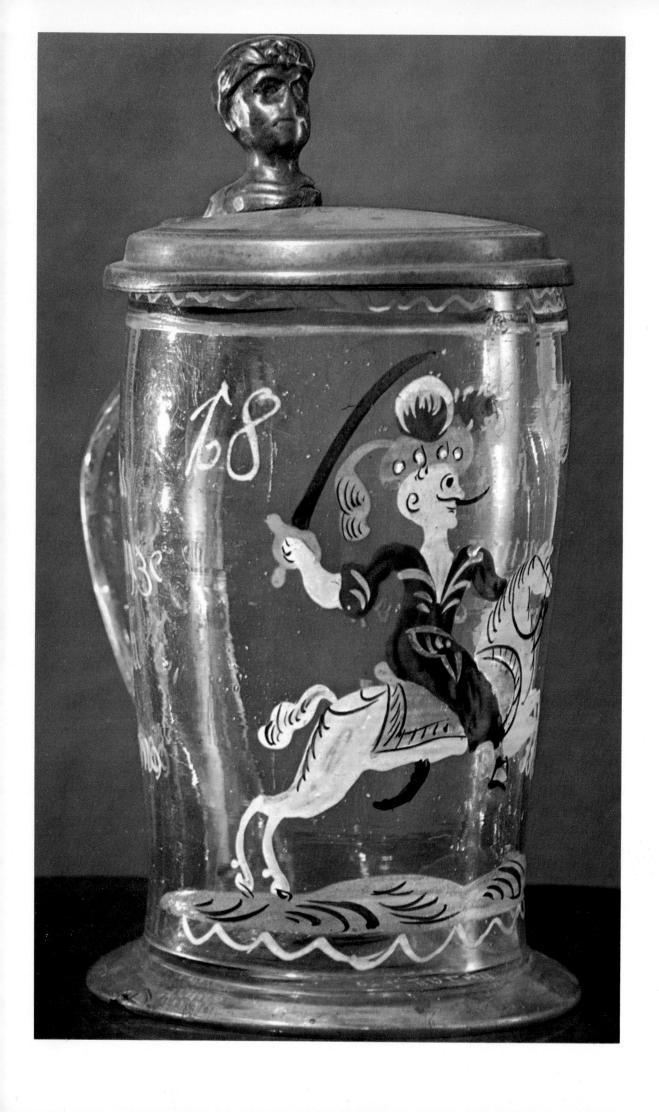

131 VIEW OF A TOWN — *part of the decoration of a wardrobe chest; Liberec, north Bohemia, about 1800.*

◄
130 BEER MUG WITH ENAMEL PAINTING AND A METAL LID.

132   DETAIL OF THE PAINTED DECORATION OF AN 18th-CENTURY WOODEN PROTESTANT CHURCH. *Paludza, central Slovakia.*

133   THE WAY TO CALVARY. *Oil on canvas, 19th century, south-eastern Moravia.*

135 A VIEW OF ŽELEZNICE by *Arnošt Rameš, oil on canvas, 1848.*

◄
134 VOTIVE PAINTING — *oil on canvas, about 1770, Rychnov nad Kněžnou, north-eastern Bohemia.*

136 ST PETER. *Oil on canvas, 19th century, south-eastern Moravia.*

137 THE HOLY FAMILY. *Painting on glass, last third of the 18th century, central Moravia.* ▶

138   PIETÀ OF ŽELEZNÝ BROD. *Painting on glass, about 1800, north Bohemia.*

139   PIETÀ OF ŽELEZNÝ BROD. *Painted wood-carving, about 1800, north Bohemia.*

140   ST BARBARA. *Painting on glass, about 1800, north Bohemia.*   ▶

165

141   THE LEGEND OF ST ISIDORE, *by the 'Painter of wavy eyebrows', first third of the 19th century, central Moravia.*

142   THE LEGEND OF ST ISIDORE, *by the 'Painter of arched eyebrows'. Painting on glass, first half of the 19th century, vicinity of Brno, central Moravia.*

143   THE CORONATION OF THE VIRGIN MARY. *Painting on glass, first half of the 19th century, central Slovakia.*

144   THE ERECTION OF THE CROSS. *Painting on glass, first half of the 19th century, vicinity of Brno, central Moravia.*   ▶

169

170

146   VIRGIN MARY THE PROTECTRESS. *Painting on glass, about 1800, south Moravia.*

145   THE BETROTHAL OF THE VIRGIN MARY. *Painting on glass, about 1850, Liptov, central Slovakia.*

147 THE CANDLEMAS MADONNA. *Painting on glass, about 1850, central Slovakia.*

To a lesser extent, these oil paintings also depict some other themes, both Czech and Slovak. Similar to the votive paintings are pictures, or rather group portraits, of different associations of the Virgin Mary and other religious societies, which again are interesting because they depict persons dressed in the local folk costume of the period. Other themes were related to liturgical services, to popular prayers and hymns, to the Catholic ceremonial and to the world of images in which the Czech and Slovak Christian once lived. Examples of this link with recited and sung prayers are presented by pictures of the Rosary, the Loreto Litany or the Passion scenes of the Stations of the Cross depicted in a serpentine manner in a single painting. Several oil paintings of this type (from Brno, Uherské Hradiště) correspond to small woodcuts probably deriving from Baroque engravings, and to a group of most interesting Moravian paintings on glass from the first third of the nineteenth century, which have the same composition. Similar links are seen in the large Brno painting on glass on the theme of the Loreto Litany with a large number of illustrated invocations written in Czech. This painting at the same time demonstrates that pictures of this type were created in the atmosphere of Czech-speaking small Moravian towns; even the once-German town of Brno had its Czech hinterland.

In the course of the process of national revival in the nineteenth century the fame and popularity of the Moravian Velehrad were restored. It was once a Cistercian place of pilgrimage with a cult of the Virgin Mary, and was linked by legend with the Slavonic mission of St Cyril and St Methodius. Pictures of these two saints exorcizing devils carrying pagan idols, or baptizing Prince Bořivoj or a group of children, are quite frequent amongst the popular oil paintings and paintings on glass produced by workshops in the Brno area and in south-eastern Moravia. The fame of Hostýn Hill, with its legend about the defeat of the Tatars in Moravia, is another theme which iconographically enriched both painting and figural folk carving.

By the time the problem of smoke in the living room had been eliminated, pictures painted on the reverse side of glass began to appear in village homes. In vivid colours, they depicted a superior protective power and in a way actually represented it. They did not require much care because they could be easily cleaned simply by wiping the unpainted side of the glass. They lasted for a long time and did not lose their bright colours. They decorated the festive corner of the room far more effectively than a woodcut or an engraving bought at a church fair. One could choose them from a large number of other such paintings according to one's need and taste. Although they were more expensive than prints, they were still within an acceptable price range.

The stylistic predecessors of the folk paintings on glass in Europe originated in the workshops of Late Gothic, Renaissance and post-Renaissance painters and craftsmen. The technique of painting on the reverse side of glass was known and used at the Prague court of Rudolf II as early as the turn of the sixteenth and seventeenth centuries. In the seventeenth and eighteenth centuries it was being used for reproducing some of the well-known works of Italian, French and German art. Soon after 1730, this technique was used in central European monasteries and convents, and in the workshops of some town painters for producing Rococo pictures representing saints and later rulers and other famous personalities. Other themes included Dutch-

PICTURES ON
GLASS

173

type landscapes, mythological, Biblical, pastoral and other genre scenes. This more sophisticated line continued around 1800 with allegorical cycles of the four seasons, so-called 'costume' portraits of girls, and other types which gradually replaced the Rococo taste with that of the Neo-Classical and Empire periods. True folk paintings began to emerge in the 1770's.

This type of painting — already fully developed by about 1800 — seems to have had two roots. One of them was the production of the 'provincial' painters already mentioned, the other was the production of paintings in glassworks. The glassmaker's or the painter's art characterized the production of the different workshops. However, this does not apply to Slovak pictures whose folk character is especially conspicuous. From the very beginning their authors never used any of the glassmaker's decorative techniques such as mirror backgrounds, cutting or matting.

The cradle of painted pictures of the glassmaker's type seems to have been the glassworks of northern Bohemia, in the vicinity of Česká Lípa and the Krkonoše (Giant) and Jizerské Mountains. German employees or ex-employees were probably the first in central Europe to produce mirror pictures with rich glassmaker's decoration. Official archives show that some of these glassmakers emigrated to the south Bohemian glass production area in the last third of the eighteenth century. This seems to have been the reason why this cottage industry moved to the vicinity of the Šumava glassworks, and to the Novohradsko district in particular. The main production centre there was the village of Pohoří na Šumavě (Buchers).

In both the north and the south of Bohemia we find an almost identical type of mirror picture — the 'cartouche' type — where the scene depicted is placed inside a richly ornamented inner frame. This frame is made up of different variants of medallions with almond- or olive-shaped cut surfaces. The white drawing of the ornament is mechanically or chemically matted. These pictures were, naturally, rather costly. They were therefore soon simplified to such an extent that, of the glassmaking techniques, only the mirror background was left. The matted themes were then usually drawn with white colour. In Pohoří pictures then appeared painted with translucent colours and having a simplified inner frame. The same type but in larger format and with some specific features was also produced in Moravia — most probably in Ždánice — in the first half of the nineteenth century. However, in the northern, southern and western parts of Bohemia popularity was long enjoyed by pictures with an ornamental inner frame, whose cut ornamentation was underlaid with gold foil while the background was painted with soot (*Kienruss* in German, which is the origin of the German name for this type of picture, *Russbild*). Technically reduced — with the gold ornament only slightly under-cut or even painted on the glass surface, and sometimes with the black background replaced by a milk-white, pink or light green one — cheap varieties of these pictures were produced with a greater selection of themes (mainly personal patron saints) especially in the Šumava region of south Bohemia.

Czechoslovak collections contain thousands of original relics of folk painting on glass but among them mirror pictures form only a minor, and not the oldest, part. In Moravia and Silesia many workshops existed producing pictures on glass, some of them as early as the eighteenth century. They display an artistic concept with obvious traces of the Baroque or Rococo tradition, often have a larger format and show some specifically Moravian themes. Such a concept also prevailed in the course of the nineteenth century in the old glassmaking areas, and the typical, mass-produced pictures from northern Bohemia and the Šumava region in the south no longer used any of the glassmaker's techniques, not even the imitation 'cartouches'.

In the last third of the eighteenth century, a surprisingly original group of painters emerged in what today is Moravian Silesia, apparently in an environment of fine provincial painting. In literature this group is provisionally called 'old Czech Silesia'. In northern Bohemia and in the Orlické (Eagle) Mountains a series of highly valuable, softly painted pictures were produced prior to 1800. Some of them made their way to collections in Wrocław and Jelenia Góra in Poland, through places of pilgrimage in the Kłodzko region, Wambierzyce in particular, because even after the Prussians had seized that region in 1742 it continued to maintain lively contacts with Bohemia. The same group includes some lovely profile portraits of women saints, whose similarity to the paintings of the Quattrocento has not yet been explained. In south-western Bohemia, on the slopes of the Šumava Mountains, the small town of Kvilda became a production centre under the influence of Bavarian painting which bases its tradition on the Augsburg school of painting. On the other hand, the village of Pohoří at the other end of the Šumava range, in south Bohemia, inspired the establishment of workshops on the Austrian side of the frontier, in Sandl and the other two communities. These workshops produced the same type of picture with a predominance of vermilion, blue modelling of fan-like forms and loops on the white parts of clothing. The south Bohemian pictures are decorated in the upper corners with roses, rose buds or rose hips, tied with a ribbon. On the other hand, the mass-produced paintings from north-eastern Bohemia always show the same stylized flower which is (incorrectly) described as a carnation. The central and southern parts of Moravia adopted many ideas from the Pohoří workshops. However, in contrast to Bohemia, the early Moravian paintings used black contours, known in the west only in Bavaria's Raimundsreut, and apparently introduced them into Slovakia and Transylvania. Moravian originality in this sphere is quite obvious in the painter's approach to his model — he apparently did not trace the graphic model exactly but transcribed it freely. The Slovak painters went even further in this respect, drawing the contours of their pictures mostly free hand. No 'tracing patterns' or records of their existence have been preserved from Moravia or Slovakia. The early Moravian paintings instead show a striking similarity to folk woodcuts. They frequently have a larger format and an unusually vivid scale of colours, as well as a great narrative quality. Particular to Moravia are cycles of large pictures telling the story of St Genevieve, the Margravine of Brabant, and richly decorated pictures depicting the legend of St Isidore, the patron saint of peasants. Moravia was the home of a number of painters with highly personal forms of expression, all of them anonymous, because in Moravia, too, we are unable to link the names of artists handed down by tradition with individual pictures. The 'Painter of arched eyebrows' achieved the greatest charm in his lyrical epic compositions. An artistically productive area was around Brno with the communities of Sloup and particularly Ždánice which was also an important centre of post-Haban faïence production. In the town of Frýdek, on the border between Moravia and Silesia, large numbers of pictures were painted and probably sold at church fairs; among them there is a prominent group with ultramarine half-wreaths surrounding each figure. The museums in the Bohemian-Moravian Highlands also have in their collections groups of paintings which could hardly have been produced in any other region.

Slovak painting on glass defies classification because the products of different regions frequently possess substantial features in common. Moreover, the two largest categories, known as the central Slovak groups, sometimes recall the Ždánice paintings in their colour composition. The east Slovak (Spiš) group is more expressive. However, the paintings produced in both these areas are, in spite of their relationship to Czech painting, highly original. They show such spontaneity in the drawing of human and animal figures and in the impact of their coloured surfaces and background flowers, that we must esteem them greatly as works of folk art. Painting in these areas is outstanding for its talented 'primitiveness' which boldly seizes any form, no matter how difficult, and creates refined formulae for mastering it. The third, west Slovak group of paintings on glass is of a later date and is, in fact, limited to the production of the Salzmann family. It mostly includes large, stylistically different pictures overflowing with floral decoration. Typical of Slovak paintings on glass is the brigand theme. Many of them depict a group of 'mountain boys' in the forest, entertaining themselves with music, shooting and dancing around a kettle of gold coins or around the fire. This scene is interpreted as representing the initiation of a new member into Jánošík's company.

Let us mention at least briefly that the pictures produced in the Czech workshops were peddled — sometimes in quite distant places — by Austrian Yugoslavs from Carinthia, who carried them in panniers on their back. Later they were packed in cases and exported to what are now Hungary, Romania and Yugoslavia. Moravian paintings were sold mostly at church fairs and markets, but they gradually found their way farther to the east and south. Slovak pictures, too, were sold by pedlars from house to house or at markets. Many of them were sold on the Polish side of the Tatra Mountains and eventually were obtained from the collections of the Tatra Museum in Zakopane, Poland. Polish scholars divide them into two categories: 'Orava' and 'Spiš' pictures.

Painting on glass continued until approximately the 1870's. Some painting was still going on in Moravia and Slovakia, in the Šumava range and the Orlické (Eagle) Mountains in the twentieth century, but its output and quality can in no way compare with traditional production and organization. An old-time Šumava family workshop with a few assistants produced as many as a hundred high quality pictures daily.

PAINTING ON FAÏENCE

Moravia and Slovakia produced many craftsmen making faïence. The jugs, dishes and plates for festive occasions, which took the place of costly tin utensils and vessels among ordinary people and were to the villager what porcelain was to the townsman, were strikingly painted. In the western part of the country faïence workshops are very rare, and the idea of a Czech origin for the 'Zittau' faïence is mere conjecture. The art of producing faïence was introduced to Moravia by the Anabaptists — Germans from Tyrol and Northern Italy who emigrated there after their church had been banned. When they were banished even from Moravia in 1622, they moved farther east to Slovakia where they once again established their 'Haban estates'

(*Haushaben*). It was only after the middle of the seventeenth century that some of them returned individually to Moravia where they gradually mixed with the local population and abandoned their strict religious principles. These Habans applied to a high-quality body, perfectly shaped from south Moravian and west Slovak clay and with a smooth, milky glaze of matte gloss, well-proportioned decorations of a floral or architectural character ('Delft' patterns), painted on by brush, always using the same four hard-fired colours — blue, yellow, green and purple.

In the eighteenth and nineteenth centuries, to the old Haban faïence manufacturing centres — Vyškov and Ždánice in Moravia, and Sobotиšte, Velké Laváre, Dechtice and Košolná in Slovakia — were added Bučovice, Prostějov, Olomouc, Šternberk, Valašské Meziříčí and some others in Moravia, and Boleráz, Smolenice, Stupava and Modra in Slovakia. Jug-makers of Haban origin settled in many of these towns and gradually merged with the local population. The decoration of their products acquired Slavonic character and slowly became rusticated. It was in this genre, before the time of hollow painted glass, that vessels suited to the needs of country people were created, upsetting the once strict rules governing the production of earthenware. The types, shapes and purposes of vessels grew in number, but their main function was aesthetic. The decoration grew to cover the entire vessel, the old motifs were relaxed and reformed, and new, increasingly figural, motifs were added to them. In the extensive collection of museums in Brno, Martin, Prague and elsewhere the most charming faïence products are undoubtedly the guild jugs with pictures showing the various craftsmen at work with their tools, or the guild insignia and patron saints. The ceremonial vessels also include jugs from the treasures of Czechoslovak synagogues, depicting processions, rituals and ceremonies of Jewish funeral fraternities. We should, in addition, mention a wide range of vessels which used to belong to wealthier households, especially those designed as wedding presents, showing pictures of a man and a woman, humorous scenes of domestic quarrels and often with sayings in Czech or Slovak. Many jugs depict ploughing with oxen in ancient types of harnesses and yokes. A fifth colour was sometimes added to the palette — red, as the colour of low flame. Tall tankards were painted with equestrian or hunting scenes, while twin cups were usually painted with flowers. Also produced were holy water receptacles, known as 'Veronicas', which combined painting with sculpture, and painted relief or flat decorative tiles, usually with pictures of saints, these becoming more numerous from the end of the eighteenth century onwards. Jugs are decorated with paintings of the Virgin Mary of Vranov, the Madonna of Křtiny and quite frequently the Austrian Madonna of Mariazell; while in Slovakia, the Madonna of Marianka (Mariatal) and the Pietà of Šaštín are most popular. All of this indicates that faïence is a genre which falls somewhere between the functional and the festive, close not only to pottery, but also to painting and sculpture, and that its function is decorative, representational and finally also religious. Moreover there are faïence works of figural sculpture from Modra of the nineteenth and twentieth centuries. Because of its happy combination of white shape with warm colour painting, this genre is one of the most popular and admired types of folk art.

At the same time, painting in enamel on glass vessels was carried on in several places but with a smaller output. In a certain sense it was the predecessor of pictures

PAINTING ON
GLASS VESSELS

painted on flat glass. It developed from the sixteenth century onwards in and around the glassworks of the Šumava, Ore and Giant Mountains as well as in the Bohemian-Moravian Highlands. Decoration was applied mostly to small, angular bottles, called *prysky*, which were used at weddings, as both the figural scenes depicted on these bottles and various inscriptions indicate. They resemble similar bottles in Germany and the Alpine countries, but are less frequent in Slovakia. The pictures differ from the paintings on pottery in the greater richness of their colours but share with them the realism and often the humour with which different situations are depicted.

PAINTED NATIVITY
SCENES

At the turn of the eighteenth and nineteenth century, folk painting began to be more popular. In the production of Nativity scenes — called 'Bethlehems' — which at that time was widespread in many areas, painted paper figures were created, similar to the sculptured figures produced elsewhere. A large area where Nativity scenes were painted, sometimes professionally but more often by amateur artists, was in the Bohemian-Moravian Highlands — in Třebíč, Třešť, Ústí nad Orlicí and other rural towns with ancient handicraft traditions. The Nativity scenes were in almost every case very large, built on a scaffolding in one corner of the room with a painted landscape background, several large wings and figures stuck in moss. The number of these figures was increased from year to year. Besides the Holy Family, the shepherds, the Magi and musicians, they included many figures in contemporary dress — gift bearers hurrying to pay homage to the Child of God with the products of the crafts common in their particular region. Nativity scenes were also painted in northern Bohemia, in the vicinity of Frenštát pod Radhoštěm in Moravia, and in Slovakia. The figures are usually faithful reproductions of ordinary people in their native environment and performing different types of work. Nativity scenes from the vicinity of Banská Štiavnica in central Slovakia, dating from the end of the nineteenth and the beginning of the twentieth centuries, differ from their Czech counterparts by their long prospects in which the figures are painted into the magnificently represented environment of mountain pastures. With a great gift of pictorial narrative they depict life around the shepherds' chalets — the watering and milking of sheep, production of cheese, a wolf being driven away, a fight with a thief, horn blowing, and playing on the shepherd's *fuyara*. Set into the dynamism and picturesqueness of this life are the stories of the birth of Christ, the angels heralding the birth, the shepherds following the Star of Bethlehem and their visit to the Manger; the legend of the birth of Christ is adopted with such naturalness that it seems as if the event had truly occurred somewhere on the Slovak slopes of the Carpathian mountains.

The painted figures in these Nativity scenes were mainly patterned on illustrations of the Bible and later also on printed sheets depicting Nativity scenes. The artists copied from one another without inhibition. A number of scenes and figures, however, were truly original, which proves how creative their makers were. In the area of Třebíč, the custom of painting Nativity scenes and placing them in the windows still survives and in the Valašsko region contemporary folk artists still use and develop these themes (see for instance the scene representing the Killing of the Innocents in the *skansen* at Rožnov pod Radhoštěm).

NAÏVE ART

The painting done by a village artist becomes a part of folk art if it acquires some generally important role in the life of a community of people and if by its form it is of a certain traditional type. There are examples from the periphery of folk culture, where the artist's work meets a new, generally still unfelt, need for which he himself must seek the proper form. We know manifestations of this kind sometimes far removed in terms of time. For example, the chronicler Beer from Dobruška illustrated many of his notes with drawings and watercolours depicting different views of a great fire which had swept his native town. Another painter in Pilsen in the seventeenth century produced the picture of a dead woman with her newly born baby, while another unknown artist depicted on a shooting target a couple of Gypsies playing the violin, and, on the signboard of an inn, Czech peasants in their typical dress. In a similar manner, today's 'primitive' painters illustrate the life of their villages and towns, and reproduce their romantic and dreamlike images of the world's beauty. This 'Sunday' art is, of course, different today to what it was at the turn of the eighteenth and nineteenth centuries or even earlier. Yet it has retained its special place on the periphery of folk culture. The position of its creators is either that of 'intellectuals' among the common people, or that of individuals who feel the urge to express themselves among intellectuals (irrespective of their lack of artistic training).

In this type of art the emotional element is sometimes especially strong and the theme plays a specific and important role, provided that the author is truly a 'primitive' painter and not a craftsman, as is the case with a large number of shooting targets. These boards, often shot full of holes, can be found in abundance in some museums, particularly in northern and north-eastern Bohemia (Jičín, Jablonec, Liberec, Litomyšl) but they also appear in the south (České Budějovice) and frequently in Moravia (Olomouc, Frenštát pod Radhoštěm). Most of them date from the 1830's to 1860's. Target shooting used to be a very popular pastime for burghers on Sundays and holidays throughout the summer, when different marksmen's societies held competitions and festivals. Some targets, in fact, depict the parades of these societies on the town square with crowds of onlookers watching them. New targets were prepared for every shooting context; these targets usually give the name of the sponsors, the date of the competition and sometimes even its results. The used targets were then kept as souvenirs. There used to be entire collections of them at the shooting ranges and only after these ranges were abolished, did the targets gradually rot away or disappear. In many cases they were utilized for other purposes. According to reports from the Horácko district of western Moravia, the burghers of Nové Město na Moravě used old targets for building an attic room and a skittles alley in the local inn, and a small cottage next to the town hall had an entire gable made of old targets.

A wide variety of themes was depicted on these targets. They were inspired by newspaper and magazine stories, period prints, illustrations of historical events and the heroes of brigand tales (*Rinaldi* by Wulpius, Schiller's *Die Räuber* and others). We find among them romantic scenes (Gypsies), views of towns and castles (Trosky), shooting practices and festivals (Jablonec, Liberec, České Budějovice), portraits of the winners of shooting competitions, etc. Many of the target paintings had no model from which they were copied, and demonstrate the independent invention of their authors. Some of the painters adapted themselves, as it was said, to the 'spirit of local humour and caricature', although their main object was different. Typical of the small-town painters was, for example, the Šír family of Nové Město na Moravě, whose members are also reported as creators of shooting targets. The founder of the family was a chronicler from the period of the issue of the Toleration Patent (1781). Other members of the family illuminated Protestant hymn-books and collections of hand-written prayers, and still later, one of the Šírs published lithographs and pilgrimage souvenir pictures. This is one example of how in the small, rural towns, folk creation and artisan production intermingled.

SIGNBOARDS

From a similar artistic milieu also came the painters of signboards, large canvases shown at fairs, illustrating different tragedies or humorous events, and the romantic and comical pictures decorating circus shooting galleries, carrousels and tents. Of all these things only a few signboards from inns, midwives' homes, tobacco shops, gingerbread-maker's shops, bakeries and other trading establishments have been preserved. These signboards were painted by urban professionals or amateurs, who were guided by tradition and their sense for making an impression on their customers, usually adding a bit of humour. Unfortunately, there is practically no documentation on the picture stories which were shown at fairs, unless we include among them a few late parodies produced in the workshops of town painters.

CIRCUS AND SHOOTING GALLERIES

As regards the circus shooting galleries, there alone the original atmosphere has not yet fully disappeared, and in a few rare cases there still exist some painted, mostly figural, targets and a few of them are even used to this day. However, most of the paintings which advertised the circus attractions at the entrance to the tent, just like most of the old carrousel decorations, are gone forever, although there are still many people who remember this romantic art. It is also recorded in old photographs or in the works of painters from the 1920's, but this entire area is, of course, outside the mainstream of folk culture and is quite a late phenomenon on the border between artisan production and 'primitive' art.

Of the traditional folk painting only some forms of decoration have survived to this day, such as the mural paintings in south-eastern Moravia and southern Slovakia, all of them ornamental and done in public and communal places rather than in places where they traditionally belong. Frequently their motifs do not respect the older types of building decoration, and instead adopt the popular ornamentation of embroideries. Figural and landscape painting have survived until today only to a small extent in the production of Nativity scenes in Slovakia, the Walachian area and also in the vicinity of Třebíč in south-western Moravia. Otherwise, painting by professionally untrained individuals takes the form of 'primitive' art, in which sphere, however, many artists have learned from the folk tradition and only to a lesser degree have been influenced by twentieth century art. These 'primitive' artists often came from villages in industrial districts or are industrial workers themselves. Today's amateur artists are interested in their environment and its values. They express it, for example, in pictures of mines or their vicinity as painted by an Ostrava miner, or in ethnographic genre scenes from the Beskydy Mountains, as painted on glass by a woman from Frenštát who remembers stories she heard from her mother and recalls her own childhood. Painting of this type belongs to the category of 'amateur creativity', promoted by competitions and exhibitions after the Second World War. Nevertheless, this amateur creativity has the same possibility of artistic discovery with a minimum of technical training, which was so fully exploited by folk art.

148 THE EMPRESS MARIA THERESA AS ST BARBARA. *Painting on glass, about 1780, Ostrava, Silesia.*

149   THE NATIVITY OF CHRIST. *Painting on glass, by the 'Painter of arched eyebrows', about 1820, Tišnov area, Moravia.*

150   JÁNOŠÍK AND HIS MEN. *Painting on glass. Mid-19th century, central Slovakia.*

▶

151   THE FINDING OF GENEVIEVE OF BRABANT. *Painting on glass, first half of the 19th century, central Moravia.*

152   THE VIRGIN MARY OF VRANOV. *Painting on glass, early 19th century. The ceramic frame dated 1863; Brno area, Moravia.* ▶

153, 154 SS BARBARA AND CATHERINE. *Paintings on glass, about 1800, north-eastern Bohemia.*

▲

▶

187

155 THE BAPTISM OF CHRIST. *Icon from the wooden church at Krivé, eastern Slovakia. First half of the 17th century.*

156 ST GEORGE. *Icon from the wooden church at Nová Sedlica, eastern Slovakia, first half of the 17th century.* ▶

190

158   PLATE WITH SCENES FROM ANIMAL FABLES. *Faïence, dated 1724, Moravia or southern Slovakia.*

◄

157   THE LAST JUDGMENT, *icon, eastern Slovakia.*

159 SLOVAK HABAN FAÏENCE. *In the foreground a ritual jug with the picture of a Jewish burial fraternity. Western Slovakia, 18th century.*

160 BEER TANKARD. *Boleráz, western Slovakia, 18th century.*

162   DETAIL OF THE DECORATION OF A JUG. *South-western Slovakia, 19th century.*

◄

161   FAÏENCE JUG. *Western Slovakia, 19th century.*

163 CENTRAL SECTION OF A NATIVITY SCENE. *Bohemian-Moravian Highlands, about 1800.*

164 DETAIL OF A NATIVITY SCENE, *Bohemian-Moravian Highlands, about 1800.*

165   MARKSMEN'S TARGET, *1839. Frenštát pod Radhoštěm, Moravia.* ▶

166 SIGNBOARD OF A SOUTH BOHEMIAN INN. *Mid-19th century.*

VI. Sculptural Works in Folk Culture

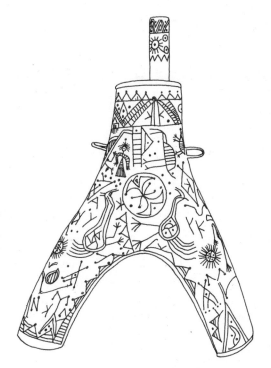

167 HUNTER'S POWDER HORN
WITH COLOURED ENGRAVING.
Central Slovakia, 18th century.

A. Relief

The communicative values and the aesthetic impact of sculptured relief can be traced in stone — most often in limestone — as far back as the early Middle Ages with their touching relics. Scholars were already attracted some time ago by certain Romanesque capitals (as, for example, in the tower of the church in Sedlec near Sedlčany) because of their emphasis on 'concept rather than creatively directed form' (Šourek), something which became typical for subsequent popular creation. Of particular interest are the tympana and the relief decoration of the portals and walls of village churches (Hrusice) or fragments incorporated in later structures (Hostinné). However, close as these relics are to folk art, the fact is that they stand apart. They are the products of medieval stone-masons rather than typical products of the contemporary folk culture, in the same way as are the woodcuts of Třeboň. The same applies to Renaissance tombstones and votive panels which again are linked with later folk creations only by the typical approach of the stone-mason with his native ability to fashion vigorous symbols and abbreviated forms of meaning and expression. The opulence of Baroque sculpture permitted the application of folk relief only at a later stage, on the socles of statues and crosses.

As shown by the relics which have survived in some regions, in the art of the eighteenth and nineteenth centuries we no longer find simple, individual expressions of an artist's native, folk background, nor abbreviations of a complex stylistic form which the artist could not master, but the products of institutionalized groups of stone-masons who worked in small towns and villages. This is true of northern and north-eastern Bohemia, the Tachov district in south-western Bohemia, and the Orava Valley in Slovakia. These stone-masons originally drew on the heritage of the great masters of the Czech Baroque (Braun) through their disciples (the Pacáks or the Mělnickýs) and were later influenced by the Empire style. The values of this stone-masons' Baroque and nineteenth-century folk relief were produced by ingenious simplification, by the addition of the common man's sense for the substantial, by the

RELIEF IN STONE

MEDIEVAL

RENAISSANCE

BAROQUE

FOLK RELIEF
ON SOCLES

transformation of the aristocratic into a more naturalistic emotion, whether deep or restrained, and by an emphasis on those elements which are essential to the meaning. This is manifested, for example, in a clear-cut distinction between the individual parts of the body, the face and the clothing, and by the stress laid on the attributes. The popular sculptured reliefs from the north and north-east of Bohemia are marked by a certain restraint of shape and colouring, as are similar stone tablets from town houses in the Tachov district. More moving and generous in expression are the reliefs on statuary and crosses found throughout the Orava Valley and the northern part of central Slovakia, casts of which were recently collected in the Orava Gallery at Slanica. They are the work of several stone-masons from the period between 1747 and 1876. They originated under the influence of the Catholic Counter-Reformation and the activities of Polish Jesuits. In their own unique way they express the opposition of the common folk to the nobility which ruled with unusual brutality in the Orava region (for example, when it suppressed an uprising of peasants in 1762 in a veritable bloodbath). Iconographically they represent a number of saints. Besides the usual patron saints, such as John of Nepomuk, Florian, Sebastian, Rosalie, Anne, Barbara, Apollonia, George, Martin, the Virgin Mary of Sorrows, or Mary Magdalene, there are many others, including SS. Adalbert, Stephen, Leonard, Andrew, Donatus, Lucy, Clare, Peter the Apostle, the evangelists Luke and Mark, and the Archangel Michael. Their creators naturally adopted the usual iconographic compositional form of the artistic style then prevalent, but its adoption indicates quite clearly that it derived from a profound emotional and artistic experience. These reliefs from the Orava region, together with a wealth of painting from the same area, are some of the most excitingly original works of folk art to be found. What we have especially in mind are the illustrations of the Ten Commandments in the church at Orávka, on the Polish side of the frontier, dating from the middle of the seventeenth century.

TOMBSTONES

Iconographically more modest and without figural themes are the Slovak tombstones, the sculptured features of which are limited to the outlining of their form, often typical of a region or a particular workshop (such as dual horseshoe-shaped family tombstones), and to a number of simple symbolical motifs. In Bohemia, rustic stone-mason's work of this type of the nineteenth century is known, but far more numerous are compositions with free-standing statues, angels, etc. Relief is found only on rare occasions. The reliefs on these tombstones were fashioned by stonemasons whose names can frequently be ascertained, especially since in many instances they were members of families in which the stone-mason's trade was passed from one generation to the next. In Moravia, too, works of this type have appeared since the end of the nineteenth century.

RELIEFS IN WOOD

Whilst ancient predecessors of reliefs in stone can be found in the surviving relics of medieval art, this cannot be said of reliefs in wood in Czechoslovakia, in spite of the extensive decorative wood-carving in the age of the Great Migrations and the early Middle Ages. The oldest preserved examples of reliefs in wood point to links with late Gothic wood-carving in central Europe, this also being true of the free-standing folk sculptures. There are, for example, relief panels such as those on display in the Domažlice Museum in south-western Bohemia (Madonna and Child surrounded by fourteen saints and the fragmentary Last Supper, both probably dating from the sixteenth century), or some Slovak reliefs in the sphere of influence of Master Paul of Levoča and other Gothic carvers from the Spiš region.

RELIEFS ON BEEHIVES

Polychromed reliefs in wood were used to a greater extent only in beehives, most of those surviving being of the eighteenth and nineteenth centuries, with only a few exceptions from the seventeenth century. These reliefs primarily decorate stump hives made of a section of tree trunk left in its original 'A' shape. Less frequently, the relief is carved directly into the stump, but in most cases it is carved in a special board fixed in front of the hive either as the silhouette of a figure or a head, or as an entire wall. The oldest surviving beehive of this type, showing the date 1691, is on display in the Šariš Museum at Bardejov. It comes from eastern Slovakia. Its slot-like opening is ringed with a relief wreath and above it is the symbolical figure of a walking bear. The same type of hive and decoration persisted in the Šariš region for a long time with only minor changes. This is indicated by the shallow carving of the biblical scene of men carrying a large bunch of grapes on the beehive from Osikov, and especially a hive bearing the date 1832 and decorated with the figure of St John of Nepomuk, which shows the later typical enlargement of the decoration whilst preserving the old principle of positioning composition and low relief, the whole being rather perfunctorily executed. Some of the relief boards of an apiary from the Orlické (Eagle) Mountains, which was eventually located in the garden of the parsonage at Bílý Újezd in north-eastern Bohemia, are perhaps from the early period as well. Some eighteenth-century stump hives are preserved in the same area, in particular those in Nové Město nad Metují and Dobruška (dated 1787). Many hives have been preserved from the nineteenth century. In the Czech Lands as well as in Slovakia these hives were decorated with religious pictures in relief (St Wenceslas, St Dominic, the Virgin Mary, the Holy Trinity, etc.) or representations of persons, both of town and village, dressed in local period costumes — monks, priests, Turkish soldiers, policemen and others. A row of stump beehives placed under one roof in the garden was often something of a private gallery which added to the bee-keeper's pleasure. A special instance of using relief to decorate stump beehives was the placing of human or animal masks on the hives; their open mouths served as the openings through which the bees entered the hive. This form of decoration is typical of north-eastern Moravia, and a large collection of such beehives can be seen in the Walachian Open-Air Museum of Folk Architecture at Rožnov pod Radhoštěm. An interesting combination using a mask and carved relief to decorate a stump beehive can be seen in the Municipal Museum in Železnice; it depicts, as the inscription says, 'The Baptism and Temptation of Our Lord, Jesus Christ'. Other hives, with secular themes of decoration, make use of Empire floral and figural motifs (as shown, for example, in the museums in Nová Paka and Teplice).

WOODEN FONTS

Some older and, indeed, some more recent articles of equipment from households, workshops, farms, vineyards, chapels and sanctuaries are decorated with floral relief which is sometimes supplemented by figural scenes. These articles include the fonts found in some village churches, vintners' columns decorated with carved spiralling vines and grapes, and especially wine presses, some of which are small, while others are of monumental size. Two such presses from Slovakia — from the vicinity of Trnava and Bratislava — are richly decorated with floral ornaments and carry the

VINTNERS' COLUMNS

WINE PRESSES

dates 1791 and 1884. The well-known wine press displayed in the museum at Uherské Hradiště, and decorated with relief caryatids, small figures on pillars, a Pietà, cherubs and the name of the owner, carries the date 1847. Also to be found are wood planes decorated with engraved or carved relief scenes, such as the eighteenth-century plane showing a cooper at work, exhibited in the Slovak National Museum in Bratislava. In the old days there used to be small wooden chapels and field sanctuaries located in the open countryside, decorated with wooden, carved reliefs of different saints.

PLANES

WOODEN CEMETERY
CROSSES

Wooden cemetery crosses from the nineteenth and twentieth centuries have been preserved in Slovakia mainly in the area between Zvolen and Detva. They are decorated with simple polychrome relief on symbolical and decorative themes — the Sun and stars, hearts, chalices, monstrances, bouquets of flowers in jugs, grape vines, etc. Similar carved wooden crosses used to stand, and can still be found in the Detva district, along roads, brooks and elsewhere. Outstanding for their wealth of symbolical ornamentation and particularly for their exacting decorative figural reliefs are the tall crosses carved by Martin Vymyslický, a farmer from Dolní Bojanovice in Slovácko in Moravia. Several of these crosses, which used to stand along the roads leading to neighbouring villages, have survived and one of them is displayed in the Ethnographical Museum in Prague. They have almost identical decorations, telling the story of Adam and Eve and depicting Passion scenes in rich colours in a simple, matter-of-fact style with a penchant for detail. These Moravian relics are the more interesting as they have no parallel elsewhere in Moravia or in Bohemia.

ROADSIDE CROSSES

RELIEF PICTURES
BY JOSEF CHVÁLA

A folk master of polychrome wooden relief still working in the south Bohemian town of Prachatice is Josef Chvála (born in 1906), a man with a colourful past. He may be classified as 'primitive' because of the specific themes of his 'wooden pictures': Chvála likes to create narrative historical scenes on long panels, such as *The Murder and Funeral of St Wenceslas*. The pictures by Josef Chvála are the products of his history-oriented mind, created without any model, simply according to his own imagination.

There are, of course, other instances of relief pictures in Czech folk creation. Thus, for example, the Municipal Museum in Český Těšín has in its collection a panel depicting Queen Sophia confessing to St John of Nepomuk. This theme, popular in northern Bohemia and Moravia, is executed with primitive straightforwardness emphasized by polychromy.

WOODEN MOULDS,
PRINTING BLOCKS

In Czech and Slovak rural towns different arts and crafts developed — in some cases from the late Middle Ages — that needed casts or printing blocks for shaping their products. These moulds had their simpler parallels in the farmer's and shepherd's butter and cheese moulds. They used to be fashioned from wood and may be classified as works of folk relief. They were made for the most part by specialist wood-carvers, but not unfrequently these moulds were produced by the wax-maker and gingerbread-maker himself (these crafts used to be combined) and in exceptional cases also by the dyer. Old blocks for blue-printing with roughly cut ornamentation are numerous in Czechoslovak collections and even more numerous are later blocks which were supplemented with pins and pieces of sheet metal. Other moulds were used for producing votive animals, figures and human limbs from wax — symbols to be offered as a sacrifice in places of pilgrimage — and also for making flat statuettes

BLUE-PRINTING

VOTIVE ARTICLES

from fresh bread, paper pulp or other materials, as were produced in the vicinity of the Holy Mountain near Příbram.

But this method was used above all for making gingerbread. This process is documented by countless types and variants of moulds. The Municipal Museum in Krnov has in its collection a rare gingerbread mould of the old type — round and two-sided — bearing the date 1640. It has shallow reliefs of the Nativity and the Adoration of the Magi, and the Crucifixion with Virgin Mary and John, all of purely folk character. The lyrical simplicity of form, full of contentment in spite of the cruel theme, ensues from the fact that these themes were close to the heart of the people, being a part of festivals, holidays, annual fairs and pilgrimages. It was, however, unusual for its time. In fact to find so early such perfect rustication and poetization of even the more usual themes of Christian art is altogether rare. For example, a later Polish mould of the same type lacks this folk character. Both moulds come from Silesia, illustrating the frequent occurrence of these articles in that region.

Many other old moulds, of a more ordinary type, point to the existence of a large number of gingerbread bakeries throughout the country. Old archive documents and surviving sign boards indicate that these bakeries existed in practically every town. The moulds used for shaping gingerbread demonstrate the imagination and the invention of their carvers, who proceeded from historical styles of art but adapted the themes and motifs employed so that their moulds would be easy to use and attractive. We find among gingerbread moulds a charming group of dancing ladies and gentlemen, a theme obviously borrowed from the Renaissance. The Baroque contributed fashionable cavaliers, horse-soldiers and servants in period dress; the Rococo added nobility in opulent costumes, sometimes riding in fancy carriages, and also harlequins and clowns; the Empire period brought in tall elegant dandies and slender girls; the realism of the nineteenth century introduced village women in traditional costumes, chimneysweeps, babies and the first locomotive. Among the saints the most popular was St Nicholas, but there were others, too, just as there were different Madonnas, sold at places of pilgrimage. Topical themes are represented by the representations of the popular Spanish dancer, Pepita de Oliva, then appearing in Prague. Toys take the form of letters of the alphabet for school beginners, small cradles, sleds, carriages, etc. which were then put together and gilded. Some collections of gingerbread moulds are especially valuable because of the carver's independent, unconventional approach to his work which on more than one occasion enriched the sculptural concept of individual themes in this medium.

Gingerbread was formed by pressing a negative relief onto a thick dough. Therefore two-sided moulds also exist. On the other hand, the baking of ceremonial and festive cakes, buns, paschal lambs and other types of pastry required a ceramic mould in which the dough was baked, necessitating a high, negative relief shaped from clay. In the Czech Lands there was a whole series of popular moulds, some of which were connected with Christmas festivities (a fish) or the Easter season (the Lamb), and others with weddings. There were also moulds connected with social customs, among them, for example, a mould shaped like a baby in swaddling clothes used in south Bohemia in the ceremony of admitting paternity of a child born out of wedlock.

Moulds were, of course, also used for shaping tiles. The figural relief decoration of these tiles sometimes lies on the borderline between professional and folk art. It would most probably be wrong to consider as folk art the late Gothic relics which somewhat bizarrely depict the Hussite campaigns, or the king with a military suite, or different patron saints, such as St George the Dragon Killer. In fact, these tiles are, as is the case of many other relics of a different kind, the products of professional potters and stove-makers, marked, however, by their rustic decoration. This was due to some extent to the techniques of production then prevalent and to the fact that the decoration of such tiles was the work of craftsmen rather than of experts in drawing and relief.

UNUSUAL
AND COMBINED
MATERIALS

In the making of reliefs, perhaps more frequently than in other products of folk culture, we meet with a quite extraordinary use of materials and thus also with unusual techniques. For example, in the case of traditional pastries which have a flat bottom, the relief is formed not only by impression with small moulds, but also by free modelling where the dough is braided or snipped by hand. Certain garments, too (fur coats), and their accessories (such as belts, handbags and purses) were decorated with ornamental or figural relief produced by layers of differently coloured and shaped pieces of leather, fabric, fibre, netting and other materials.

METAL-PLATE
BOOK COVERS

Book covers from brass plate were produced by an exacting technique approaching that of jewellery production. By moulding and working the metal, a basic relief decoration in the form of different saints was created on the plate (Madonnas, Pietàs, or Crucifixions). In the medieval fashion, popular in folk culture, this basic form was supplemented by setting into the plate Bohemian garnets and coloured cut-glass pieces imitating gems. Precious relics of this type can now be seen in museums in western Bohemia.

CHRIST'S BODIES
FOR CRUCIFIXES

Metal-plate shaped in relief also forms the bodies of Christ for crucifixes, both the small ones designed for home use, and the large ones placed in chapels or at crossroads. Of those that have been preserved perhaps the most remarkable is the large body of Christ now displayed in the church in the Walachian Open-Air Museum of Folk Architecture at Rožnov pod Radhoštěm. It originally came from a former wooden church in Rožnov. Several other bodies of Christ of this type, more flat and of lesser quality, are still in their original places, mostly in small towns and villages in northern Bohemia.

CAST METAL
RELIEF

Cast figural reliefs with rustic groups which decorate metal combs for horses and horse harness are to be found in collections in southern and western Bohemia.

168   ST APOLLONIA. *Polychrome relief, end of the 18th century, Železný Brod, north Bohemia.*

169   BEEHIVE WITH A RELIEF CARVING OF ADAM AND EVE. *Dated 1867. Železnice, north Bohemia.*

170 RELIEF WITH THE BAPTISM
AND TEMPTATION OF JESUS CHRIST
FROM A BEEHIVE DATED 1867.
Železnice, north Bohemia.

171   THE MURDER AND FUNERAL OF ST WENCESLAS. *Polychrome relief, about 1967. Made by Josef Chvála of Prachatice, south Bohemia.*

172   ADAM AND EVE. *Polychrome relief from a tall crucifix from the vicinity of Uherské Hradiště, south-eastern Moravia, 19th century.*

173   CHRIST ON THE MOUNT OF OLIVES. *Polychrome relief from the same crucifix as No. 172.*

174 TWO MEN WITH HATS. *Polychrome relief from a beehive. Železnice, north Bohemia, about 1880.*

175 FRONTAL PANELS OF BEEHIVES WITH POLYCHROME RELIEF DECORATION. *Apiary of the parsonage at Bílý Újezd, north-eastern Bohemia.*

176 DECORATED STUMP BEEHIVES. *Walachian area, Moravia, 19th century.*

177 BEEHIVE WITH A RELIEF OF ST JOHN OF NEPOMUK. *Walachian area, Moravia, 19th century.* ▶

179   WINE-PRESS WITH FIGURAL RELIEFS, DATED 1847. *Made by Jura Švestka, Havřice near Uherský Brod, south-eastern Moravia.*

◄

178   HEAD OF A MAN WITH A HAT. *Mask decorating a stump beehive from the Walachian area, Moravia, 19th century.*

180 **CHEESE MOULD, DATED 1886.** *Orava Valley, north-western Slovakia.*

181 **BABY. GINGERBREAD MOULD FROM NORTH-EASTERN BOHEMIA,** *18th century.* ▶

182　THE SPANISH DANCER, PEPITA DE OLIVA, ON A GINGERBREAD MOULD. *North Bohemia, about 1855.*

183 GINGERBREAD MOULD WITH THE RELIEF OF A LOCOMOTIVE. *Pilsen area, western Bohemia, about 1850.*

B. Free-standing Sculpture

NATURAL FORMS

We have become accustomed to retracing the origins of the formation of materials into three-dimensional shapes back to those natural growths fashioned by shepherds in their leisure hours. This is especially true of the Slovak walking sticks known as *palice* (and their Czech equivalents, the 'Žižka sticks'), serving as supports when hiking in the mountains or used for herding sheep or chasing away wolves. Large museum collections in Bratislava and Martin contain numerous expressive and sometimes even caricature-like variants of human and animal heads shaped by shepherds from the hard knots of suitably gnarled branches. Twisted roots were also fashioned by shepherds and peasants into serpentine forms called *kluky* in Silesia and used mostly as symbols of office (for example, mayoral staffs). The same early stage of development of free-standing figural sculpture can be seen, for example, in the stone *mamlas* from Prague — a boulder protecting the corner of a house. Its roughly conical shape was chiselled to resemble a head or bust. In the same category belong the beehives made of twisted and braided straw, whose jug-like bodies were often shaped to form a devil's head or the half-figure of a girl. Thus the folk artist of any period could find himself once again at this starting point in time, irrespective of the previous historical development of form, to which he then, knowingly or unknowingly, contributed through his work.

WALKING STICKS

KLUKY

An important form of three-dimensional expression was also the shaping of ceremonial objects, figures and toys from natural materials, sometimes combined with artificial ones. These include a wide assortment of figures made of dried fruit, known from the former St Nicholas's Fairs in Klatovy and Prague and made in a less developed form by children during their holidays, as well as the dolls made from maize husks, straw or pieces of rag, and toy animals made of chestnuts and acorns.

CEREMONIAL
FIGURES AND TOYS

Some of these objects (for instance, the wedding *vrkoče*, 'wreaths of dough', magic dolls and figurines) were used in various ceremonies and for magic. Aesthetically, the most complex among them were figurines representing Death (*Smrtka*, *Mařena*) as a symbol of winter and the temporary death of vegetation. On the Sunday before Easter, girls used to carry these figurines in procession from the village and either throw them into a river or brook, or burn them. A masterpiece of this kind is the Death figure called *čaramara*, from Ořechovičky near Brno, which is on display in the Prague Ethnographical Museum. Its straw body is dressed in white linen cloth, the face is covered with red drawing, and the whole figurine is richly decorated with egg and snail shells. Quite interesting, too, is another figure displayed in the same museum — the 'golden hag' from the Pardubice area in eastern Bohemia, a straw maiden with plaits. This was the shape given to the last sheaf for the harvest festival. The same principles were applied to all such figures — a body was made of straw and decorated with pieces of different fabrics and various symbols. The Moravian *slaměňák* (straw-man) or the Slovak *obilník* (corn-man) from village carnival processions differed from them only in the fact that a live man was wrapped up in straw. Even the more complicated *pohřebenář* from the Nedašov area in Moravia was basically dressed up in the same manner. Fancy costumes, often replaced by a white sheet, and the face masks which supplemented them, developed great variety and

FIGURINES

MASKS

expressiveness throughout Czechoslovakia due to the tradition of Shrovetide carnivals and the similar festivities which took place before Christmas. Such carnivals with parades of masked villagers are still held in many communities, especially in south Bohemia, south Moravia and Slovakia. Although the masks that have been preserved date only from the nineteenth and twentieth centuries, we may presume that their tradition is much older, going back to the medieval and Renaissance buffoons' processions and perhaps even as far as ancient magic rituals. Rarely, however, do we detect in their form the influence of the different art styles — only, perhaps, in the case of harlequins and the south Bohemian 'Mother of the Shrovetide'. Usually, even such figures as Bacchus, Sweepers, who ceremonially cleaned the living rooms before Christmas and Easter, or Lucias, the personifications of St Lucia, the patron saint of weavers, are constructed with the directness of the popular approach. Their main features are simply, often naïvely, accentuated (white sheet, stuffed belly, conical beak, bloody mask) and they bear other necessary attributes (goose pinion, blood-stained knife, or sack). The sculptural character of the masks is noticeable particularly in the case of figures which are meant to evoke fear and horror *(Bloody Perchta)*, which are mysteriously silent (the Slovak *Lucia*) or excessively tall (the goat-like *Turoň* in Slovakia). The face masks or entire heads, fashioned from starched paper or linen and accentuated by polychromy, bits of fur, real horns, etc., and stuck out on a pole from a sheet cloaking the body, often showed a highly ingenious design.

NATIVITY FIGURES

In the case of these face masks — and still more frequently in the case of the little figures for Nativity scenes, toys, dolls, etc. — the creators sometimes produced a more sculptural form by modelling some parts from different pasty materials (paper pulp, bread dough). However, most three-dimensional Nativity figures were carved from wood and their dress, accessories and tools, etc., were painted on them or were made of other materials and attached to them. As far as the motifs are concerned, the same applies to these figures as to those painted on paper, except that the wooden figures are artistically more original because they are less easily copied than their paper counterparts. The Nativity scenes made of such figures are often very large and colourful and in some cases are fitted with ingenious mechanical equipment which sets some groups of figures into motion. Individual figures were occasionally produced for sale. Some Nativity figures, and frequently also larger group compositions, are attractive for the qualities of their sculptural conception, their appropriate characterization in scenes of everyday life or the impressiveness of their simple, quiet emotional impact, set in their idyllic, pastoral scenes.

PUPPETS
(MARIONETTES)

By their being fitted for movement, these Nativity figures are sometimes very close to marionettes, which were usually carved or shaped from other materials and dressed, also by amateurs. Folk puppeteers, as exemplified by Matěj Kopecký (1775 -1847), played a major role in village cultural life — especially in Bohemia — in the eighteenth and nineteenth centuries. Puppet carvers shared in the creation of the typical characters of the native or adopted repertoire of marionette theatres. The puppets were usually half a metre tall. The smaller ones, used in small home theatres, were carved by the father of the family or were even painted and cut out from cardboard or made from other materials by the children themselves. The north Bohemian *Krakonoš* was also a puppet — although usually not used in marionette plays. He was the legendary ruler of the Giant Mountains and his figure was fashioned from natural materials — pieces of wood, bark, moss, etc. — and displayed in the windows of cottages. Thus literature and folklore often inspired the creation of a work of art.

The peak of Czech and Slovak sculptural folk creation was surely the polychrome wooden statues displayed in niches and rooms of houses, in chapels and field sanctuaries, in mine altars and other places, where protection was sought. St Florian was supposed to protect the house against fire, St John of Nepomuk against flood and dishonour; St Anne and the Virgin Mary were protectresses of children and of women at childbirth as well as at the time of death; St Barbara protected miners and lumberjacks against accident, SS Wendelinus and Leonard were the patron saints of cattle threatened by the plague, while people sought protection against epidemics from SS Sebastian, Roch and Rosalie; St Apollonia helped against toothache, etc. The Czechs and Slovaks shared the popularity of this genre to some extent with the Germans and Austrians, but mainly with the Poles. The artistic value of the Czech and Slovak statuettes is similar to that of their Polish parallels. However, in contrast to the Polish, Czech figural wood-carving of saints was more affected by mass production. This was especially true of statues of the most popular patron saints, such as SS Florian and John of Nepomuk, and of sculptural reproductions of famous pilgrimage Madonnas — those of Svatá Hora, Vambeřice, Vranov, Křtiny, Hostýn, the Pietà of Šaštín, and others.

These sculptures, most often small but in some instances of considerable size, do not usually have their stylistic and typological predecessors in the Baroque, as one might expect, but rather in the Late Gothic from which they are separated by several centuries. In the Czech Lands, as much as in Slovakia, the pilgrimage statues representing Our Lady of Grace were mostly works of Gothic art. The village carver, however, usually did not have them as direct models, but instead used a graphic reproduction — a Baroque engraving, woodcut or lithograph printed in pilgrimage pamphlets. Even so, he reproduced faithfully their customary features — their posture and bent knee, their dress with the traditional system of folds, the shape of head and type of crown, as well as all the accepted attributes. Thus, the outer form of these sculptures closely approaches the Gothic models and, moreover, even the content, the inner meaning, of these creations in many cases has something which is quite close to the Middle Ages. There existed, of course, similarities in the life of the villager in the period of the second serfdom to that of medieval man. There are many parallels in his attitude to the religious content of the forms presented to him during church ceremonies, festivals and devotional exercises, which he himself then tried to express. Even the medieval tone in the Baroque (the revival of places of pilgrimage, medieval religious plays, the tradition of hermits, and many other features), when it eventually penetrated into post-Baroque village culture, was probably very close to the heart of those peasants who were poor, most open to emotional influences, and who were capable of submitting to the excitement of their creative talent, of believing in their artistic mission. Strong emotional qualities with mystic overtones are manifested chiefly in those works which were original and were not produced in series. Their creators were not heads of family (or any other) workshops which reproduced one or several types in an identical form. They were usually paupers, individuals who were not infrequently objects of derision and contempt. They differed from the farmer or even the farmhand by certain divergencies from the conventions of village life. While the exterior form of their work, the established type, reflects characteristically rural features, some of its expressive elements also reflect the creators' own spiritual feelings. These powerful works, reminiscent of primitive art, have attracted considerable attention at exhibitions — in Prague, Warsaw, Brussels, Paris — as have other, modest sculptures of rounded and subdued form, expressing a desire for peace and contentment even when treating cruel themes.

SERIAL CARVING

Nevertheless, even carvings produced in large numbers on a commercial basis have their specific aesthetic values arising from the perfection to which, by repetition, the particular canon was brought. The best known of these sculptures is the Madonna of Svatá Hora near Příbram, whose carved images became popular even in neighbouring countries. This statuette, usually carved from a piece of spruce or limewood, was a product of an extensive cottage industry with an interesting economic organization, in villages around the mining town of Příbram, especially in Zálany, in the nineteenth and early twentieth centuries. The Příbram area was the largest of the centres where wood-carvings were produced in series, and documents and information on the range of products and production techniques have been preserved. The local carvers also produced toys, Nativity figures and small figures of miners in their traditional costume, holding mining lamps in their hands. Unfortunately, the other centres were not registered in time by scholars and thus today we only know their typical products but not their exact location.

WOODEN HEADS FOR BONNETS

In a number of cases the wooden busts which were used for stretching bonnets in production or after washing may be considered as sculptural works. Those that have been preserved show different concepts of form which, in spite of the workaday purpose of these objects, are artistically ingenious, ranging from a lovely gentleness underlined by a slight touch of colour, to strict, stylized expressions which approach some of the best products of modern sculpture.

PUPPETS (TOYS)

A similar expressiveness of form, confined and stiff, is found in some wooden dolls for children — babies in swaddling clothes known from Bohemia (Pilsen, Humpolec) and Moravia (Valašské Klobouky). Even an ordinary rocking horse sometimes displays this efficacy of profile drawn with the best possible line, as does a small toy horse shaped from a roughly worked piece of wood with a strand of horsehair added.

HUMAN HEADS AS DECORATION

Slovakia can boast of several relics with grandly sculpted human heads. Two such heads top the posts of a farmstead gate; one belongs to the figure of a 'wedding man', which had a ceremonial function, and another one decorates a shingle-cutting bench. We see here not only the products of the same extraordinary talent which characterizes many Slovak statuettes of saints, but also a sense of form which is highly effective even for modern man.

FIGURAL BEEHIVES

Slovakia, too, is the locale of most nineteenth and twentieth-century figural beehives where the entire stump is cut into the shape of a human or animal figure — a saint, a monk, a priest, the patron saint of bee-keepers — St Ambrose, a Turkish soldier, a farmer and his wife, a townsman and his wife, a man with a pannier, a bear, etc. A Polish scholar speaks in this connection of works of monumental folk sculpture. What he probably has in mind is the type rather than the value, but some of these

Czech and Slovak beehives may be thus described even from the viewpoint of their artistic quality. They include so-called 'stretchers' in the shape of reclining lions, which are reminiscent not only of the lion supports of Romanesque portals but also of the stone animals decorating the pillars of the gates of some farmsteads in northern Bohemia and the Orava Valley.

Free-standing stone sculpture is the pride of folk art in Czechoslovakia and is not as rare as was formerly believed. For some time now, we have known several Slovak statues of folk origin, such as that of St Wendelinus of Húl, dating from 1871, or the Crucifixion with the Virgin Mary and St John from Nové Mesto nad Váhom, dating from the early nineteenth century, and some attractive smaller stone sculptures. Research carried out in recent years has also produced more information on stone-masonry in Bohemia (the north, north-east and south-west) and Moravia. Primacy in this respect is held by northern Bohemia (the vicinity of the towns of Turnov, Jablonec and Jičín) with interesting relics, the oldest of which reflect a rustication of the Rococo style. The entrances to north Bohemian farmsteads were sometimes decorated with painted stone sculptures of saints, in particular the regionally popular St Wenceslas, but also St Anne and others. In some instances these works imitated on a smaller scale the statues standing in the village green. The landscape was enlivened, too, with roadside crosses and field sanctuaries. However, several family workshops specializing in stone-masonry of folk character were established in this area only in the nineteenth century when experience with the already familiar Baroque and Rococo styles of sculpture was further enhanced by the great impact of the new forms of the Empire style and by demands for the decoration in stone of houses and the open landscape, the products of these busy workshops being geared to the needs of small towns and villages. The best known of the master stone-masons of this period was Jan Zeman, who was working about the middle of the nineteenth century. Northern Bohemia still has many examples of the work of these folk artists, mostly in villages and along roads, often in their original situations. Besides numerous crosses they include statues with polychrome relief on their socles, such as that of the Holy Trinity crowning the Virgin Mary, one of the works of Jan Zeman, located in Lhota Bradlecká. Field sanctuaries, too, often have rich figural decoration. Also preserved is some narrative statuary of folk origin, such as the *Christ Bidding Farewell to His Mother in Bethany* or the *Apostles Sleeping on the Mount of Olives*, now located in the garden of the old parsonage in Jablonec nad Nisou.

Outside these areas where stone statues are most frequent one may now also find smaller stone sculptures in museums. Thus, for example, we find a remarkable statue of an older woman with a baby in swaddling clothes in her arms in the south Bohemian town of Nové Hrady. It is thought to have been originally a house sign which stood on a column in front of the house of a midwife. It does, indeed, seem to represent a secular theme. The monumental concept of this figure contrasts in a bizarre way with the tiny feet on which the half-figure stands. In the case of other relics, too, such as the statue of St Catherine from Olomouc, the difficulty of shaping stone produced poorly differentiated forms and a block-like effect.

These and many other features of the folk approach to form still offer researchers the opportunity to study and define its specific character in greater detail.

184 A SHEPHERD'S STICK. *Central Slovakia, 19th century.*

185 WOMAN. *Unpainted wood-carving by Pavol Bavlna, central Slovakia, 1967.*

186 VOTIVE ANIMALS OF WROUGHT IRON. *South Bohemia, 19th century.*

188 'MOTHER OF THE SHROVETIDE'. MAN'S CEREMONIAL
MASK. *Dobrkovská Lhotka, south Bohemia, about 1950.*

189 'CORN MAN'. *Carnival mask from Omšenie, western Slovakia, late
19th century. Detail.*

190 HEAD AND TAIL OF THE CARNIVAL MASK CALLED *ŠIMLA. Doudleby area of south Bohemia, late 19th century.*

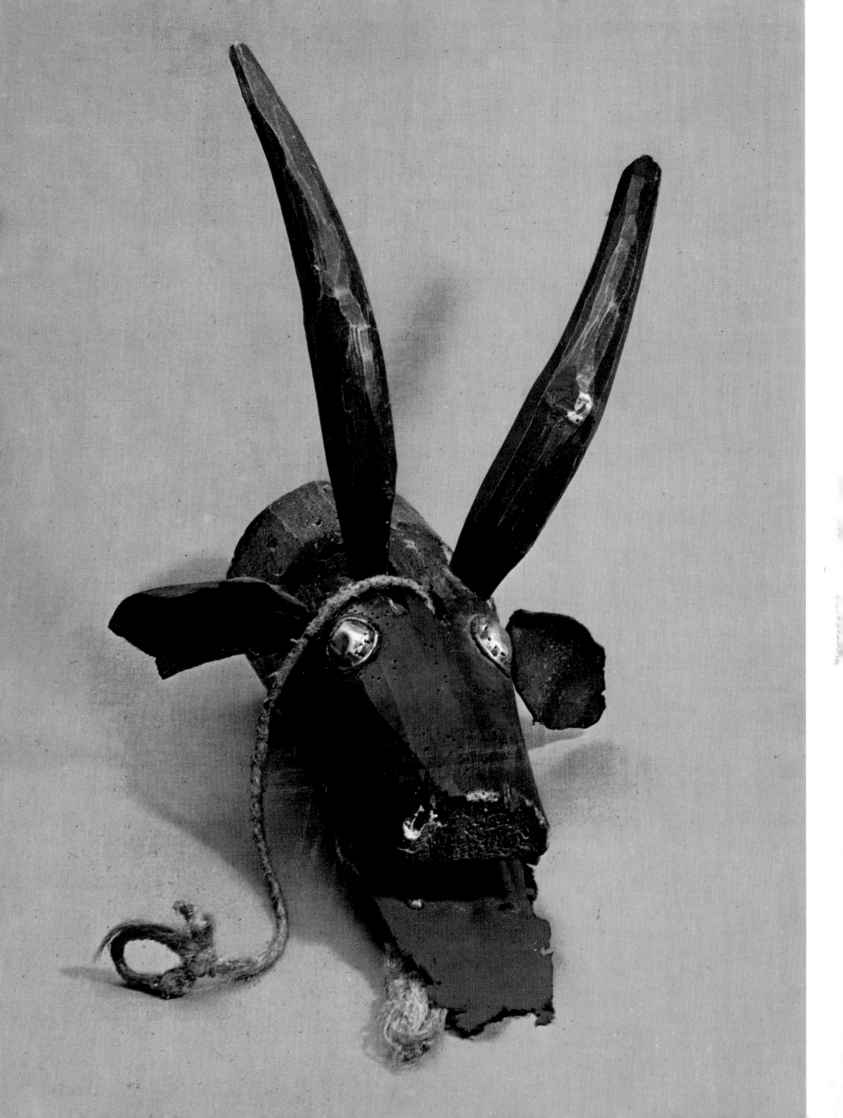

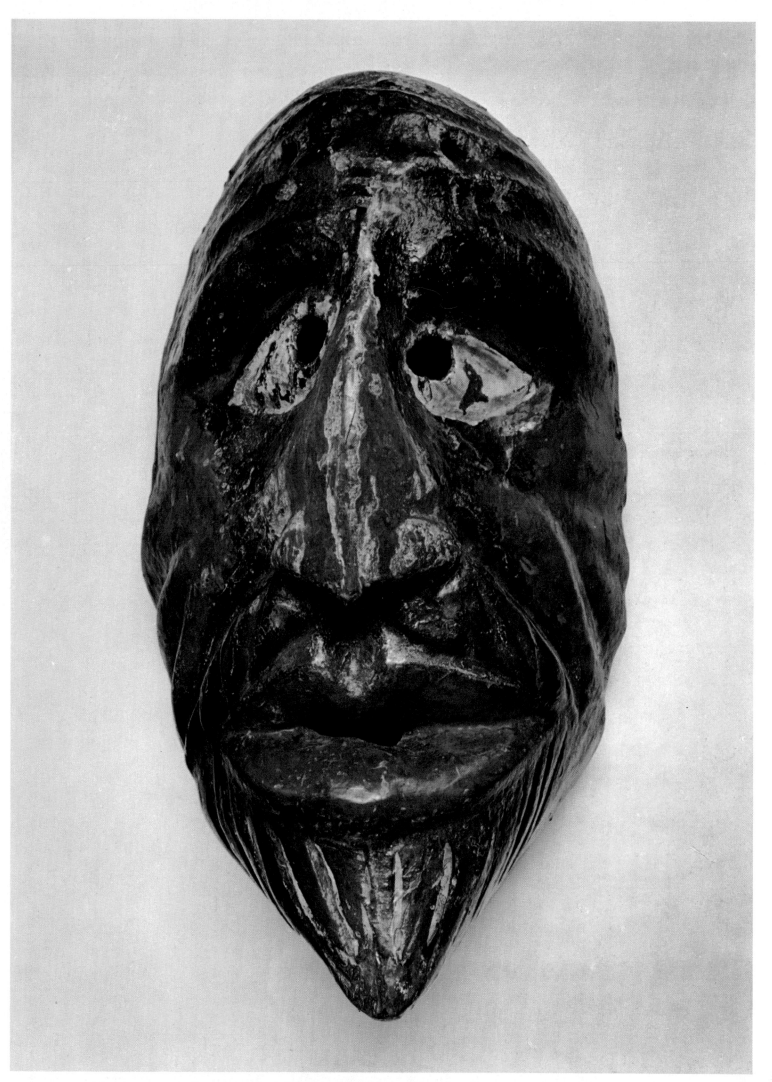

192   FACE MASK OF THE DEVIL FROM A CARNIVAL PROCESSION AT HLUK IN 1890. *South Moravia.*

193   FIGURAL CERAMIC FLOWERPOT. *Made by Martin Fremr, a potter from Losiná, District of Pilsen, in the middle of the 19th century.*

▼

194 FIGURES FROM A NATIVITY SCENE. *Bohemian-Moravian Highlands, first half of the 19th ce*

BY THE
CE, *eastern Moravia, 1970.*

UGH BY THE

196 VERONICA. FAÏENCE WALL STOUP FROM THE VICINITY OF LUHAČOVICE, *eastern Moravia, 18th-19th century.*

198 CAROLLERS' NATIVITY SCENE. *Orava Valley, north-western Slovakia,*
19th century.

199 BAGPIPER FIGURES FROM A MINERS' NATIVITY SCENE. *Painted*
wood; vicinity of Banská Štiavnica, central Slovakia, 19th century.

◄ 197 MARY'S HEART. *Frenštát pod Radhoštěm or its vicinity, north-eastern*
Moravia, mid-19th century.

200 BAKER'S WIFE. *Wood and dough toy from Příbram area, central Bohemia, second half of the 19th century.*

201 WOODEN TOY HORSE. *Central Slovakia, 20th century.* ▶

202 MERRY-GO-ROUND. *Wooden toy carved by*
Václav Žákovec of Dobříč, south-western Bohemia,
mid-20th century.

204 **MERMAID HOLDING SCALES.** *Detail. Rychnov nad Kněžnou, north-eastern Bohemia, second half of the 18th century.*

203 **STRIDING LION.** *Wooden beehive from Stropešín, western Moravia, about 1930.*

248

206a, b ST JOHN OF NEPOMUK AND THE VIRGIN MARY. *Wooden statuettes; central Slovakia, 19th and 20th century.*

207 ST FLORIAN. *Painted wood-carving; early 20th century, Pstruží, eastern Moravia.*

◄

205 CARRYING THE MADONNA OF SVATÁ HORA. *Pilgrimage souvenir toy of wood and dough, Příbram area, central Bohemia, second half of the 19th century.*

209   CRUCIFIX FROM A SANCTUARY. *Painted wood, Kostelec nad Orlicí, north-eastern Bohemia, after 1800.*

◄

208   WOODEN CRUCIFIX FROM THE AREA OF KAŠPERSKÉ HORY, *south Bohemia.*

210   CRUCIFIX. *Detail. Painted wood, Hartmanice near Sušice, south Bohemia, about 1800.*   ►

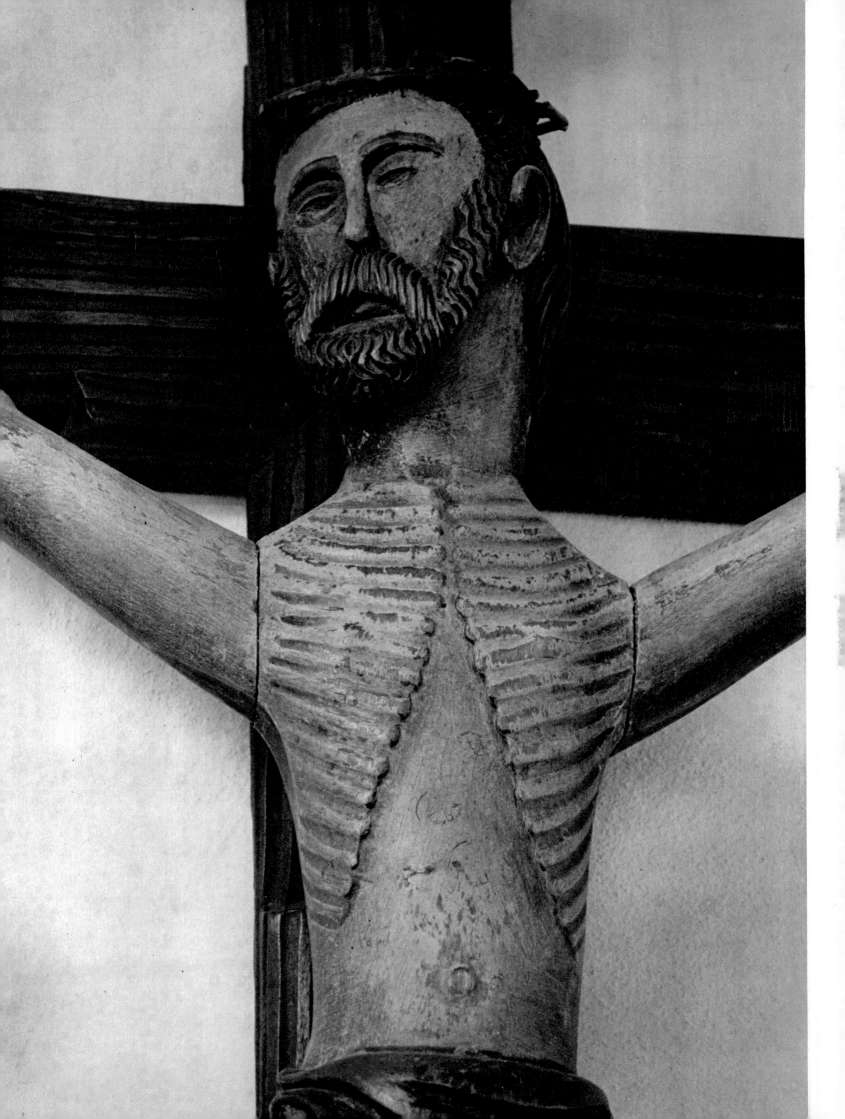

252

211 **CHRIST ON THE MOUNT OF OLIVES.** *Statuette from a niche at Stará Bělá near Ostrava, Silesia, about 1820. Painted wood.*

◄

212 **CHRIST FALLING UNDER THE CROSS.** *Painted wooden statue from a chapel in Osada, Orava Valley, north-western Slovakia, late 19th century.*

213 SANCTUARY WITH A STATUE OF ST JOHN OF NEPOMUK.
Wood-carving from south Bohemia, about 1800.

214 ST JOHN OF NEPOMUK. *Painted wood-carving, Bohemia.* ▶

215   THE PIETÀ OF ŠAŠTÍN. *Painted wood-carving of serial production. Western Slovakia, late 19th century.*   ▶

216   THE CORONATION OF THE VIRGIN MARY. *Painted sandstone statue by Jan Zeman, dated 1850. Lhota Bradlecká, District of Jičín, north-eastern Bohemia.*

258

217 MADONNA AND CHILD WITH BRANCHES.
Painted wood-carving from central Slovakia, late 18th century.

◄

218 MADONNA AND CHILD. *Painted wooden statue
from Pstruží, eastern Moravia, probably late 18th century.*

219 MADONNA AND CHILD.
*Painted wood-carving from western
Slovakia, first half of the 19th century.*

220 STANNE TEACHING MARY.
*Wood-carving from south Bohemia,
19th century.*

221 PIETÀ. *Painted wood-carving adapted for placement in a niche. Těšín*   222 PIETÀ. *Painted wooden statue, probably of Slovak origin, 19th century.*
area of Silesia, late 18th or 19th century.

▶

223 MADONNA AND CHILD. *Painted wooden statue from western Slovakia, 19th century.*

224 MADONNA AND CHILD. *Painted wood-carving, south Moravia, 19th century.*

225 MIDWIFE. *Granite house sign from Nové Hrady, south Bohemia.*

226 ST CATHERINE. *Sandstone statue from a niche; Olomouc or its vicinity, central Moravia.*

227 ST ANNE WITH THE VIRGIN MARY AND INFANT JESUS.
*Painted wood; Frenštát pod Radhoštěm or its vicinity, north-eastern
Moravia, mid-19th century.*

228 THE HOLY TRINITY. *Painted wooden statue.* ▶

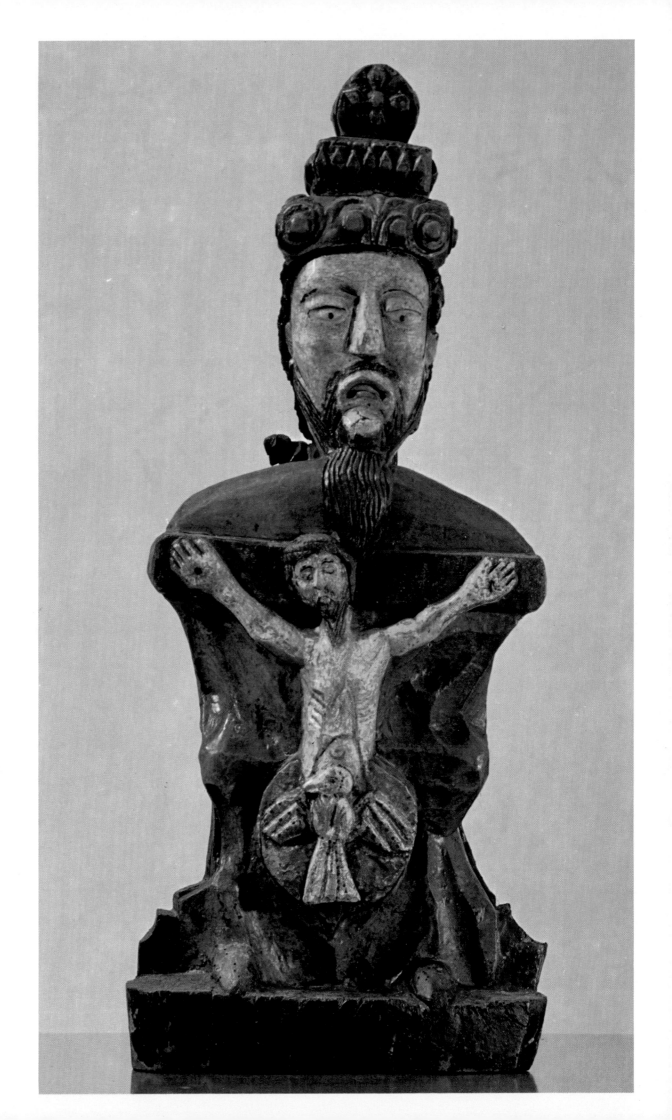

229   THE VIRGIN MARY. *Painted sandstone statue from a niche in a farmstead gate at Kalužník, north Bohemia.*

230 MADONNA AND CHILD. *Painted wooden statue from the Dlask farmstead at Dolánky, north Bohemia, first half of the 19th century.*

◀

231 HEAD FOR SHAPING BONNETS. *Painted wood. Pilsen area, western Bohemia, after 1800.*

232 HEAD FOR SHAPING BONNETS. *Pear wood with traces of polychromy. Turnov, north Bohemia, first half of the 19th century.*

233 'WEDDING OLD MAN'. *Wood-carving. Pekelník, Orava Valley (Poland), about 1900.*

234 HEAD FROM A CARPENTER'S WORKBENCH. *Wood-carving from Zakamenné, District of Dolný Kubín, Orava Valley, central Slovakia, about 1930.*

235 FIGURAL STUMP BEEHIVE FROM HORNÝ TURČEK,
District of Martin, central Slovakia, 1940.

VII. The Specific Character of Czech and Slovak Folk Art in a European Context

236 EASTER EGG WITH SCRATCHED DECORATION

from the southern part of the Walachian area,

north-eastern Moravia, mid-20th century.

As at the beginning we mentioned the role played by folk art and culture in the history of the Czech and Slovak nations, we should now outline at least briefly their place and significance in the context of European folk art in general. This is not a matter that can easily be settled, for it requires more information than has previously been available. No monographs exist dealing with this subject as it applies to individual countries, nor is there a satisfactory comparative synthesis of the material from Europe as a whole. Therefore, what we say here can in no way be considered as definitive. It is rather an outline, the individual aspects of which must be traced further by comparative study, and if necessary, corrected. It will also be necessary to abandon many nineteenth-century prejudices which have become firmly entrenched in some interpretations of folk art. In many respects it will be essential to correct the beliefs in a national or local uniqueness of certain types and forms of this art which still prevail. Against arguments of 'national originality' we must recognize and appreciate the fruitful impact of neighbouring cultures, the contacts and intermingling of different ethnic groups, on the formation of creative folk expression.

We may assume that the development of the surviving forms of folk art in Czechoslovakia began somewhat later than, for example, in Scandinavia, Ireland or Scotland, where some elements of folk art form developed directly from production which was typical of the period of the Great Migrations. This applies, for example, to such features as braided ornaments in carved decoration. In the Nordic regions — Iceland is a typical example — tradition extended the life of these characteristic forms by many centuries. This was due perhaps to the fact that Romanesque and Gothic art did not have such a profound impact there as it had in central Europe. In what is now Czechoslovakia such pronounced changes occurred in the way of life, and thus also in the field of art, in the first half of the second millennium A.D. that the old, tribal forms were forgotten and only folklore documents the numerous phenomena which may be remnants of ideas and beliefs prevalent in the age preceding the adoption of Christianity. In this connection we might consider whether this does not also apply to some objects from the sphere of folk art which were used at different annual and family ceremonies and for certain acts which undoubtedly have their origins in magic. What we have in mind are the different figures of Death, maypoles, wreaths and wedding table cakes, Easter eggs, magic dolls, figural sheafs, etc. So far, however, this question has remained open, for we know how profoundly the form of these objects was influenced by the medieval and Renaissance folk festivals, and we also know that the Baroque revival of these festivals produced further new forms.

Only a few, isolated relics reminiscent of folk art are known from the period when the feudal system was beginning to develop, but they have no place in its subsequent evolution. The beginning of the entire system, as we study it today, for example with respect to folk costume and its decoration, may be taken to be the late Middle Ages and the Renaissance. The antiquity of forms in ethnographic material, in architecture, dress, implements and vessels, seems to be confirmed by their occurrence in other territories and continents. They could thus have belonged to the general European or to the general human culture, perhaps even before the spread of Christianity. This is especially true of the use of large sheets as dresses, the forms of different vessels, tools and implements, as well as some principles of human habitation. It has not yet been demonstrated whether these cases involve an uninterrupted tradition (and if so, of what time) or rather what is often called the 'eternal recurrence' of types.

In tracing the evolution of folk culture, a simple developmental sequence leading from the simplest to the most complicated is not sufficient, because by identifying it with a chronological sequence we would run counter to the actual course of development. We know that it was a complex process in which we find the adoption of already developed, finished forms, as well as many reversions to the primitive under the influence of wars and for various other reasons, both general and local, and over long periods of time.

The Thirty Years War was a major hiatus which, for Czech and Moravian villages, produced a divergence from some other European cultures. As we are increasingly discovering, Czech folk culture was relatively well-developed already prior to that war, but under the impact of the unprecedented holocaust, from the second half of the seventeenth century on, folk art transformed the stylistic heritage of the Renaissance whilst at the same time adopting the Baroque way of life and art. Thus the growing Baroque Counter-Reformation frequently made use of features reminiscent of medieval art. In figural folk art this meant an inspiration by Gothic statues and their graphic reproductions which often preserved the medieval stylistic character of their models. In this sphere numerous similarities with German folk art exist, both on the territory of present-day Czechoslovakia and outside its borders, and with Austrian folk art. The unification of states, which in the decisive period brought the Czech Lands and Slovakia into the central European Habsburg monarchy, only strengthened these common features.

One remarkable aspect of folk art in Czechoslovakia is the great wealth of traditional folk dress, which in some places is unusually diverse, as well as the fact that in some parts of the country the present-day form of historical 'folk costumes' is still worn on special occasions or even every day — in the Chodsko district in Bohemia, the Slovácko region of south-eastern Moravia, and in quite a number of places in Slovakia. In this respect there is some similarity to the southern parts of the former Austro-Hungarian monarchy, where the rural population continued to wear richly decorated traditional dress for a long time. The great diversity of folk dress, and the great variety of other forms of folk art, may be attributed to the present great boom in handicrafts in Czechoslovakia today.

During the nineteenth century some aspects of folk art changed in the sphere of cottage industry both in the Czech Lands and in Slovakia. Additional fields of this semi-professional work made use of traditional forms and ornaments. The initial prosperity of some industrial branches (glass production, for instance) promoted the emergence and growth of new types of folk creation. Czechoslovakia is the centre of folk painting on glass in Europe and its collections contain an immense wealth of such works. In other cases, older production organized in workshops or in the form of cottage industry — lace-making is one example — made its contribution to folk dress and village house interiors, and thereby spurred a new upsurge of popular creativeness. This oscillation between handicrafts, cottage industry and native folk art might be considered typical of Czechoslovakia, did it not have parallels in other central European countries and in the Balkans.

The large-scale production of carved wooden sculptures of saints, crucifixes, Nativity scene figures and toys, so typical of Bohemia and Moravia — though less so of Slovakia — also has its links with central Europe, in particular with Austria and Bavaria. There is a less pronounced similarity to Poland where figural carvings of this type were rarely reproduced in large numbers, and where original creation was preferred. Typical of the Czech Lands and Slovakia in the nineteenth century was the great development of the production of Nativity scenes, with both originally created figures and figures produced on a serial basis.

Thus creative folk culture in Czechoslovakia is inseparably a part of the central European context. It is one of the most highly diversified cultures in terms of genre and form, with a wide range of types and a great wealth of surviving relics. Amongst the Slavonic cultures, Polish and Lusatian folk art is closest to it while among the non-Slavonic cultures Austrian and German, and in Slovakia Hungarian folk creations are very similar to it. In some aspects Slovakia in particular has close links with the southern parts of the former Austro-Hungarian Empire. The folk art of the Carpathian Ukrainians, which is most remarkable and rich, has its continuation in the same ethnic group on the territory of former Galicia in Poland and in Soviet Trans-Carpathian Ukraine.

The development of some artistic forms and the decline of others were also influenced by the religion professed by the village population. It was — at the time of the greatest flowering of folk art — most often Roman Catholic but in both nations — Czech and Slovak — there were also Protestant minorities and in eastern Slovakia, among the Carpathian Ukrainians, Russian Orthodox and Greek Orthodox denominations. The Protestants usually had less decorated and more subdued dress and home interiors, whilst vividly colourful fabrics and richly painted icons are typical of the Greek Orthodox.

There is no doubt that the people of Czechoslovakia made many prominent and original contributions to the folk art of Europe. We find remarkable types and individual designs of high artistic value, especially in the treatment of framed dwellings, wooden churches and their decoration, in figural wood-carving as well as in stone-masonry, in embroidery, fabrics and lace. Nor can we ignore the sphere of ceremonial and ritual objects, while the charming works of different genres of painting would undoubtedly gain prominence in any all-European exhibition.

Taken as a whole, this art definitely belongs to the past. But no definition would be complete without mentioning that some of its types and manifestations continue to be created — Easter eggs, pottery, decorative fabrics, wickerwork, etc. Thus, even under new conditions of life, these ancient popular crafts still participate in the development of Czechoslovakia's creative culture, contributing to it an inspiring depth of feeling.

LIST OF ILLUSTRATIONS

1 THE CHURCH OF ST JOHN THE BAPTIST IN SLAVOŇOV NEAR DOBRUŠKA was built of wood in 1553. Joined to its single nave is a rectangular presbytery with a sacristy and narthex. The flat ceiling is covered with paintings dating from 1705. Nearby stands a belfry built at the same time, partly of masonry and partly of planking. The two structures may be said to fall within the sphere of folk creation.

2 BATIK-DECORATED EASTER EGG with a carmine red drawing of a plant and a bird on a black background. It was made by Mrs. Anselmová from Bohuslavice, District of Valašské Klobouky, south Moravia, about 1950.
Archives of the Centre for Folk Arts and Crafts, Uherské Hradiště.

3 DETAIL OF A WEDDING BANNER from the community of Meziříčko, showing scenes of wedding preparations; flat embroidery of red and blue thread on white linen cloth. The figures on the original are 12 cm high. Bohemian-Moravian Highlands, dated 1850.
Ethnographical Institute of the Moravian Museum, Brno.

4 BRASS HAIRPIN, west Bohemian type, 19th century.
Ethnographical Department of the Historical Museum, National Museum, Prague.

5 MOTHER-OF-PEARL BROOCHES, known as *kotuly*, for Walachian men's shirts.
National Museum, Prague.

6 BYŠIČKY, DISTRICT OF NYMBURK. Farmsteads built in the Elbe River basin were characterized by a frontal arcade formed by ornamentally shaped queen posts and straining beams supporting the triangular gable of a thatched saddleback roof. The plastered and whitewashed timber-framed frontal wall emphasized the vigour of the façade which was usually broken by a pair of windows, indicating the ancient origin of this structural type. This particular house dates from the 18th century, after the founding of the village in 1717.

7 SÁDEK, DISTRICT OF SVITAVY. Farmsteads in villages formed around strip-fields were separated from each other. This affected their construction, and they usually enclosed a small yard. The Sádek farmstead is a typical example, made of timber-framed walls with technically perfect joints at the corners. Some structural and ornamental elements, the use of rounded beams and the hipped roof, indicate the relative antiquity of this structure. One of its chief qualities is its position on the hillside and its harmonious blending with the surrounding landscape.

8 PŘÍŠOVICE, DISTRICT OF LIBEREC. A timber-framed two-storey farmstead. The upper floor is held up by a supporting structure of posts which provides the front walls with a decorative blind arcade. There is a triangular, decorative gable and a thatched saddleback roof. The window-frames of the granaries on the top floor are most interesting.

9 TCHOŘOVICE, DISTRICT OF STRAKONICE. This farmstead illustrates the characteristic type of farm buildings of south-western Bohemia with the timber-framed walls of the house made of unshaped, whitewashed beams, and the saddleback thatched roof ending in trapezoid gables.

10 PODZÁMČÍ, DISTRICT OF DOMAŽLICE. A typical example of the corner joints below the eaves of a log house in the Chodsko district. Note the ornamental shaping of this construction, which underlines its structural function.

11 BŘESTEK, DISTRICT OF UHERSKÉ HRADIŠTĚ. At the back of this farmyard in southern Moravia stands a timber-framed wooden barn in which the horizontal beams of the walls fit into grooves cut in the supporting posts. This structural principle, which was replaced by others in more recent times, is evidence of the age of this building, the origin of which may be in the 17th but not later than the early 18th century.

12 JEŠETICE, DISTRICT OF BENEŠOV. Polygonal barns are common in most parts of present-day Czechoslovakia. Their relatively low, skilfully made timber-framed walls were built on a ground-plan with six to twelve sides. Their interior is usually divided into three parts, it being possible to drive through the central one. The earliest known barns of this type have been traced to the beginning of the 17th century.

13 LYSOVICE, DISTRICT OF VYŠKOV. The entrance porch, or *žudr*, projecting from the façade of farmsteads in the Haná region of central Moravia is an original way of articulating the street front of houses and the characteristic shape of the opening adds a rhythm to the structures facing the village square. In contrast to the two-storey *žudr* to be found in other parts of the Haná region, in the Vyškov area it is an exclusively one-storey structure. The attic houses the granary.

14 LECHOTICE, DISTRICT OF KROMĚŘÍŽ. Timber-framed houses with clay walls and with a two-storey granary incorporated in the main body of the house, which is covered with a thatched hipped roof, are typical of the folk architecture of central Moravia. Their interior lay-out evolved from the usual three-room plan of a living room, hall and granary.

15 DOUBRAVY, DISTRICT OF GOTTWALDOV. This two-storey granary from the vicinity of Luhačovské Zálesí is a relic of this ancient type of building with all its characteristic structural and architectural features. It is typical, however, only of the territory of central Moravia of which Luhačovské Zálesí is a part. In most parts of Bohemia two-storey granaries were separated from the house and played a quite different role in the development of village architecture.

16 SVINKY, DISTRICT OF TÁBOR. The façade of this farmstead with its two-storey granary and richly decorated gable, dating from 1841, is a remarkable composition and represents an important relic of south Bohemian village architecture. The less decorated outline of the house on the right, built in 1894, helps to emphasize the fine architecture of the granary. The farmstead has three wings around a rectangular yard which opens into the village green through a vaulted entrance gate with double doors.

17 KOMÁROV, DISTRICT OF TÁBOR. A typical example of the architectural decoration of a granary in the south Bohemian region demonstrates well the manner in which the village masons shaped and composed architectural elements into a remarkable, artistically compact and effective form. The use of three-dimensional elements is underlined with colour. This façade of a granary in Komárov built in 1863, dates from a period in which south Bohemian villages were given their characteristic architectural vivacity.

18 UNHOŠŤ, DISTRICT OF KLADNO. Late Baroque forms used in folk architecture demonstrate a growing prosperity for a part of the village population in the 18th century. However, many of these buildings were erected by the inhabitants of larger towns, who turned increasingly to farming. Their architectural value varies according to the skill of the builders, who were also mostly of urban origin. The façade of this house in Unhošť illustrates the exact form and rich decoration of the Baroque manner, including a sculpture with a religious theme.

19 PALUDZA, DISTRICT OF LIPTOVSKÝ MIKULÁŠ. The design of this façade demonstrates the creative standards attained in a village setting by master masons who had worked on major building projects in the cities or for the nobility. The architectural elements of the structural system, with their pronounced three-dimensional design, break up the wall surface by an interplay of light and shade which is emphasized by the white colouring of the wall.

20 VALAŠSKÁ POLANKA, DISTRICT OF VSETÍN. This cottage from the Walachian region of eastern Moravia shows the type of house built by the poorer inhabitants of the mountain areas. The structural and architectural elements are similar to those found in the Carpathian region. The high standard of the carpentry work even in these dwellings for the very poor is quite remarkable.

21 ŽÍTKOVÁ, DISTRICT OF UHERSKÉ HRADIŠTĚ. The system of heating in the living area, consisting of an open fire in front of an oven with a chimney hood above, is evidence of the antiquity of this type of hill farmstead. Owing to the lack of contact with more advanced neighbouring areas and to the low standard of living of the population, the development of these hill farms lagged behind until the end of the 19th century. The addition of a stove represents something of a later influence, but many archaic features persisted in the homes of the older and more conservative inhabitants of this area until the middle of the 20th century.

22 VALAŠSKÁ BYSTŘICE, DISTRICT OF VSETÍN. The table in the living room was a centre of family life, this role often being reflected in the shapes of its different parts and in the attention paid to its maintenance. In many a village household the table was the most important piece of furniture in the living room.

23 VELKÉ KARLOVICE, DISTRICT OF VSETÍN. A mountain cottage of the type which indicates that it belongs to the Carpathian architectural region. The buildings in the mountains of the Valašsko region blend with a particular harmony into the surrounding landscape.

24 MARTOVCE, DISTRICT OF KOMÁRNO, CADASTRAL PLAN. The clustered arrangement of the houses is determined by the low-lying ground in a flat area with numerous streams. The lay-out of the village is not dependent upon the distribution of the fields but rather upon the specific conditions created by the meandering river.

25 NYNICE, DISTRICT OF PILSEN-NORTH, CADASTRAL PLAN OF 1839. A lay-out based on the village green to which the façades of the houses and the granaries of the farmsteads are turned; the irregular arrangement creates a picturesque skyline.

26 BÁNOV, DISTRICT OF UHERSKÉ HRADIŠTĚ, CADASTRAL PLAN OF 1827. A street-type plan in which the farmsteads are ranged in close sequence with no space between them. The small two-storey granaries are in the street which is terminated by a church, the landmark of the village. Cottages are positioned around a rocky slope behind the church and at the other end of the village street where it turns almost a full right angle. Outside the village stand the house and farm buildings of the former landlord.

27 DETVA, DISTRICT OF ZVOLEN, CADASTRAL PLAN. A street-type plan in which the gabled ends of the farmsteads face the street, ranged closely one beside the other. This Slovak type of street-based village differs markedly from the Czech and Moravian types.

28 VLKOŠ, DISTRICT OF HODONÍN, CADASTRAL PLAN OF 1832. A street-type plan with a street-like green and with smaller cottages built on the outskirts of the village and on the village green. The limits of the built-up area are marked by barns.

29 OSTRÝ KÁMEN, DISTRICT OF SVITAVY, CADASTRAL PLAN OF 1835. A village with a strip-field lay-out of the farmsteads, the buildings of which enclose yards. Smaller cottages were built between the larger farmsteads at a later date.

30 JÍVOVÍ, DISTRICT OF ŽĎÁR NAD SÁZAVOU, CADASTRAL PLAN OF 1835. This type of village with a strip-field lay-out and a green is one of the characteristic forms of internal colonization in the Middle Ages. The village green is the centre onto which converge radially divided strips of land. The farmsteads are constructed around a yard enclosed by the house and farm buildings.

31 BYŠIČKY, DISTRICT OF NYMBURK, CADASTRAL PLAN. The almost circular village green is the result of a colonization project directed by feudal landlords and realized in 1717.

32 PASEKY, DISTRICT OF CHRUDIM, PLAN OF THE GROUND-FLOOR. A farmstead in a village of the strip-field type. The house, the cowshed and tool shed, the barn and a two-storey granary completely enclose a small yard. Most of the wooden walls are built of rough, rounded beams.

33 KACEŘOV, DISTRICT OF PILSEN-NORTH, CADASTRAL PLAN OF 1839. Village with a street-type ground-plan, adjoining a feudal manor. The original plan of this village was not deformed by the subsequent construction of smaller cottages.

34 BOROVÁ, DISTRICT OF SVITAVY. In the strip-field system of villages the free-standing farmsteads stand out prominently because of the colourful horizontal decoration of their external walls, due to the jointing of their timber-framed construction. The combination of the white surfaces of their masonry with timber-framed and whitewashed walls produces harmonious compositions.

35 HOŘÍNĚVES, DISTRICT OF HRADEC KRÁLOVÉ. This old inn, dating from 1720, is a striking landmark on the edge of the village. The design is notable, with a large number of structural and carved wooden architectural elements. The horizontally jointed framework of the walls gives a distinctive colour decoration.

36 VELKÁ NAD VELIČKOU, DISTRICT OF HODONÍN. The characteristic colour schemes of the street fronts of houses in southern Moravia are based on the rich colour tones of the plaster which is sprayed onto surfaces enclosed within a white frame. A sequence of façades in several striking colours is a major factor in the architectural pattern of villages in this region.

37 KLEČATY, DISTRICT OF TÁBOR. The spacious greens of villages in south Bohemia are characterized by abundant vegetation, ponds and small chapels. All this is framed by farmsteads whose façades are decorated with fine stucco ornaments and form graceful silhouettes against the sky. The low-key colour patterns of the façades are based primarily on white, light blue and ochre, and also, but less frequently, on the contrasting colours of the architectural details.

38 PLÁSTOVICE, DISTRICT OF ČESKÉ BUDĚJOVICE. The architecture of village masons in south Bohemia developed an originality of form about the middle of the 19th century. Especially noteworthy is their method of articulating the façades by a sequence of buildings and fence walls. Situated in the open space of the village was usually a small religious structure, a belfry or a smithy.

39 KUŽELOV, DISTRICT OF HODONÍN. A windmill of the Dutch type on a mountain ridge on the Moravian-Slovak frontier is a prominent landmark dominating the surrounding countryside.

40 RYMICE, DISTRICT OF KROMĚŘÍŽ, AN ANALYSIS OF THE DEVELOPMENT OF A GROUP OF FARMSTEADS. An analysis of the development of a group of farmsteads, made on the basis of an on-the-spot survey and archive studies, demonstrates the dynamic character of building activity carried out since the Baroque period. Major reconstructions were due to several large fires and inspired a more advanced spatial arrangement. However, the most significant change in the original plans took place in the middle of the 19th century, when the formerly traditional three-room house forming a single structure was abandoned and was enlarged to include rooms built in a new wing in the yard.

41 ZLÁMANEC, DISTRICT OF UHERSKÉ HRADIŠTĚ, ELEVATION AND GROUND-PLAN OF A FARMSTEAD. The central Moravian type of farmstead built of adobe bricks preserves the three-room lay-out on the ground-floor and has a built-in kitchen. There are two granaries on the upper floor. At the side of the living quarters there is a passageway leading to the yard, which serves at the same time as a shed.

42a, b HORNÍ BEČVA, DISTRICT OF VSETÍN, VERTICAL CROSS-SECTION AND GROUND-PLAN OF A SMALL FARMSTEAD. This Walachian mountain farmstead shows the type of architecture found in hilly country. An important feature of the lay-out is the cowshed directly connected with the house, in which the dominant feature is the heating system. The cottage blends with its natural setting, helped by the pattern of the adjoining roads and other auxiliary structures built of natural materials.

43 ŽDIAR, DISTRICT OF POPRAD. The houses in the mountain area on the eastern slopes of the Tatra range belong to the architecture of the Carpathian region by virtue of the pattern of their composition and their structure. A notable feature is their

ornamentation, which adds to the character of their architectural design, carved and painted decorations being much used.

44 HUBOVÁ, DISTRICT OF LIPTOVSKÝ MIKULÁŠ. A group of timber-framed cottages plastered with clay, situated at right angles to the roadway. Several dwelling units are ranged one after another in a single block. Features of special interest are the gambrel roofs with triangular gables and the corner joints with extending beams which support the roofs.

45 ZUBEREC, DISTRICT OF DOLNÝ KUBÍN. Timber-framed cottages in the Orava Valley have their own characteristic silhouette, due mainly to their gambrel roofs with small gables and wide projecting eaves. The houses are placed close together, end-on to the road.

46 VYŠNÉ RUŽBACHY, DISTRICT OF POPRAD. The community is located in a shallow valley beneath the Belanské Tatry mountains and only the church spire projects upwards from its horizontal silhouette. The limit of the built-up area is marked by a group of barns. In the flat terrain the street-type plan of the village could develop fully, with smaller cottages being built later along the edges.

47 VYŠNÉ RUŽBACHY, DISTRICT OF POPRAD. A typical outline of a house in an area of timber-framed structures, although in this case the living area is built of masonry. A special feature of the lay-out of village farmsteads in the area of the Tatra foothills is a covered gateway forming the entrance to the house. The façade is often distinctively decorated by a triangular gable which has small eaves at the bottom and a conical projection at the top. The surface of the gable is made of planking with spiked lathwork and ornamentally carved lattices on the sides.

48 ZÁVADKA NAD HRONOM, DISTRICT OF BANSKÁ BYS-TRICA. Houses in central Slovakia frequently have cellars and are therefore built on foundations of masonry. Their characteristic feature is the gable with eaves facing the street. The gable is of decorative lathwork and its top is protected by a conical rooflet topped with a wooden pin. The façade includes a covered wooden gate and wicket.

49 JAKUBANY, DISTRICT OF POPRAD. In the mountains archaic architectural types with gables facing the street survived for a long time. Until the middle of the 20th century their heating systems still had no chimneys. This ancient form contrasts with the relatively advanced design and execution of the timber-framing and the high standard of shaping of the buildings, with their triangular gables, eaves and conical projections at the top.

50 DAČOV LOM, DISTRICT OF ZVOLEN. In the low-lying parts of central Slovakia single-block clay houses were topped by straw-covered hipped roofs which softened the outline of the whole structure. The ornamentally shaped metal window shutters and doors are a reminder of the almost ceaseless warring in this area in the past.

51 DOBRÁ NIVA, DISTRICT OF ZVOLEN. The traditional interior of the village home was furnished for everyday needs in keeping with customs of the period and with the owner's financial and material position. In spite of the undeniably functional character of every piece of furniture, some items were gaily — often lavishly — decorated but still with a sense of colour and of the overall effect.

52 TERŇA, DISTRICT OF PREŠOV. An example of the archaic design of granaries in which the upper space is formed by a false vault made of wooden beams. On this vault the light construction of a thatched saddleback roof rests freely. A more advanced version of this type of granary from the point of view of carpentry can be found in most parts of Czechoslovakia, except in those areas where clay structures originally prevailed and in areas affected by external cultural influences.

53 VELKÁ TRŇA, DISTRICT OF TREBIŠOV. In the eastern part of Slovakia clay houses were built at right angles to the road. They were covered by thatched hipped roofs. The structural form is based on a very simple arrangement of the individual parts and the houses are relatively undecorated.

54 PRUŠÁNKY, DISTRICT OF HODONÍN. Extensive viticulture is reflected in architecture. Structures housing wine-presses and wine cellars were located on the edges of the vineyards. Their purpose dictated their design, but the natural environment and the treatment of their surfaces were frequently additional important factors affecting their construction.

55 SUCHÁ HORA, DISTRICT OF DOLNÝ KUBÍN. In the northernmost part of the Orava Valley, in north-western Slovakia, timber-framed houses face the road with their gable ends and are ranged in an irregular sequence along the street. Their form is of the Carpathian architectural type, but their character distinguishes them from the buildings found in other Orava villages.

56 PRUŠÁNKY, DISTRICT OF HODONÍN. This group of buildings housing wine-presses was built in basically the same manner as were other structures in the southernmost corner of Moravia. The walls made of clay or adobe bricks support a thatched hipped roof. Behind these buildings there are cellars dug into a slope and in most cases strengthened by brickwork vaulting. The façades were usually whitewashed with a blue strip painted along the base. Occasionally a modest but colourful ornament was added.

57 ČIČMANY, DISTRICT OF ŽILINA. The life and cultural environment of the village of Čičmany are products of the natural conditions which isolated this community from the outside world. The remarkable ornamentation which today covers the walls of the Čičmany houses, which have storage rooms in the attic or on upper floors, is the result of reconstruction after a fire which swept the village in the 1920's. The decoration of the older houses was more subdued, although the same ornamental elements and painting techniques were used.

58 TASOV, DISTRICT OF HODONÍN. The *žudro* in the Slovácko region of southern Moravia is built of unbaked clay. Entrance porches of this type characterize folk architecture in a large area covering central, south-eastern and southern Moravia as well as western and south-western Slovakia, and are specific to areas where clay structures predominate. The ornamentation of façades has a parallel in the other products of folk art of this area and is not exceptional in the architecture of the Czechoslovak countryside.

59 TRAKOVICE, DISTRICT OF TRNAVA. Clay houses in the lower part of the Váh River lowlands are related to structures typical of the Danubian architectural region. The house is built parallel to the street while the farm buildings, with separate, architecturally shaped entrances, are placed at right angles.

60 KÁTOV, DISTRICT OF SENICA. In the area of clay buildings in southern Moravia and western Slovakia most houses were built parallel to the street and had thatched hipped roofs. The auxiliary farm facilities were housed in a side wing. Narrow alleys separated individual houses, many of them being used as entrances to the yards.

61 SALAJNA, DISTRICT OF CHEB. In this strip-field village located in a valley the mill buildings are partially half-timbered and partially stone built. This structural system developed, in the vicinity of Cheb, into a rich decoration of the façade applied mainly to the gables. The exceptional importance of this complex of buildings is shown not only by their large size, but also by a small belfry on the top of the rear gable.

62 LADOMÍROVÁ, DISTRICT OF BARDEJOV. The wooden church of the Archangel Michael, dated 1742, with a typical three-part spatial arrangement. The roof of each of the three parts ends in a separate spire. In front rises the tower with a complex, onion-shaped roof. The cemetery surrounding the church is enclosed by a roofed, wooden fence with a covered entrance gate. The tall trees are an integral part of the scene.

63 KOČÍ, DISTRICT OF CHRUDIM. Adjoining the medieval Church of St Bartholomew, built in 1397, is a wooden pyramidal belfry of polygonal plan, reconstructed in 1666. The cemetery around the church is surrounded with a fence of wooden beams, protected by a moat. The church is entered by a covered, wooden bridge supported on stone piers, built in 1721, probably on the foundations

of an older bridge and quite possibly from some parts of the older structure.

64 BULHARY, DISTRICT OF BŘECLAV. The yard fronts of farmsteads in the lower Dyje and Morava basin and in the Danubian area are frequently decorated with arcades which shelter the walk between the entrance and the different parts of the single-block houses. The clay used as building material makes a great variety of forms possible, and many interesting compositions have been created.

65 TEKOVSKÉ LUŽANY, DISTRICT OF LEVICE. In southern Slovakia houses have arcades sheltering a walk along the inner side of the long wall facing the yard, onto which open the doors of both the dwelling part of the building and the farm part. Many variations of architectural shapes occur.

66 A WROUGHT-IRON SEPULCHRAL CROSS FROM SOUTH BOHEMIA, decorated with spirals and acanthus leaves with a motif of birds on a skull and crossbones at its base. 19th century.
South Bohemian Museum, České Budějovice.

67 A WROUGHT-IRON SEPULCHRAL CROSS FROM THE KLATOVY AREA with a heart in the place of the Corpus Christi. Height 92 cm. Early 19th century.
Regional Museum, Klatovy.

68 WEATHER COCK. Wrought iron. Height 94 cm. From Velké Karlovice. District of Vsetín. 19th century.
Ethnographical Institute of the Moravian Museum, Brno.

69 IRON CROSS WITH SYMBOLS OF THE PASSION. Originally this cross, made in 1890, was located in an open mountain landscape near Nicov, District of Vimperk. Now it stands by the church in the town square in Kašperské Hory.

70 THE BINDING OF A PRAYER BOOK CALLED THE *KEY TO HEAVEN*. Brass plate with embossed figural motifs (cross with the Pietà and cherubs) and ornaments (hearts), enriched with inset red, green and blue pieces of cut glass. 18×10.5×4 cm. Klatovy area, 1839.
Regional Museum, Klatovy.

71 DETAIL: CUPBOARD WITH PAINTED AND CARVED DECORATION. Northern Bohemia, about 1800.
Ethnographical Department of the Historical Museum, National Museum, Prague.

72 PAINTED CUPBOARD WITH ST. BARBARA AND THE MADONNA. 50×120×180 cm. Samšín, District of Sobotka, north Bohemia, first half of the 19th century.

73 WARDROBE CHEST WITH PAINTED BOUQUETS AND A MADONNA INSIDE A WREATH. 74×58×102 cm. Šaštín, District of Senica, western Slovakia, 1874.
Slovak National Museum, Bratislava.

74 TOY CRADLE WITH COLOURFUL PAINTED DECORATION. 30×44×48 cm. Northern Bohemia.
Municipal Museum, Železný Brod.

75 BACK OF AN OAK CHAIR WITH CARVED ROCAILLES, ENGRAVED FLORAL DECORATION AND A BIRD. Eagle Mountains, north-eastern Bohemia, 1799.
Eagle Mountains Museum, Rychnov nad Kněžnou.

76 DETAIL OF THE PAINTED DECORATION OF A WOODEN PEW OF THE 18TH CENTURY. The pew is in the wooden parish church of St John the Baptist at Slavoňov, District of Nové Město nad Metují, north-eastern Bohemia.

77 DETAIL: BRIDE AND GROOM WITH A PRIEST. From the painting *Wedding in the Cheb Area*. Watercolour, 36×205 cm; the figures are 20 cm high. The painting is in three parts and shows, besides the detail reproduced here, the wedding procession and the carrying of the bride's trousseau, in which the most prominent feature is the eiderdown covered with a blue-print. The bride and groom both wear crowns and the bride is dressed in an ancient, black, ceremonial cape of a type which was usually lined with red. In the centre of the scene the mineral spring in Františkovy Lázně is shown. From the Cheb area in western Bohemia, early 19th century.
West Bohemian Museum, Pilsen.

78 EMBROIDERY FROM THE COLLAR OF A WOMAN'S CHEMISE from around Uherské Hradiště in the Slovácko area of south-eastern Moravia. The background embroidery is in a warm yellow which contrasts with the heavy, flat embroidery of the main, repeating motif of a stylized petalled flower with two tulips. The embroidery is edged with an openwork design. About 1900.
Private collection, Prague.

79 WOMAN'S APRON OF BLUE-PRINT CLOTH DECORATED WITH SILK AND WOOL EMBROIDERY. The bobbin lace is made of flax thread, the tie of rough wool. From the vicinity of Kyjov in the Slovácko region of south-eastern Moravia. About 1900.
Ethnographical Department of the Historical Museum, National Museum, Prague.

80 PILLOWCASE OF A HOME-MADE FABRIC (*ČINOVAŤ*). Linen warp and cotton weft. Ždiar, District of Poprad, northern part of eastern Slovakia, early 20th century.
Ethnographical Department of the Historical Museum, National Museum, Prague.

81 A BRIDE FROM THE BECHYNĚ AREA OF SOUTH BOHEMIA. Gouache on paper. Probably 1836. Painted after a participant in the coronation parade.
Municipal Museum, Bechyně.

82 A BRIDEGROOM FROM THE BECHYNĚ AREA. Counterpart of No. 81.
Municipal Museum, Bechyně.

83 A YOUNG GIRL FROM MORAVSKÉ LIESKOVÉ, Trenčín area of western Slovakia, in a white linen, home-made dress. Mid-20th cent.

84 DETAIL OF A MAN'S GREAT-COAT OF CREAM WOOLLEN CLOTH decorated with appliqué and embroidery in blue and yellow. Brass clasp. Hungarian influence. Eastern Slovakia or southern part of central Slovakia, 20th century.
Slovak National Museum, Bratislava.

85 DETAIL OF EMBROIDERY ON A WEDDING SCARF with the motif of a bouquet of petalled flowers and tulips, tied with a ribbon. Flat stitches of cotton thread (which was originally yellow) on white linen, outlined in silver thread, today blackened. Dated 1706. Kostelec nad Vltavou, District of Písek, south Bohemia.
West Bohemian Museum, Pilsen.

86 BOUQUET OF POMEGRANATE, CARNATIONS AND TULIPS, tied with a ribbon, from the corner of a wedding scarf from Kostelec nad Vltavou. Same material, technique and colours as in No. 85.

87 CREAM-COLOURED SILK EMBROIDERY ON A WHITE LINEN SQUARE, emphasized by details in black. From the borderland between the Walachian and Haná areas, 19th century.
Municipal Museum, Valašské Meziříčí.

88 BLUE-PRINTED COTTON APRON WITH A TWO-COLOURED PATTERN. Detail of bouquets and border. Liptov, northern Slovakia, late 19th century.
Ethnographical Department of the Historical Museum, National Museum, Prague.

89 EMBROIDERED NET INSERTION DEPICTING ABRAHAM'S SACRIFICE WITH A BOBBIN LACE BORDER. Detail of the lower part of an antependium made of white, home-woven linen. 65×156 cm, width of network 45 cm, of lace 14 cm. The embroidery on the net was done with flat stitches of white, cream, yellow and black cotton thread; the lace is cream-coloured. The theme of the embroidery is incorporated in an ingenious composition of two alternating motifs — two sheep on either side of a tall, stylized flower, and a group with Abraham and Isaac and the approaching angel. Gemer, southern part of central Slovakia, 19th century.
Slovak National Museum, Martin.

90 DETAIL OF THE INSERTION FROM CORNER HANGINGS, embroidered on white home-made linen. The basic theme of cocks — their outline and decoration — is embroidered in flat stitches of green, ochre and cream-coloured silk thread, the background, some details and both parallel border lines are done in openwork. Size of the insertion is 20×72 cm. Gemer, about 1800.
Slovak National Museum, Martin.

91 DETAIL OF THE INSERTION FROM CORNER HANGINGS embroidered in white thread on white, home-made linen with alternating motifs of a large parrot and a spiral with a pomegranate. Needlework techniques: flat stitch, Holbein stitch, reticella, openwork. Height of strip 39 cm. Central Slovakia, 18th century.
Ethnographical Institute of the Moravian Museum, Brno.

92 CORNER EMBROIDERY FROM A LARGE SCARF CALLED A *VYVAZOVAČKA*. White thread on fine, white, home-made linen. Flat stitches and openwork. Walachian area, north-eastern Moravia, 19th century.
Walachian Open-Air Museum, Rožnov pod Radhoštěm.

93 LEATHER SATCHEL, CALLED A *CÍGR*, decorated with textile appliqué of tree motifs and embroidery, dated 1826. Vertical strips made of woven reedmace. Size roughly 30×60 cm. Doudleby area, south Bohemia.
South Bohemian Museum, České Budějovice.

94 TWO LARGE CLASPS — *SPINKY* — FROM THE JABLUNKOV AREA OF MORAVIAN SILESIA. Goldsmith's work with motifs of petalled flowers and a stylized tulip. Silver filigree with gilded centres. 6×3 cm. Mid-19th century.
Municipal Museum, Ostrava.

95 SILVER CHAIN BELT WITH INSET ROSETTES on square platelets with chain pendants and tiny oval ringlets. Mostly silver filigree with some gilded details. Length of belt 83 cm, diameter of the rosettes 6 cm. Těšín area, 19th century.
Municipal Museum, Ostrava.

96 SEPULCHRAL CRUCIFIX WITH RICH ORNAMENTATION. Wrought iron, height 175 cm. Originally from the old cemetery at Dolany, District of Klatovy, late 18th century.
Regional Museum, Klatovy.

97 A WINE-PRESS OF DOMESTIC MANUFACTURE with carved decoration of tulips and spiral ornaments, the monograms of Jesus Christ and the Virgin Mary, the initials of the owner and the date. Southern part of western Slovakia, 1791.
Private collection.

98 WOODEN WALL SCULPTURE FROM A MOUNTAIN CHALET, representing the crucified Christ placed against the background of a shallow dish in the shape of a butter mould with engraved leaves as ornament. Unpainted wood. Height 33 cm. Central Slovakia, 20th century.
Slovak National Museum, Bratislava.

99 WOODEN SEPULCHRAL CARVING with a circular lobed disc capped with a stylized tulip and decorated with a stylized flower and leaves and with geometric ornaments. It shows the engraved dates 1889 and 1891. Height 102 cm. Vicinity of Krupina in central Slovakia.
Slovak National Museum, Martin.

100 MANGLING BAT DECORATED WITH ENGRAVED FIGURAL SCENES: Pietà with a crowning angel; a man, woman and child; birds; a heart; rosettes and flowers. The border is decorated with a geometric pattern of zig-zags, crosses and triangular notches. Jan Bor (Janbor?) 1890 is inscribed near the handle. Unpainted wood, length 71 cm. Osuské, District of Senica, western Slovakia.
Slovak National Museum, Bratislava.

101 CARPATHIAN CORN BIN (*SÚSEK*) of columnar construction with an arched lid. Traditional carpentry work with ornamentation engraved with compasses on smoke-blackened wood. Length 38 cm, height 50 cm. Luhačovské Zálesí, eastern Moravia.
Luhačovice Museum.

102 A *SÚSEK* richly decorated with ornaments engraved with compasses. The motifs are repeated or alternate in strips on the sides and the legs. Domestic carpentry work with wooden pegs. The wood was darkened by fire to a brownish red colour; the engraved ornament is yellowish. Size 102×101×63 cm. Kyjatice. District of Rimavská Sobota, 19th century.
Slovak National Museum, Bratislava.

103 SALT BOX CARVED AND CUT FROM WOOD. Shepherd's work of Carpathian type decorated with animal heads and notched ornaments. Height 30.5 cm. Zázrivá, District of Dolný Kubín, Orava region of central Slovakia, 19th century.
Slovak National Museum, Bratislava.

104 WOODEN TANKARD. Cooper's work, natural wood with an inlay of deeper colour, lid with a combination closure. Height 30 cm. Probably the product of the Brož family workshop in Železnice. District of Jičín, north Bohemia, mid-19th century.
Municipal Museum, Železnice.

105 WOODEN MUGS (*ČRPÁKY*) OF THE DETVA TYPE with decorative profiled and cut handles and with fully three-dimensional figural (a shepherd playing his pipe) and animal motifs. The jug with the stag is also decorated with a notched ornament. Central Slovakia, early 20th century.
Slovak National Museum, Bratislava.

106 *ČRPÁKY* OF THE DETVA TYPE:
(a) Handle decorated with a pair of rams and with carved and notched spirals; maplewood, metal hoop, inset bottom. Height of handle 16 cm, of mug 9 cm, diameter of mug 10.5 cm. Upper Hron Valley, second quarter of the 20th century.
(b) Handle of architectural type (small turret with step-like roof) and two circular openings for fingers; cherry wood, hoop of hazelnut twigs, inset bottom. Height of handle 18 cm, of mug 10 cm, diameter of mug 11 cm. Ábelová, District of Lučenec, end of the 19th century.
(c) Handle, decorated at the top with figures of a shepherd playing the *fuyara* and a bagpiper, has the shape of a lyre and is ornamented with notches. Maplewood, brass hoop, inset bottom. Height of handle 18.5 cm, of vessel 9.5 cm, diameter of mug 13 cm. Central Slovakia, early 20th century.

ČRPÁK OF THE LIPTOV TYPE:
(d) Mug of conical shape with a handle carved in the form of a serpent's head with a bird perching on top and with a turret-like form behind the serpent's head. Notched ornamentation; cherry wood, brass hoop, inset bottom. Height of handle 19.5 cm, of mug 11 cm, diameter of mug 13 cm. Krpeľany, District of Martin, Turiec, central Slovakia, early 20th century.
Slovak National Museum, Martin.

107 JUG OF CLEAR GLASS DECORATED WITH ENGRAVED ORNAMENTS of floral and spiral themes. Height 22.5 cm. Jiříkovo údolí, Nové Hrady area of south Bohemia, first half of the 19th century. Tumbler of clear glass with engraved decoration (Madonna and wavy lines). Height 13.5 cm. South Bohemia, first half of the 19th century.
South Bohemian Museum, České Budějovice; exposition 'South Bohemian Glass' at the State Castle of Nové Hrady.

108 PRISM-SHAPED CANDLE-MAKER'S EARTHENWARE VESSEL decorated with relief ornamentation in the form of an upturned heart and chainlike frame, with inscriptions and the date 1775. Height 38 cm, width 47 cm. Eastern Slovakia.
Slovak National Museum, Bratislava.

109 FAÏENCE JUG WITH PAINTED DECORATION depicting a ploughman, buildings, vegetation and a bird perched on a branch. Dated 1820. Height 30 cm. Stupava, District of Bratislava, western Slovakia.
Slovak National Museum, Bratislava.

110 FAÏENCE JUG WITH LID, decorated with a painting of a team of oxen in a wooden yoke, with floral and geometric ornaments, and with the owner's personal data. Height 32 cm. Western Slovakia, second half of the 19th century.
Museum of Moravian Slovakia, Uherské Hradiště.

111 SMOKE-BLACKENED CERAMIC JUG decorated with simple, polished ornamentation. Height 27 cm. Pozdišovce, District of Michalovce, eastern Slovakia, 19th century.
East Slovak Museum, Košice.

112 GROUP OF SMALL GINGERBREAD TOYS: sled, horse-drawn carriage, cradle, open carriage, cups, slippers. Reconstructed in

plastic from impressions of original gingerbread moulds, decorated with gilding. Height 3 to 7.5 cm. Moulds from north Bohemia, 18th and 19th centuries.
Municipal Museum, Železný Brod.

113 STORAGE POT WITH TWO HANDLES. Smoke-blackened ceramic decorated with chains relief and simple, polished patterns. Height 40.5 cm. Jablonové, District of Bratislava, 19th century.
Private collection.

114 STORAGE POT WITH TWO HANDLES. Smoke-blackened ceramic decorated with chains in relief, wavy lines and polished spirals. Height 41 cm. South Moravia, first half of the 19th century.
Museum of Moravian Slovakia, Uherské Hradiště.

115 GROUP OF EASTER EGGS FROM MORAVIA, 19th and 20th centuries, from the collections of the Ethnographical Museum in Olomouc:
(a) Red with scratched drawing of a seated woman holding a child in her lap, a standing woman with upraised arms, and stylized flowers. Vlachovice in the Walachian area of eastern Moravia.
(b) Black with scratched design of a church and a cross, leaf ornaments and a bird. Ježov near Kyjov, south-eastern Moravia.
(c) Brownish-red with scratched decoration of the Lamb and the symbols of the Passion, a chalice placed on a book, the Host, and the inscription 'Hallelujah'. The Highlands of western Moravia.
(d) Rose-violet with scratched decoration of three squirrels climbing a tree and a bunch of flowers in a pot.
(e) Brownish-red with a scratched Biblical scene at a well. The Highlands of western Moravia.
(f) Black with batik decoration consisting of a white and pink drawing of a man, woman and two children holding hands. The children hold a rake, a scythe and a spade. Between the figures is a stylized tree. Bojkovice, south-eastern Moravia.
(g) Dark violet with scratched ornament of lilies-of-the-valley, a jug with a tulip and the inscription 'In Remembrance'. Mistřín, south-eastern Moravia.

116 POT WITH TWO HANDLES AND SIMPLE ORNAMENT. Pozdišovce, District of Michalovce, eastern Slovakia, about 1910.
Ethnographical Department of the Historical Museum, National Museum, Prague.
EAST SLOVAK BATIK-DECORATED EASTER EGGS. After 1960.
Ethnographical Department of the Historical Museum, National Museum, Prague.

117 BASKET WITH BATIK-DECORATED EASTER EGGS of different colours from eastern Slovakia. Čertižná, District of Humenné, 1970.
Ethnographical Department of the Historical Museum, National Museum, Prague.

118 TITLE PAGE OF A STALL-KEEPERS' PRINT with a woodcut of St Anne with the Virgin Mary and Infant Jesus. Page size 15×9 cm. North Bohemia, 19th century.
Private collection, Jablonec nad Nisou.

119 TITLE PAGE OF A STALL-KEEPERS' PRINT ABOUT 'THE LATEST STEAM ENGINE FOR REHASHING SPINSTERS' with a woodcut of two women in conversation. Page size 10.6×7.8 cm. Printed by S. Pospíšil in Chrudim, 19th century.
Private collection, Jablonec nad Nisou.

120 SINGLE-SHEET PRINT WITH AN ILLUSTRATION OF A HUMOROUS STORY. Woodcut, 22×18 cm, probably printed at Štípa near Gottwaldov, eastern Moravia, 19th century.
Luhačovice Museum.

121 TITLE PAGE OF THE STALL-KEEPERS' PRINT 'A LOVERS' GRAVE — BEWARE OF UNFAITHFULNESS' with the woodcut depicting a horseman with drawn sword in front of a town gate. Page size 10.4×7.8 cm, woodcut 4.3×5.9 cm. Printed by S. Pospíšil, Chrudim, in 1864.
Private collection, Jablonec nad Nisou.

122 WOODCUT ILLUSTRATING THE LEGEND OF THE HOLY BLOOD (reproduction of a pilgrimage painting from Walldürn in southern Germany) from the title page of St. Augustine's Prayer to Jesus Christ. Page size 13.3×8.6 cm, woodcut 11.4×6.6 cm. Printed by S. Pospíšil in Chrudim, about 1850.
Private collection, Jablonec nad Nisou.

123 WAFER IRON WITH AN ENGRAVING DEPICTING JOHN HUSS AT THE STAKE. Humpolec, eastern Bohemia.
Municipal Museum, Humpolec.

124 TEAMSTER'S LEATHER BELT colourfully embroidered with peacock's feather. Width 17 cm. The centre of the decoration is a waggon drawn by two pairs of horses with a fifth horse in front and the teamster riding one of the four horses. The edges are decorated with bands of tiny geometrical patterns, while the decorative metal buckle has two small tablets on each side, embroidered with themes of petalled flowers, tulips and apples, and edged with the same ornament as the belt itself. Beside the horse-drawn waggon is embroidered in large figures the date 1803. Doudleby area, south Bohemia.
South Bohemian Museum, České Budějovice.

125 SINGLE-SIDED WOOD-ENGRAVER'S BLOCK WITH FLAT CARVING (engraving and notches) depicting the standing figure of the Infant Jesus; this is probably a reproduction of the pilgrimage statue of the Infant Jesus from the Church of Our Lady of Victories in Prague. The dress and the spaces on both sides of the figure are richly decorated with floral design. The museum also possesses an original print made from this block in 1905, which is coloured by hand in red, blue, green and yellow watercolours. Size 39×27×1.3 cm. Pezinok, District of Bratislava, western Slovakia.
Slovak National Museum, Martin.

126 DOUBLE-SIDED WOOD-ENGRAVER'S BLOCK WITH FLAT CARVING (engraving and notches) depicting the crucified Christ, with two tall plants with petalled flowers and tulips on each side of the cross and canopies above it. The museum also has an original print made from the block in 1901, which is coloured by hand in red, blue, green and brown watercolours. Pezinok, District of Bratislava, western Slovakia.
Slovak National Museum, Martin.

127 CALLIGRAPHIC DECORATION OF A DOUBLE-PAGE OF A HANDWRITTEN PRAYER BOOK of 1820 with ornamental framing of the pages and decorative initials. Owned by Ludmila Pokorná of Libčice near Prague. Size 22×17 cm.
Ethnographical Department of the Historical Museum, National Museum, Prague.

128 PAINTED DECORATION OF THE INTERIOR OF THE WOODEN CHURCH OF ST JOHN THE BAPTIST IN SLAVOŇOV, north-eastern Bohemia. The beamed ceiling on the north side (scrolls with flowers) was painted with greasy tempera colours at the time of the building of the church in 1553. The figures of saints on the cornice, taking the place of a triumphal arch, were repainted in 1705. The photograph was taken in 1970 after the painting had been cleaned.

129 DOCTOR VISITING A PATIENT — oil painting on wood. Detail of the decoration of a framed attic room in an old distillery in Lab near Malá Skála, District of Turnov, north Bohemia. Dated 1709. The room, the four walls and ceiling of which are all covered with paintings, is the oldest document of folk painting of this kind in the Jizera Valley, and was transferred to the Museum of the Bohemian Paradise in Turnov. Size of the room 340×330×190 cm, of the painting shown here 103×74 cm.

130 BEER MUG OF CLEAR GLASS decorated with an enamel painting of a Turkish warrior with drawn sabre on a white horse. The metal lid is decorated with a small sculpture of a man's head. 18th century, Slovakia.
Ethnographical Department of the Historical Museum, National Museum, Prague.

131 VIEW OF A TOWN WITH A STORK'S NEST ON THE TOP OF A TOWER. Detail of the decoration of a painted wooden wardrobe chest from Liberec, north Bohemia, about 1800. Size of painting

27×40 cm, with a blue church, red roofs, grey tower, and pink background.
Municipal Museum, Železný Brod.

132 ADAM AND EVE. Detail of the painted decoration of a wooden Protestant church, dating from 1773 to 1781. Paludza near Liptovský Mikuláš, central Slovakia.

133 THE WAY TO CALVARY. A serpentine composition popular in some Moravian folk prints and paintings on canvas, paper and glass. Oil on canvas, size of painting 71×89 cm, width of frame 3.5 cm. South-eastern Moravia, 19th century.
Museum of Moravian Slovakia, Uherské Hradiště.

134 VOTIVE PAINTING FOR VÁCLAV PRAUS, the miller and later postmaster of Rychnov nad Kněžnou, north-eastern Bohemia, who sponsored the construction of the statue of Christ tied to a column above the town. The picture shows the statue, the Church of the Holy Trinity in Rychnov and the Piarist School; its lower part depicts the postmaster's kneeling family in period costume. Oil on canvas, 35.5×30 cm, without frame, artist unknown, about 1770.
Eagle Mountains Museum, Rychnov nad Kněžnou.

135 A VIEW OF ŽELEZNICE. Oil on canvas, 78×93 cm. Amateur painting of 1848 by Arnošt Rameš, a dyer from Železnice. District of Jičín, north-eastern Bohemia.
Municipal Museum, Železnice.

136 ST PETER REGRETTING HIS DENIAL OF CHRIST. Oil painting on canvas. It depicts the usual symbols associated with the saint, a portrait of Christ and the inscription 'And Peter went out, and wept bitterly.' It also shows the intentionally contrasted picture of St John of Nepomuk hearing the confession of the Queen in the small gallery at the bottom of the painting. Size of painting 77.5× ×60 cm, width of frame 1 cm. Anonymous work from south-eastern Moravia, 19th century.
Museum of Moravian Slovakia, Uherské Hradiště.

137 THE HOLY FAMILY WITH ST ANNE AND ST JOACHIM. Painting on glass, 53×37 cm, in its original black, flat frame. 'Painter of Oriental faces', central Moravia, last third of the 18th century.
Ethnographical Museum, Olomouc.

138 PIETÀ OF ŽELEZNÝ BROD. Painting on glass, 40×27.5 cm, reproducing a Gothic pilgrimage sculpture, with a small scarf in Mary's hand. Železný Brod, north Bohemia, about 1800. The painting is based on a print of the late 18th century, which is also in the possession of the museum. The folk sculpture illustrated below (No. 139) was also based on this print.
Municipal Museum, Železný Brod.

139 PIETÀ OF ŽELEZNÝ BROD. Polychrome wood sculpture, height 31.7 cm, rounded and painted at the back. This carved folk reproduction of a Gothic pilgrimage statue in Železný Brod, north Bohemia, was based on a late 18th-century engraving which also served as the model for the painting on glass No. 138 above. Besides showing the typical motif of the little scarf in Mary's hand, the sculpture depicts Christ with the lower part of his body covered, as do also the print and the painting on glass.
Municipal Museum, Železný Brod.

140 ST BARBARA. Painting on glass in its original black, profiled frame within an inner oval painted frame with floral decoration. Opaque paints and gold-foil. Size 32×21 cm, with frame 43× ×30.5 cm. North Bohemia, about 1800.
Private collection, Jablonec nad Nisou.

141 ST ISIDORE (in the scene of the legend with ploughing angels, set in a landscape with a church). Painting on glass, 34.5×49.5 cm, in its original black, profiled frame. Opaque paints and gold-foil. 'Painter of wavy eyebrows', probably from the vicinity of Sloup in the Brno region, Moravia, first third of the 19th century.
Ethnographical Institute of the Moravian Museum, Brno.

142 ST ISIDORE (in the scene of the legend with ploughing angels in a field against a landscape with a castle on a hill and a church). Painting on glass, 31×47 cm, in its original black, profiled frame, opaque paints and gold-foil. 'Painter of arched eyebrows', probably

working at Ždánice in the vicinity of Brno, Moravia, in the first half of the 19th century.
Ethnographical Institute of the Moravian Museum, Brno.

143 THE CORONATION OF THE VIRGIN MARY BY THE HOLY TRINITY. Painting on glass in its original frame, 49×39.5 cm. Unidentified central Slovak workshop. Dubové, District of Zvolen, central Slovakia, first half of the 19th century.
Slovak National Museum, Martin.

144 THE ERECTION OF THE CROSS. Painting on glass, 46×30 cm, in its original, brown profiled frame. 'Painter of arched eyebrows', probably working at Ždánice in the vicinity of Brno in the first half of the 19th century.
Ethnographical Museum, Olomouc.

145 THE BETROTHAL OF THE VIRGIN MARY. Painting on glass, 41×29 cm, opaque paints and gold-foil, original flat, brown frame. Liptov area. Work of an unidentified central Slovak workshop, about 1850.
Slovak National Museum, Martin.

146 VIRGIN MARY THE PROTECTRESS. Painting on glass, 41× 30 cm, in its original dark, profiled frame. Work of an early central Moravian group, with black outlines and floral decoration of roses and tulips, about 1800.
Museum of Moravian Slovakia, Uherské Hradiště.

147 THE CANDLEMAS MADONNA with the Infant Jesus in swaddling clothes on her right arm and a candle in her left hand, and with decoration on her dress and in the upper corners; black contours and black background. Painting on glass, 41×28.5 cm. Central Slovakia, mid-19th century.
Slovak National Museum, Martin.

148 EMPRESS MARIA THERESA AS ST BARBARA. Painting on glass, 34×28 cm, original frame 42×35 cm. Opaque paints (red, white, blue), and gold-foil. Altarpiece from the Hermenegild Mine in Ostrava-Hranečník. Third quarter of the 18th century.
Municipal Museum, Ostrava.

149 THE NATIVITY OF CHRIST. Nativity scene with the adoration of the shepherds, a bagpiper and women bringing gifts. Painting on glass, 36×52 cm, opaque paints and gold-foil. Inspired by cut-outs of Nativity scenes on paper. 'Painter of arched eyebrows', probably active at Ždánice, in the vicinity of Brno, in the first half of the 19th century. Drásov, near Tišnov, Moravian Highlands.
Regional Museum, Tišnov.

150 JÁNOŠÍK AND HIS MEN (Jánošík on the right, standing at the wine cask) DRINKING, PLAYING THE BAGPIPES AND DANCING WITH AN AXE. Painting on glass, 39×46.5 cm, opaque paints and gold-foil. Flat, brown frame. Vicinity of Rimavská Sobota, central Slovakia, mid-19th century.
Slovak National Museum, Martin.

151 THE FINDING OF ST GENEVIEVE — from a cycle based on the Legend of St Genevieve of Brabant. Painting on glass, 31.5× 47.5 cm; original recessed frame decorated with small carved ornamentation. 'Painter of arched eyebrows', probably working at Ždánice, vicinity of Brno, in the first half of the 19th century.
Ethnographical Museum, Olomouc.

152 THE VIRGIN MARY OF VRANOV (reproduction of a Late Gothic pilgrimage statue of the Virgin Mary of the Corn) CROWNED BY ANGELS. Painting on glass with floral decoration and the black outlines which were typical of the early Moravian group. Opaque paints and gold-foil. After 1800. The ceramic frame with dark glazing is of a later date (1863). The size of the combined picture and frame is 55×32 cm.
Luhačovice Museum.

153—154 SS BARBARA AND CATHERINE. Two matching paintings on glass. 28×18 cm, opaque paints and gold-foil in original dark, profiled frames. North-eastern Bohemia (Eagle Mountains), about 1800.
Eagle Mountains Museum, Rychnov nad Kněžnou.

155 THE BAPTISM OF CHRIST IN THE RIVER JORDAN. Icon, oil painting on wood, 130×107 cm. Wooden Church of St Luke the

Evangelist, Krivé, eastern Slovakia, first half of the 17th century.

156 ST GEORGE. Icon, oil painting on wood in carved and painted Baroque frame, from the wooden church at Nová Sedlica, eastern Slovakia, 18th century.
Slovak National Gallery, Bratislava.

157 THE LAST JUDGMENT. Icon with folk motifs of social criticism; oil painting on wood. Eastern Slovakia.
Museum of Ukrainian Culture, Svidník.

158 LATE HABAN FAÏENCE PLATE WITH THEMES FROM ANIMAL FABLES. Diameter 28.5 cm. Colours: cobalt, manganese, yellow, greyish-green. Dated 1724. Moravia or southern Slovakia.
Ethnographical Institute of the Moravian Museum, Brno.

159 GROUP OF SLOVAK-HABAN FAÏENCE JUGS; in the foreground is a Jewish ritual jug with a picture of a burial fraternity, a Hebrew inscription and floral ornamentation. Height 41 cm. Western Slovakia, 18th century.
Slovak National Museum, Bratislava.

160 BEER TANKARD WITH PAINTED BATTLE AND HUNTING SCENES. Faïence, height 18.5 cm. Colours: manganese, green, yellow, blue. Boleráz, western Slovakia, 18th century.
Ethnographical Institute of the Moravian Museum, Brno.

161 FAÏENCE JUG DECORATED WITH BANDS OF FLORAL AND GEOMETRICAL ORNAMENTATION, with farming implements, figures of saints and inscriptions. Probably made in western Slovakia in the 19th century.
Ethnographical Institute of the Historical Museum, National Museum, Prague.

162 DETAIL: FAÏENCE JUG DECORATED WITH A PASTORAL SCENE AND A STAG. Rich floral ornamentation. South-western Slovakia, 19th century.
Ethnographical Institute of the Historical Museum, National Museum, Prague.

163 DETAIL: CENTRAL PART OF A NATIVITY SCENE of painted and cut paper figures, buildings, trees and flowers, set in moss. Bohemian-Moravian Highlands, about 1800.
Ethnographical Institute of the Historical Museum, National Museum, Prague.

164 DETAIL: AN ELEPHANT AND ITS MOORISH KEEPER, from the suite of the Magi whose figures were added to the Nativity scene at Epiphany. Painting in opaque colours on paper. Bohemian-Moravian Highlands, about 1800.
Ethnographical Institute of the Historical Museum, National Museum, Prague.

165 MARKSMEN'S TARGET with a painting of a Gypsy violin-player and a gypsy woman wrapped in a shawl against a landscape background. The tempera colours on wood are vivid, especially the greens (the woman's skirt and the man's waistcoat and jacket) and yellows (the woman's shawl, the man's boots). The target was donated to the Shooters' Society active in Frenštát pod Radhoštěm between 1835 and 1900 by a member, Josef Bumbala, in 1839.
Municipal Museum, Frenštát pod Radhoštěm.

166 SIGNBOARD OF THE 'THREE CZECH FARMERS' INN in the Písek area of south Bohemia. Oil painting on wood, 95×113 cm, mid-19th century.
South Bohemian Museum, České Budějovice.

167 A HUNTER'S POWDER HORN decorated with engraved and coloured figural and animal motifs, various objects and symbols. Central Slovakia, 12×9 cm, 19th century.

168 ST APOLLONIA (formerly venerated as a patron saint against toothache); polychrome relief from the stone pedestal of a statue or a cross, 86×36 cm. Fragment. Traces of polychromy: red mantle, yellow palm frond, brown head. Železný Brod, north Bohemia, end of the 18th century.
Municipal Museum, Železný Brod.

169 CABINET BEEHIVE FOR TWO COLONIES OF BEES decorated with a relief carving of Adam and Eve, originally painted. In the gable under the shingled roof, shaped as the symbol of the Trinity, a cage for a thrush was built. 147×65 cm, dated 1867. Originally from the apiary of Jan Řepka of Železnice, District of Jičín, north-eastern Bohemia, who had twenty carved beehives. Between 1923 and 1967 this hive was in use at Zámezí near Železnice. Its creator is unknown.
Municipal Museum, Železnice.

170 FRONT PANEL OF A STUMP HIVE with the engraved inscription 'The Baptism and Temptation of Jesus Christ' and the date 1867. Between the figures of St John the Baptist and Christ the unknown creator placed a mask of the devil, whose eyes, nostrils and mouth form the entrance for the bees. The original polychromy was destroyed. 110×50 cm. The hive, like the hive shown under No. 169, comes from the apiary of Jan Řepka in Železnice.
Municipal Museum, Železnice.

171 THE MURDER AND FUNERAL OF ST WENCESLAS. Polychrome wooden relief used as a wall picture; 63×102.5 cm. In the bottom right corner is the signature 'Chwala'. This is a work by the contemporary folk carver Josef Chvála, born in Prachatice, south Bohemia, in 1906. The picture was carved in about 1967.
South Bohemian Museum, České Budějovice.

172 ADAM AND EVE. One of the polychrome reliefs from a tall, richly decorated wooden crucifix. Height 6 m, dated 1895. Dimensions of the relief 70×20 cm. Several of these from the vicinity of Uherské Hradiště, where they used to stand in the open countryside, have been preserved. The artist was František Vymyslický of Dolní Bojanovice in the Slovácko region of south-eastern Moravia.
Ethnographical Institute of the Historical Museum, National Museum, Prague.

173 CHRIST ON THE MOUNT OF OLIVES. Polychrome relief from the same crucifix as No. 172. 63.5×21 cm.

174 CABINET BEEHIVE FOR THREE COLONIES OF BEES. Detail of painted carved relief of two men in hats. 130×95 cm, the figures are 63 cm high. Made in the 1870's for the apiary of the Bílek family of carpenters in Železnice, north-eastern Bohemia. Still in use.
Municipal Museum, Železnice.

175 FRONTAL PANELS WITH PAINTED RELIEFS FROM BEEHIVES IN THE GARDEN OF THE PARSONAGE AT BÍLÝ ÚJEZD, District of Rychnov nad Kněžnou, north-eastern Bohemia. The reliefs depict St Sebastian, Madonna and Child, St Aloysius, St John of Nepomuk, the Guardian Angel and St Catherine. The hives, originally from north-eastern or north Bohemia, were probably moved twice. In recent years they have been used in the garden of the parsonage at Bílý Újezd. Since 1970 the panels have been stored separately.

176 GROUP OF THREE STUMP BEEHIVES covered with a shingled roof. The entrances to the two side hives are decorated with simple openings in the shape of hearts and stars, the middle hive is decorated with a roughly carved face and the painted outline of a man's figure. Walachian region, eastern Moravia, 19th century.
Walachian Open-Air Museum, Rožnov pod Radhoštěm.

177 BEEHIVE FOR FOUR COLONIES OF BEES with a painted relief of St John of Nepomuk. Walachian region, 19th century.
Walachian Open-Air Museum, Rožnov pod Radhoštěm.

178 HEAD OF A MAN WITH A HAT — mask on the opening of a stump beehive. High polychrome relief, Walachian area, eastern Moravia, 19th century.
Walachian Open-Air Museum, Rožnov pod Radhoštěm.

179 WINE-PRESS DECORATED WITH FIGURAL RELIEFS (male figures as caryatids and, on the pillars, a Pietà and cherubs), a simple ornamental line and engraved dates and names emphasized with red colour. Probably made by Jura Švestka, signed on the press. 225×210×95 cm. Havřice, District of Uherský Brod, south-eastern Moravia, dated 1847.
Museum of Moravian Slovakia, Uherské Hradiště.

180 CHEESE MOULD IN THE FORM OF A RESTING SHEEP. Shepherd's carving, dated 1886. Orava Valley, north-western Slovakia.
Slovak National Museum, Bratislava.

181 BABY IN SWADDLING CLOTHES — gingerbread mould from north-eastern Bohemia, 18th century.
Eagle Mountains Museum, Rychnov nad Kněžnou.

182 TWO-SIDED GINGERBREAD MOULD WITH A LOW RELIEF OF THE SPANISH DANCER PEPITA DE OLIVA. On the other side of the mould is the figure of St John of Nepomuk. Limewood, 26.5 × 14 cm. Turnov area, northern Bohemia, about 1855, when the dancer was in Prague.
Private collection, Jablonec nad Nisou.

183 TWO-SIDED GINGERBREAD MOULD WITH A LOW RELIEF OF ONE OF THE FIRST LOCOMOTIVES IN BOHEMIA. On the other side is a vase with a bouquet of flowers. Hard wood, 14.5 × 19.5 cm. Pilsen area, western Bohemia, about 1850.
West Bohemian Museum, Pilsen.

184 A NATURAL BRANCH ADAPTED TO FORM A SHEPHERD'S STICK with a carving of a monkey's face with bared teeth. Length 98 cm. Central Slovakia, 19th century.
Slovak National Museum, Bratislava.

185 WOMAN RAISING HER ARMS IN A GESTURE OF INVOCATION — unpainted wood-carving made in 1967. Pavol Bavlna, born at Štiavnik, District of Žilina, central Slovakia, in 1896.
Slovak National Museum, Bratislava.

186 VOTIVE ANIMAL FIGURES (cow, goat, sheep and pig). Wrought iron, length 7 to 12 cm. Šumava area in south Bohemia, 19th century.
South Bohemian Museum, České Budějovice.

187 DOLL REPRESENTING DEATH FOR PRE-EASTER RITUALS. Made of straw, textiles, colourful trinkets; height 55 cm. Ořechovičky, Brno area, central Moravia, early 20th century.
Ethnographical Institute of the Moravian Museum, Brno.

188 'MOTHER OF THE SHROVETIDE' — a man's ceremonial mask made of straw, wood, textiles and fur. Dobrkovská Lhotka, District of Český Krumlov, south Bohemia, mid-20th century.
South Bohemian Museum, České Budějovice.

189 DETAIL OF THE CARNIVAL MASK OF THE 'CORN-MAN'. The male figure is wrapped from head to foot in straw bands with little bells. The head is covered with a conical straw hat topped with two arching straw plaits. Height 200 cm. Omšenie, District of Trenčín, western Slovakia, late 19th century.
Slovak National Museum, Martin.

190 HEAD AND TAIL OF THE CARNIVAL MASK KNOWN AS *ŠIMLA* — the white mare. Polychrome wood, textiles, straw and tow. Doudleby area of south Bohemia, late 19th century.
South Bohemian Museum, České Budějovice.

191 HEAD OF A GOAT CARNIVAL MASK. Soft wood painted black, with a red cloth tongue, leather ears, and eyes made from metal pipe-lids. Length of head 27 cm. Bezděkov near Klatovy, south-western Bohemia, early 19th century.
West Bohemian Museum, Pilsen.

192 DEVIL FACE MASK. Polychrome on paper, 36 × 20 cm. Used in a carnival procession at Hluk, District of Uherské Hradiště, south-eastern Moravia, in 1890.
Museum of Moravian Slovakia, Uherské Hradiště.

193 WOMAN IN A HAT CARRYING TWO PAILS. Red ceramic flowerpot with white and brown decoration. 36 cm. Made by Martin Fremr, a potter from Losiná, District of Pilsen, who died about 1859.
West Bohemian Museum, Pilsen.

194 GROUP OF FIGURES FROM A NATIVITY SCENE, carved from wood, painted and embellished. The Nativity scene includes 60 figures, castles and palaces, a windmill and a painted landscape background. Bohemian-Moravian Highlands, first half of the 19th century.
Ethnographical Institute of the Historical Museum, National Museum, Prague.

195a CRUCIFIX ON A PEDESTAL OF FERNS AND BLOSSOMS MADE OF DOUGH, height 15 cm, produced in the Lutonský workshop in Vizovice, southern Walachian area, in 1970.
Private collection, Prague.

195b ADAM AND EVE, made of dough, height 13 cm, from the Lutonský workshop in Vizovice, 1970.
Private collection, Prague.

196 VERONICA, WALL STOUP. Faïence, 24 × 12 cm, Luhačovské Zálesí, south Moravia, 18th or 19th century.
Luhačovice Museum.

197 THE VIRGIN MARY (Mary's Heart). Polychrome statuette with silver and gold, simply carved from a single piece of limewood, flat at the back; height 25 cm. Frenštát pod Radhoštěm or vicinity, Walachian area, north-eastern Moravia, about the middle of the 19th century.
Municipal Museum, Frenštát pod Radhoštěm.

198 CAROLLERS' NATIVITY SCENE. Painted wood, height 40 cm. Orava Valley, north-western Slovakia, 19th century.
Slovak National Museum. Martin.

199 TWO BAGPIPERS — CARVED FIGURES FROM A MINERS' NATIVITY SCENE. Painted wood, height 39.5 and 34 cm. Vicinity of Banská Štiavnica, central Slovakia, 19th century.
Slovak National Museum, Bratislava.

200 BAKER'S WIFE SELLING BREAD AND CAKES. Toy made of turned wood with dough additions (hands and arms, scarf, ribbon, the baked goods). Painted (red dress, blue scarf with white polka dots, light green stand) and lacquered. Size of supporting board 5.8 × 12 cm, height of doll 14.6 cm. Příbram, central Bohemia, second half of the 19th century. Sold at Christmas fair in Klatovy, south-western Bohemia.
Regional Museum, Klatovy.

201 WOODEN TOY HORSE. Roughly carved with knife, domestic production, with painted eye and tail of tow; length 46 cm. Upper Hron Valley, central Slovakia, 20th century.
Slovak National Museum, Bratislava.

202 MERRY-GO-ROUND — A MOBILE TOY MADE OF PAINTED WOOD. Diameter 67 cm, height 71 cm; colours: white, green, red and yellow. Made by Václav Žákovec (1874—1965) of Dobříč in the Plasy area of south-western Bohemia, about 1950.
West Bohemian Museum, Pilsen.

203 STRIDING LION — WOODEN BEEHIVE, 95 × 152 cm, grey and ochre. Stropešín, District of Třebíč, south-western Moravia, about 1930.
Ethnographical Institute of the Moravian Museum, Brno.

204 DETAIL: MERMAID HOLDING SCALES ABOVE A SHOP COUNTER; painted wood, 60 × 240 cm. From the R. Vostřebal food-shop in Rychnov nad Kněžnou, north-eastern Bohemia, second half of the 18th century.
Eagle Mountains Museum, Rychnov nad Kněžnou.

205 CARRYING THE MADONNA OF SVATÁ HORA — a pilgrimage souvenir toy. The figure of the Madonna was made of dough in a mould and painted; the figures of the four maidens carrying it were turned from wood, with arms, hair, collars and scarves of dough. Polychrome: white dresses with red dots and red scarves. Size of supporting board 12 × 10.5 cm, height of dolls 12.5 cm, total height 23 cm. Made at Příbram in the second half of the 19th century, sold at Klatovy Christmas fair, south-western Bohemia.
Regional Museum, Klatovy.

206 PAINTED CARVED SCULPTURES FROM THE SLOVAK NATIONAL MUSEUM IN MARTIN:
(a) St John of Nepomuk, carved from a single piece of wood; Muráňska Zdýchava, District of Rožňava, central Slovakia, 19th century.
(b) The Virgin Mary praying; height 15.5 cm. Face and upper part of the body gilded, details outlined in black. Orava Valley, north-western Slovakia, first quarter of the 20th century.

207 ST FLORIAN — painted wooden statuette made of several pieces of primitively shaped wood, flat at the back. Coloured with light oil paints without any ground layer. The cape, banner and part of the house are red, the hair and boots black, the helmet, top of banner and socle green; the dress, body parts and parts of the house whitish. Height 34.5 cm. Carving of serial production of the

early 20th century. Pstruží, District of Frýdek-Místek, north-eastern Moravia.
Municipal Museum, Frenštát pod Radhoštěm.

208 CRUCIFIX FOR DISPLAY AT HOME. Painted wood-carving with the kneeling Mary Magdalene on the socle at the foot of the cross.
Municipal Museum, Kašperské Hory.

209 CRUCIFIX. Painted wood; height 132 cm, probably after 1800. The crucifix comes from a sanctuary in Kostelec nad Orlicí, north-eastern Bohemia, which was torn down in 1912.
Eagle Mountains Museum, Rychnov nad Kněžnou.

210 CRUCIFIX. Detail of the upper part of the body of Christ with ornamental stylization of the beard and chest; painted wood, height of the body of Christ 67 cm. Hartmanice, District of Sušice, South Bohemia, about 1800.
Municipal Museum, Kašperské Hory.

211 CHRIST ON THE MOUNT OF OLIVES. Carved probably from limewood; 42.5 × 28 cm, with remnants of original polychromy. The statuette was originally placed in a niche in the farmstead of M. Varvasová at Stará Bělá No. 502, near Ostrava, Silesia; first quarter of the 19th century.
Private collection, Jablonec nad Nisou.

212 CHRIST FALLING UNDER THE WEIGHT OF THE CROSS. Painted wood-carving, fully rounded, 23 × 105 cm, coloured blue, red and brown. Originally from a small chapel in Osada, District of Dolný Kubín, Orava Valley, north-western Slovakia. Work of the self-taught carver Rudolf Hrabula from Osada. Late 19th century.
Slovak National Museum, Martin.

213 SANCTUARY WITH THE STATUE OF ST JOHN OF NEPO-MUK. Wood-carving, with none of the original polychromy surviving. Height of sanctuary 160 cm, of figure 30 cm. From the vicinity of Trhové Sviny or the Doudleby area, south Bohemia, about 1800.
South Bohemian Museum, České Budějovice.

214 ST JOHN OF NEPOMUK. Painted wooden statuette, height 58 cm. From Střížov, Bohemia.
Ethnographical Department of the Historical Museum, National Museum, Prague.

215 THE PIETÀ OF ŠAŠTÍN. Painted wooden statuette; height with pedestal 52.5 cm. Serial folk production of the pilgrimage statue in Šaštín, District of Senica, western Slovakia. This particular piece comes from the village of Vyhne, District of Žiar nad Hronom, central Slovakia, late 19th century.
Slovak National Museum, Martin.

216 THE CORONATION OF THE VIRGIN MARY. Painted sandstone. On the socle are painted reliefs of SS John of Nepomuk, Wenceslas, Anthony of Padua and Florian. On the back is the inscription: 'Erected in 1850 by the honourable Community of Lhota Bradlec. Made by Jan Zeman of Žernov'. Lhota Bradlecká, District of Jičín, north-eastern Bohemia.

217 MADONNA AND CHILD WITH BRANCHES. Flat painted carving with rich relief decoration of the dress. Height 46.5 cm. Čausa, District of Prievidza, late 18th century.
Slovak National Museum, Martin.

218 MADONNA AND CHILD. Painted statue made from several pieces of limewood, worked also at the back; height 78.5 cm. Coloured with oil paints without any ground layer. Pstruží, District of Frýdek-Místek, Silesia, probably end of the 18th century.
Municipal Museum, Frenštát pod Radhoštěm.

219 MADONNA AND CHILD. Wood-carving coloured dark red and dark blue, height 26 cm. Terchová, District of Žilina, north-western Slovakia, first half of the 19th century.
Slovak National Museum, Martin.

220 ST ANNE TEACHING THE YOUNG MARY. Wood-carving with traces of brownish-red polychromy, decorated with ornamental metal discs and hobnails. Height 41 cm. South Bohemia, 19th century.
Municipal Museum, Humpolec.

221 PIETÀ. Painted wood-carving, shaped to fit into a niche in a house or chapel; 28 × 18 cm, flat and without paint at the back. Colours:

carmine red, green, beige complexion. Těšín area in Silesia, late 18th or 19th century.
Municipal Museum, Ostrava.

222 PIETÀ. Painted wooden statue, height 72 cm. Mary's robe red with yellow bands at the neck, blue cape, Christ's loin cloth yellowish. Both crowns were originally gilded. Probably from Slovakia, 19th century.
Ethnographical Institute of the Moravian Museum, Brno.

223 MADONNA AND CHILD. Flat, painted wooden statue, height 44.5 cm; western Slovakia, 19th century.
West Slovak Museum, Trnava.

224 MADONNA AND CHILD. Painted wooden statue, height 52 cm; dress and crowns red, cape blue. South Moravia, 19th century.
Museum of Moravian Slovakia, Uherské Hradiště.

225 WOMAN WITH A BABY IN SWADDLING CLOTHES — stone sculpture without polychromy, originally a house sign marking the home of a midwife at Nové Hrady in south Bohemia. Granite, 86 × 61 cm. 17th-18th century.
State Castle of Nové Hrady.

226 ST CATHERINE. Sandstone without polychromy, height 33 cm. The statuette is flat, unworked at the back. Originally placed in a house or chapel niche in Olomouc (central Moravia) or its vicinity.
Ethnographical Museum, Olomouc.

227 ST ANNE WITH THE VIRGIN MARY AND INFANT JESUS. Carved from a single piece of limewood with knife and chisel, flat back. Painted, without any ground layer, with rich, light oil paints: Anne's cape and Mary's skirt blue, Anne's dress red, flowers on the dress white, complexion white with red cheeks. Height 35 cm. Frenštát pod Radhoštěm or its vicinity (north-eastern Moravia), probably mid-19th century.
Municipal Museum, Frenštát pod Radhoštěm.

228 THE HOLY TRINITY. Painted wood, height 67 cm. From Rychnov nad Malší, south Bohemia, 18th-19th century.
National Museum, Prague.

229 THE VIRGIN MARY IN PRAYER. Painted sandstone statue, probably a pilgrimage type from Horní Police, 63 × 26 cm. Originally placed in a niche at the gate to the Loutchan farmstead in Kalužník, District of Turnov, north Bohemia.
Museum of the Bohemian Paradise, Turnov.

230 MADONNA AND CHILD. Wood painted in oils, height 55 cm. From the Dlask farmstead at Dolánky near Turnov, north Bohemia, first half of the 19th century.
Museum of the Bohemian Paradise, Turnov.

231 HEAD FOR SHAPING BONNETS. Painted wood, height 39 cm. Pilsen area, western Bohemia, after 1800.
West Bohemian Museum, Pilsen.

232 HEAD FOR SHAPING BONNETS. Pear wood with traces of polychromy; 32 × 17.5 cm. Turnov, north Bohemia, first half of the 19th century.
Museum of the Bohemian Paradise, Turnov.

233 DETAIL: 'WEDDING OLD MAN' Wood-carving; moustache of hemp, fixed on a naturally forked stick. Total height 165 cm. Ceremonial artefact interpreted as a relic of an ancestors cult. Pekelník, Orava Valley (Poland), about 1900.
Slovak National Museum, Martin.

234 HEAD FROM A CARPENTER'S WORKBENCH. Wood-carving, height 62 cm. Zakamenné, District of Dolný Kubín, Orava Valley, north-western Slovakia, about 1930.
Slovak National Museum, Martin.

235 STUMP BEEHIVE ROUGHLY SHAPED IN THE FORM OF A STANDING MAN. The carved and painted head with a hat serves as the lid. Wood and oil paints, height 227 cm. Horný Turček, District of Martin, central Slovakia, 1940.
Slovak National Museum, Martin.

236 EASTER EGG WITH A SCRATCHED DECORATION OF STYLIZED POMEGRANATES on a dark-blue base. Brumovice, southern Walachian region, north-western Moravia, mid-20th century.
Archives of the Centre for Folk Arts and Crafts, Uherské Hradiště.

BIBLIOGRAPHY OF BOOKS IN THE CZECH LANGUAGE

Bečák, Jan R., LIDOVÉ UMĚNÍ NA HANÉ (Folk Art in Haná), *Velký Týnec u Olomouce, 1941.*

Bednárik, Rudolf, ZVYKOSLOVNÉ PRAMENE VÝTVARNÉHO PREJAVU SLOVENSKÉHO (Traditional Sources of Slovak Artistic Expression), *Turčiansky svätý Martin, 1942.*

'Hmotná kultura' (Material Culture), SLOVENSKÁ VLASTIVĚDA (Slovak Studies), *Vol. II, Bratislava, 1943.*

ĽUDOVÉ NÁHROBNÍKY NA SLOVENSKU (Folk Gravestones in Slovakia), *Turčiansky svätý Martin, 1948.*

ĽUDOVÝ NÁBYTOK (Folk Art Furniture), *Martin, 1949.*

MALOVANÉ OHNIŠTIA V OBLASTI MALÝCH KARPÁT (Painted Fire-places in the Lesser Carpathians), *Martin, 1956.*

PASTIERSKE REZBÁRSKE UMENIE (The Shepherd's Art of Wood-Carving), *Bratislava, 1956.*

SLOVENSKÉ ÚLE (Slovak Beehives), *Bratislava, 1957.*

Benža, Mojmír and Kaňová, M., ĽUDOVÉ KOŽUCHY (Traditional Fur Coats), *Martin, 1970.*

Bíbová, Regina and Smolková, Marie, KRAJKY A KRAJKÁŘSTVÍ LIDU SLOVANSKÉHO V ČECHÁCH, NA MORAVĚ, VE SLEZSKU A UHERSKÉM SLOVENSKU (Lace and Lace-making by the Slav People in Bohemia, Moravia, Silesia and Hungarian Slovakia), *Prague, 1907.*

Bogatyrev, Peter, FUNKCIE KROJA NA MORAVSKOM SLOVENSKU (Traditional Costume and Its Role in Moravian Slovakia), *Motica slovenská, 1937.*

Buchner, Heinrich, HINTERGLASSMALEREI IN DER BÖHMERWALDLANDSCHAFT UND IN SÜDBAYERN, BEITRÄGE ZUR GESCHICHTE EINER ALTEN HAUSKUNST, Munich, 1936.

Černohorský, Karel, MORAVSKÁ LIDOVÁ KERAMIKA (Moravian Folk Ceramics), Prague, 1941.

ČESKOSLOVENSKÁ VLASTIVĚDA (Czechoslovak Studies), *Series II, Ethnography, Prague, 1936.*

ČESKOSLOVENSKÁ VLASTIVĚDA (Czechoslovak Studies), *Vol. II, Folk Culture, Orbis, Prague, 1968.*

Chotek, Karel, 'Staré typy valašského domu' (Old Types of Walachian Houses), NÁRODOPISNÝ VĚSTNÍK ČESKOSLOVANSKÝ (Czecho-Slavonic Ethnographical Bulletin), *Vol. XI, 1916, pp. 133—145.*

'O slovenském domě' (The Slovak House), NÁRODOPISNÝ VĚSTNÍK ČESKOSLOVANSKÝ (Czecho-Slavonic Ethnographical Bulletin), *Vol. XVII, 1922, pp. 38 ff.*

'Poznámky k národopisu Slovenska' (Comments on Slovak Ethnography), NÁRODOPISNÝ VĚSTNÍK ČESKOSLOVANSKÝ (Czecho-Slavonic Ethnographical Bulletin), *Vol. XVII, pp. 38 ff.*

LIDOVÁ KULTURA A KROJE V ČESKOSLOVENSKU (Folk Culture and Folk Costumes in Czechoslovakia), *Prague, 1937.*

HLAVNÍ OBLASTI ČESKÉHO SELSKÉHO DOMU V ČECHÁCH A NA MORAVĚ (Principal Areas of Czech Farmsteads in Bohemia and Moravia), *Prague, 1940.*

'Pletené stavby na Slovensku' (Wicker Structures in Slovakia), SLOVENSKÝ NÁRODOPIS (Slovak Ethnography), *Vol. II, 1954, Nos. 3—4, pp. 237—284.*

Duša, Ferdyš, LIDOVÝ DŘEVORYT 18. A 19. STOLETÍ (Folk Woodcuts in the Eighteenth and Nineteenth Centuries), *Nový Jičín, 1938.*

Frický, Alexander, IKONY Z VÝCHODNÉHO SLOVENSKA (East Slovak Icons), *Košice, 1971.*

Güntherová-Mayerová, Alžběta, SLOVENSKÁ KERAMIKA (Slovak Ceramics), *Turčiansky svätý Martin, 1942.*

SLOVENSKÉ ĽUDOVÉ SOŠKY (Slovak Folk Statuettes), *Bratislava, 1944.*

Hasalová, Věra, 'K ikonografii, formě a obsahu slezských lidových skulptur v českých muzejních sbírkách' (The Iconography, Form and Content of Silesian Folk Sculptures in Czech Museum Collections), RADOSTNÁ ZEMĚ (Happy Land), *Vol. X, 1960, pp. 33—49.*

'Lidové sakrální sochařství, jeho evidence a katalogizace' (Sacred Folk sculpture, Its Registration and Catalogues), MUZEJNÍ A VLASTIVĚDNÁ PRÁCE (Museum and Ethnographical Work), *Vol. IV, 1966, No. 3, pp. 136—150.*

'Moravská lidová malba na skle' (Moravian Painting on Glass), 'Die mährische Hinterglassmalerei' (Summary in German), ETHNOGRAPHICA, *VII—VIII, 1965—1968, Moravian Museum, Brno, pp. 42—81 and 30—41.*

Havrlík, Svatopluk, LIDOVÉ UMĚNÍ NA PŘÍBRAMSKU (Folk Art in the Příbram Area), *Pardubice, not dated.*

Herain, Karel, 'Lidový projev v českém sklářství' (Folk Expression in Czech Glassmaking), VĚCI A LIDÉ (Things and People), *No. 4/1952—53, pp. 1—17.*

Hercík, Emanuel, ČESKOSLOVENSKÉ LIDOVÉ HRAČKY (Folk Toys in Czechoslovakia), *Prague, 1951.*

HORŇÁCKO. ŽIVOT A KULTURA LIDU NA MORAVSKO-SLOVENSKÉM POMEZÍ V OBLASTI BÍLÝCH KARPAT (The Horňácko Area — The Life and Culture of the People in the Moriavan-Slovak Borderland in the White Carpathian Region), *edited by Václav Frolec, Dušan Holý and Richard Jeřábek, Blok Publishing House, Brno, 1966.*

Hrbková, Růžena, 'Olmützer und Sternberger Fayencen', ETHNOGRAPHICA, *I/1959, pp. 100—109.*

Jeřábek, Richard, 'Identifikace obličejových česen z východní Moravy' (Identification of Face-like Beehives from Eastern Moravia), ČESKÝ LID (The Czech People), *Vol. 53, 1966, No. 2, pp. 95—102.*

Johnová, Helena, 'Lidové šperky československé' (Folk Jewellery in Czechoslovakia), VĚCI A LIDÉ (Things and People), *Vol. 5, 1953, Nos. 7—8, pp. 311—357.*

LIDOVÉ JESLIČKY (Traditional Nativity Scenes), *National Museum, Prague, 1967.*

'Sponky jako součást lidového oděvu' (Clasps as Parts of Traditional Folk Costume), SLOVENSKÝ NÁRODOPIS (Slovak Ethnography), *Vol. VI, 1958, pp. 3—126.*

Kalesný, František, ĽUDOVÉ UMENIE NA SLOVENSKU (Folk Art in Slovakia), *Osveta, Martin, 1956.*

Kovačevičová, Soňa, ĽUDOVÝ ODEV V HORNOM LIPTOVE (Folk Costume in the Upper Liptov Area), *Bratislava, 1955.*

'Volkstümliche Friedhöfe und Grabmäler der Slowakei', ETHNOGRAPHICA, *VII—VIII, 1965—1968, Part One, pp. 131—158, Moravian Museum, Brno.*

ĽUDOVÉ PLASTIKY (Folk Sculptures), *Slovak Academy of Sciences, Bratislava, 1971.*

Kunz, Ludvík, 'Quellen und Forschungen zur volkstümlichen Hinterglassmalerei in der Tschechoslowakei', ETHNOGRAPHICA, *VII—VIII, 1965—1968, Part Two, pp. 13—29, Moravian Museum, Brno.*

Kunz, Ludvík, and Vydra, Josef, MALEREI AUF VOLKSMAJOLIKA, *Artia, Prague, 1956.*
   PAINTING ON FOLK CERAMICS, *Artia, Prague, 1956.*
Landsfeld, Heřman, LIDOVÉ HRNČÍŘSTVÍ A DŽBÁNKAŘSTVÍ (Folk Pottery and Jug-Making), *Prague, 1950.*
Langer, Juraj, and Svobodová, Júlia, ORAVSKÉ KAMENNÉ RELIÉFY 1749—1876 (Stone Reliefs from Orava 1749—1876), *Orava Gallery, Oravský Podzámok, 1969.*
Láznička, Zdeněk, 'Typy vesnického osídlení na Moravě' (Types of Village Settlement in Moravia), SPISY ODBORU ČESKÉ SPOLEČNOSTI ZEMĚPISNÉ V BRNĚ (Annals of the Czech Geographical Society in Brno), *1946.*
LIDOVÁ KULTURA VÝCHODNÍ MORAVY (Folk Culture in Eastern Moravia), *Vol. I (1960) and Vol. II (1961), Gottwaldov—Brno.*
Ludvíková, Miroslava, 'Kroj brněnského venkova v letech 1748—1848' (Village Costume in the Brno Area in 1748—1848), ČASOPIS MORAVSKÉHO MUZEA (Journal of the Moravian Museum), *Vol. XLIX, 1964, pp. 169—198.*
Máčel, Otakar, ZÁKLADNÍ PROBLEMATIKA URBANISTICKÉ STRUKTURY VESNICE V ČECHÁCH A NA MORAVĚ (Basic Problems of the Structure of Czech and Moravian Villages), *VÚVA, Brno, 1954.*
Máčel, Otakar, and Vajdiš, Jaroslav, SLOVÁCKO, ARCHITEKTONICKÝ VÝVOJ VESNICE (The Architectural Development of Villages in the Slovácko Area), *Prague, 1958.*
Markov, Jozef, SLOVENSKÝ ĽUDOVÝ ODEV V MINULOSTI (Slovak Folk Costume in the Past), *Bratislava, 1955.*
Marková, Ema, SLOVENSKÉ ČIPKY (Slovak Lace), *Bratislava, 1962.*
Melniková-Papoušková, Naděžda, ČESKOSLOVENSKÉ LIDOVÉ MALÍŘSTVÍ NA SKLE (Czechoslovak Folk Painting on Glass), *Prague, 1938.*
   PUTOVÁNÍ ZA LIDOVÝM UMĚNÍM (Journeys In Search of Folk Art), *Prague, 1941.*
   ČESKOSLOVENSKÉ LIDOVÉ VÝTVARNICTVÍ (Folk Art in Czechoslovakia), *Prague, 1948.*
   LIDOVÉ HRAČKY (Folk Toys), *Prague, 1948.*
   'Těsto jako sochařský materiál' (Dough as a Sculptural Material), TVAR (Shape), *Vol. II, 1949, pp. 220—226.*
   'Horníci a lidové umění' (Miners and Folk Art), VĚCI A LIDÉ (Things and People), *Vol. II, 1949/50, pp. 213—222.*
   'Kovové oplatnice a pečení oplatek' (Wafer Irons and Wafer Baking), VĚCI A LIDÉ (Things and People), *Vol. VI, 1954, pp. 446—473.*
   'Figurálně zdobené úly' (Beehives with Figural Decoration), VĚCI A LIDÉ (Things and People), *Vol. VI, 1954, pp. 342—368.*
   'Několik myšlenek kolem lidového dřevořezu' (A Few Thoughts on Folk Woodcuts), HOLLAR, *Vol. 31, 1961, pp. 6—21.*
   'Lidový dřevořez' (Folk Woodcuts), UMĚNÍ A ŘEMESLA (Arts and Crafts), *1965, pp. 217—222.*
   'Lidové a periferní sklo' (Folk and Peripheral Glass), VĚCI A LIDÉ (Things and People), *Vol. IV, 1952/53, pp. 18—57.*
Mencl, Václav, 'Gotická tvář české vesnice' (The Gothic Face of the Czech Village), UMĚNÍ (Art), *Vol. XVI, 1944, Nos. 3—4, pp. 129—148.*
   'Lidová architektura' (Folk Architecture), ZPRÁVY PAMÁTKOVÉ PÉČE (Bulletin for the Care of Monuments), *Vol. IX, 1949, pp. 1—43.*
MORAVSKÉ SLOVENSKO (Moravian Slovakia), *2 vols., ed. Lubor Niederle, Prague, 1918 and 1922.*
NÁRODOPISNÁ VÝSTAVA ČESKOSLOVANSKÁ V PRAZE 1895 (The Czechoslovak Ethnographical Exhibition in Prague, 1895).
Niederle, Lubor, SLOVANSKÉ STAROŽITNOSTI (Slavonic Antiquities), *Vol. II,* 'Život starých Slovanů' (Life of the Ancient Slavs) I/2, 'Slovanský příbytek a dvůr' (The Slav Dwelling and Yard), *Prague, 1911.*
   'Starý selský dům na Moravském Slovensku' (The Ancient Farmstead in Moravian Slovakia), NÁRODOPISNÝ VĚSTNÍK ČESKOSLOVANSKÝ (The Czecho-Slavonic Ethnographical Bulletin), *Vol. VII, 1912, pp. 97—113.*
   RUKOVĚŤ SLOVANSKÉ ARCHEOLOGIE (A Manual of Slavonic Archaeology), *Prague, 1931.*
Nosáľová, Viera, ĽUDOVÝ ODEV V HEĽPE A POHORELEJ (Folk Costume in Heľpa and Pohorelá), *Bratislava, 1966.*
Okálová, Edita, ĽUDOVÉ DREVENÉ SOŠKY V SLOVENSKOM NÁRODNOM MÚZEU (Wooden Folk Statuettes in the Slovak National Museum), *Catalogue, Collections of the Ethnographical Division of the Slovak National Museum in Martin, III, 1964.*
Pátková, Jarmila, ĽUDOVÝ ODEV V OKOLÍ TRNAVY (Folk Costume in the Trnava Area), *Bratislava, 1957.*
Pišútová, Irena, Z KLENOTNICE SLOVENSKÉHO ĽUDOVÉHO UMENIA (From the Treasury of Slovak Folk Art), *Catalogue, Bratislava-Martin, 1968.*
Plessingerová, Anna, SOUČASNÍ LIDOVÍ ŘEZBÁŘI — PAVOL BAVLNA A JOSEF CHVÁLA (Contemporary Folk Carvers — Pavol Bavlna and Josef Chvála), *Exhibition catalogue, Ethnographical Department of the National Museum, Prague, 1966.*
Plicková, Ester, HRNČIARSTVO V POZDIŠOVCIACH (Pottery in Pozdišovce), *Bratislava, 1959.*
Plicková, Ester, and Scheufler, Vladimír, LIDOVÁ HRNČINA V ČESKOSLOVENSKU (Folk Pottery in Czechoslovakia), *Uherské Hradiště, 1966.*
Pranda, Adam, SÚČASNÍ MODRANSKÍ FIGURALISTI (Contemporary Figural Painters from Modra), *Martin, 1957.*
Pražák, Vilém, K DĚJINÁM SLOVENSKÉHO VÝŠIVKOVÉHO ORNAMENTU (History of Slovak Embroidery Ornamentation), *Bratislava, 1933.*
   SLOVENSKÉ LIDOVÉ VÝŠIVKY (Slovak Folk Embroidery), *Bratislava, 1936.*
   'Problém vzniku jednoposchoďového domu v Čičmanoch' (The Origin of the Two-Storey House in Čičmany), NÁRODOPISNÝ SBORNÍK (Ethnographical Miscellany), *Vol. II, 1941, pp. 23—71.*
   'Valašský dům pod Makytou' (Walachian Houses Under the Makyta), NÁRODOPISNÝ SBORNÍK (Ethnographical Miscellany), *Vol. VIII, 1947, pp. 189—200, and Vol. IX, 1950, pp. 68—161.*
   'Vliv sociálně-hospodářského faktoru na vznik štítu v lidové architektuře' (The Influence of the Socio-Economic Factor on the Origin of the Gable in Folk Architecture), NÁRODOPISNÝ VĚSTNÍK ČESKOSLOVANSKÝ (Czecho-Slavonic Ethnographical Bulletin), *Vol. XXXI, 1949/50, pp. 217—238.*
   'K problematice základních půdorysných typů lidových staveb v Československu' (The Problem of Basic Types of Ground-Plans of Folk Structures in Czechoslovakia), ČESKOSLOVENSKÁ ETNOGRAFIE (Czechoslovak Ethnography), *Vol. VI, 1958, pp. 219—236 and 331—360.*
   'Die böhmische Stickerei', ETHNOGRAPHICA, *III—IV, 1961/62, pp. 429—471.*
   'K problematice vzniku jizby a síně v čs. obydlí a jejich vztahu k staroslovanskému a franskému domu' (The Origin of the Living Room and the Hall in Czechoslovak Dwellings and Their Relationship to the Ancient Slavonic and Frankish Houses), ČESKÝ LID 52 (The Czech People 52), *1965, pp. 267—275.*
Scheufler, Vladimír, DĚJINY CHODSKÉ KERAMIKY (The History of Chod Pottery), *Pilsen, 1959.*
   LIDOVÉ HRNČÍŘSTVÍ V ČESKÝCH ZEMÍCH (Folk Pottery in the Czech Lands), *in print.*
   BĚLNINY V ČESKÉ LIDOVÉ KULTUŘE (White Pottery in Czech Folk Culture), *in print.*
SLOVENSKÉ ĽUDOVÉ UMENIE (Slovak Folk Art — Album of photographs by Alexander Paul), *2 vols., Bratislava, 1953 and 1954.*
SLOVENSKÝ ĽUDOVÝ TEXTIL (Slovak Folk Textiles), *Martin, 1957.*

Soukupová, Zora, and others, KATALOG VÝSTAVY JIHOČESKÁ LIDOVÁ PLASTIKA (Catalogue of the Exhibition of South Bohemian Folk Sculpture), *České Budějovice—Jindřichův Hradec—Soběslav, 1968.*

Staňková, Jitka, 'Lidové tkaniny v tradičním oděvu a interiéru' (Folk Fabrics in Traditional Costume and Interior Decoration), ČESKOSLOVENSKÁ ETNOGRAFIE (Czechoslovak Ethnography), *Vol. 8, 1960, pp. 384—413.*

Staňková, Jitka, and others, LIDOVÉ VÝTVARNÉ UMĚNÍ, ČECHY A MORAVA (Folk Painting and Sculpture, Bohemia and Moravia), *State Pedagogical Publishing House, Prague, 1967.*

Starý, Oldřich, and others, ČESKOSLOVENSKÁ ARCHITEKTURA OD NEJSTARŠÍ DOBY PO SOUČASNOST (Czechoslovak Architecture from Ancient Times to the Present), *Prague, 1965.*

Stránská, Drahomíra, LIDOVÉ KROJE V ČESKOSLOVENSKU (Folk Costumes in Czechoslovakia), *Vol. I — Bohemia, Prague, 1948.*

'Lidový nábytek a jeho historické vzory' (Folk Furniture and Its Historical Models), NÁRODOPISNÝ VĚSTNÍK ČESKOSLOVANSKÝ (Czecho-Slavonic Ethnographical Bulletin), *Vol. XXXII, 1951, pp. 111—127.*

'Lidové šperky ve Slezsku' (Folk Jewellery in Silesia), ČASOPIS NÁRODNÍHO MUZEA (Journal of the National Museum), *Vols. CXVII—CXIX, 1948/50, pp. 79—94.*

'Tvůrci lidového umění' (The Creators of Folk Art), ČESKÝ LID (The Czech People), *Vol. XXXXIII, 1956, pp. 67—76 and 124—130.*

Svoboda, Josef F., MORAVSKÉ HORÁCKO, LIDOVÉ UMĚNÍ VÝTVARNÉ (Moravian Highlands — Folk Art), *Prague, 1930.*

Šourek, Karel, LIDOVÉ UMĚNÍ V ČECHÁCH A NA MORAVĚ (Folk Art in Bohemia and Moravia), *Prague, 1940.*

'Rubens a Šír — dva příklady filiace lidového malířství na skle' (Rubens and Šír — Two Examples of the Affiliation of Folk Painting on Glass), ČESKÝ LID (The Czech People), *No. 4, 1946, pp. 55—59.*

VOLKSKUNST IN BILDERN (ed. Hana Volavková). *Die Natur, der Mensch, die Arbeit, die Religion, die Farbe, Prague, 1956.*

Tyršová, Renáta, and Kožímová, A., SVÉRÁZ V ZEMÍCH ČESKÝCH (Folk Motifs Used for the Decoration of Products in the Czech Lands), *Pilsen, 1921.*

Vachová, Zdena, NÁRODOPISNÉ SBÍRKY SLEZSKÉHO MUZEA (The Ethnographical Collections of the Silesian Museum), *Ostrava, 1962.*

'Slezské lidové malby na skle' (Silesian Folk Paintings on Glass), *Catalogue,* ČASOPIS SLEZSKÉHO MUZEA (Journal of the Silesian Museum), *XVI, 1967, Series B, Nos. 1, 2, 17 (1968).*

'Slezská lidová malba na skle' (Silesian Folk Painting on Glass), with a German summary "Die Hinterglasmalerei in der schlesischen Volkskunst", ETHNOGRAPHICA, *VII—VIII, 1965/68, pp. 92—108 and 82—91, Moravian Museum in Brno.*

Václavík, Antonín, PODUNAJSKÁ DEDINA (The Danubian Village), *Bratislava, 1925.*

'Příspěvky k vývoji malovaných ohnišť (Notes on the History of Painted Fire-Places), SBORNÍK K PRAVĚKU, DĚJINÁM A NÁRODOPISU SLOVENSKA (Miscellany on the Prehistory, History and Ethnography of Slovakia), *1924—1931, pp. 190 ff.*

LUHAČOVSKÉ ZÁLESÍ, *Luhačovice, 1930.*

TRADÍCIE ĽUDOVEJ DREVOREZBY. PRÍSPEVKY K VECNEJ A ORNAMENTÁLNEJ GENEZI SLOVENSKÝCH PRACICH A VALKA-CÍCH PIESTOV (Traditions of Folk Wood-Carving. Notes on the Objective and Ornamental Genesis of Slovak Laundering and Mangling Bats), *Bratislava, 1936.*

SLOVENSKÉ PALICE (Slovak Sticks), *Turčiansky svätý Martin, 1938.*

VÝROČNÍ OBYČEJE A LIDOVÉ UMĚNÍ (Anniversary Customs and Folk Art), *Prague, 1959.*

VĚCI A LIDÉ (Things and People), *Vol. II, 1949, Nos. 3—5,* entirely devoted to folk lace.

Vydra, Josef, LIDOVÉ STAVITELSTVÍ NA SLOVENSKU (Folk Architecture in Slovakia), *Prague, 1925.*

'Lidová hračka' (Folk Toys), VĚCI A LIDÉ (Things and People), *Vol. IV, 1952/53, pp. 211—235.*

ĽUDOVÁ MODROTLAČ NA SLOVENSKU (Traditional Blue-Printing in Slovakia), *Bratislava, 1954.*

ĽUDOVÁ ARCHITEKTÚRA NA SLOVENSKU (Folk Architecture in Slovakia), *Bratislava, 1958.*

Zíbrt, Čeněk, VESELÉ CHVÍLE V ŽIVOTĚ LIDU ČESKÉHO (Merriment in the Life of the Czech Village People), *Prague, 1950.*

BIBLIOGRAPHY OF BOOKS IN THE ENGLISH LANGUAGE

Hetteš, Karel and Pravoslav Rada, MODERN CERAMICS, *Spring Books, London, 1966.*

Husa, Václav, Petráň, Josef and Petráňová, Alena, TRADITIONAL CRAFTS AND SKILLS, *Hamlyn, London, 1967.*

Kybalová, Ludmila, CONTEMPORARY TAPESTRIES FROM CZECHOSLOVAKIA, *Alan Wingate, London, 1965.*

Markov, Jozef, THE SLOVAK NATIONAL DRESS THROUGH THE CENTURIES, *Artia, London, 1956.*

Pohribný, Arsen and Tkáč, Stefan, NAIVE PAINTERS OF CZECHOSLOVAKIA. *Artia, London, 1967.*

Skrobucha, Heinz, ICONS IN CZECHOSLOVAKIA, *Hamlyn, London, 1971.*

Šourek, Karel, FOLK ART IN PICTURES, *Spring Books, London, no date.*

Václavík, Antonín, and Orel, Jaroslav, TEXTILE FOLK ART, *Spring Books, London, no date.*

Volavková, Hana, A STORY OF THE JEWISH MUSEUM IN PRAGUE, *Artia, London, 1968.*

Vydra, Josef, PAINTING ON FOLK CERAMICS, *Spring Books, London, no date.*

Vydra, Josef, FOLK PAINTING ON GLASS, *Artia, London, no date.*

Ethnographical Regions of Czechoslovakia

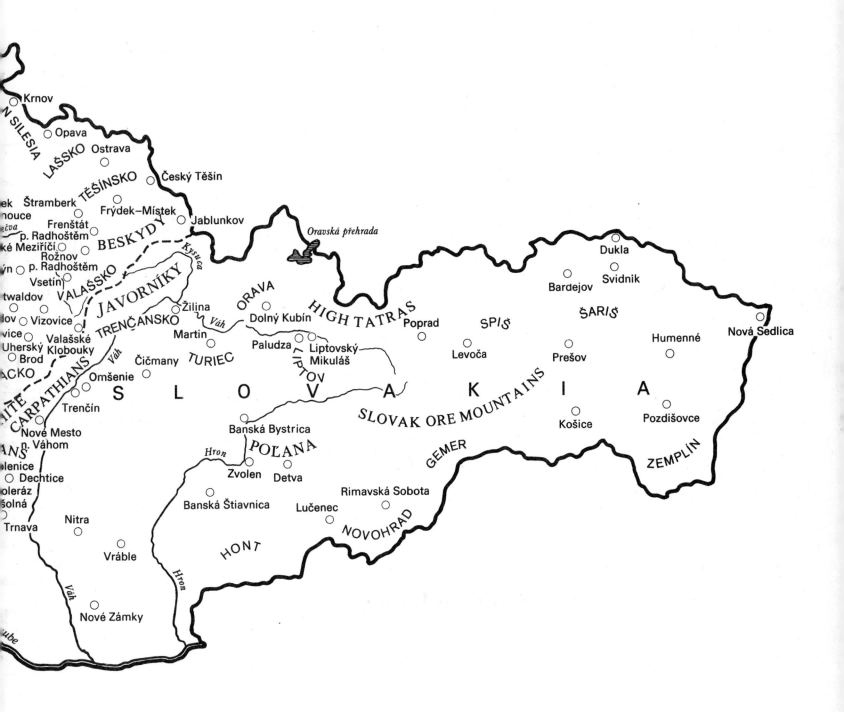

0   20   40   60   80   100 km

Krnov

N SILESIA

Opava

LAŠSKO   Ostrava

TĚŠÍNSKO   Český Těšín

ek   Štramberk

nouce   Frýdek-Místek   Jablunkov

Frenštát   Oravská přehrada

čva   p. Radhoštěm

ké Meziříčí   BESKYDY

Rožnov   Dukla

ýn   p. Radhoštěm   Svidnik

Vsetín   Bardejov

twaldov   VALAŠSKO   Žilina   ORAVA   ŠARIŠ

JAVORNÍKY   Dolný Kubín   HIGH TATRAS

lov   Vizovice   Váh   Poprad   SPIŠ   Humenné   Nová Sedlica

vice   TRENČANSKO   Martin   Paludza   Liptovský   Levoča   Prešov

Uherský   Valašské   Mikuláš

Brod   Klobouky   Čičmany   TURIEC   LIPTOV

ACKO   CARPATHIANS   Omšenie   SLOVAKIA   Košice   Pozdišovce

ITE   Trenčín   SLOVAK ORE MOUNTAINS

ANS   Nové Mesto   ZEMPLÍN

n. Váhom   Banská Bystrica   GEMER

lenice   Hron   POĽANA

Dechtice   Zvolen   Detva

oleráž   Rimavská Sobota

šolná   Banská Štiavnica   Lučenec

Trnava   Nitra   NOVOHRAD

Vráble   HONT

Váh

Nové Zámky   Hron

ube

Acknowledgements

The authors hereby express their appreciation to the following museums for their permission to photograph their exhibits and for assistance rendered in gathering the necessary information:
Eagle Mountains Museum, Rychnov nad Kněžnou
East Slovak Museum, Košice
Ethnographical Department of the Historical Museum, National Museum, Prague
Ethnographical Institute of the Moravian Museum, Brno
Ethnographical Museum, Olomouc
Luhačovice Museum, Luhačovice
Municipal Museum, Bechyně
Municipal Museum, Frenštát pod Radhoštěm
Municipal Museum, Humpolec
Municipal Museum, Kašperské Hory
Municipal Museum, Valašské Meziříčí
Municipal Museum, Ostrava
Municipal Museum, Železnice
Municipal Museum, Železný Brod
Museum of the Bohemian Paradise, Turnov
Museum of Moravian Slovakia, Uherské Hradiště
Museum of Ukrainian Culture, Svidník
Regional Museum, Klatovy
Regional Museum, Tišnov
Slovak National Museum, Bratislava
Slovak National Museum, Martin
South Bohemian Museum, České Budějovice
Walachian Open-Air Museum, Rožnov pod Radhoštěm
West Bohemian Museum, Pilsen
West Slovak Museum, Trnava

The authors also wish to thank private collectors in Jablonec nad Nisou and Prague and, in particular, the following institutions:
The Archives of the Centre for Folk Arts and Crafts in Uherské Hradiště
The Parish Offices in Slavoňov and Bílý Újezd
The Slovak National Gallery in Bratislava
The State Castle of Nové Hrady.

Photographic Credits:

Ladislav Neubert, Prague — 1, 70, 71, 73—82, 84—166, 168—235
Jaroslav Vajdiš, Prague — 6—18, 20—23, 34—37, 39, 44—49, 52, 54—55, 57—58, 60—64
Alexander Paul, Prague — 19, 43, 50, 51, 53, 59, 65
Karel Plicka, Prague — 83
Jan Líkař, Prague — 72

Pen-drawings:
Jaroslav Vajdiš, Prague — 24—33, 40—41, 42a, b
Otakar Máčel, Brno — 38, 56

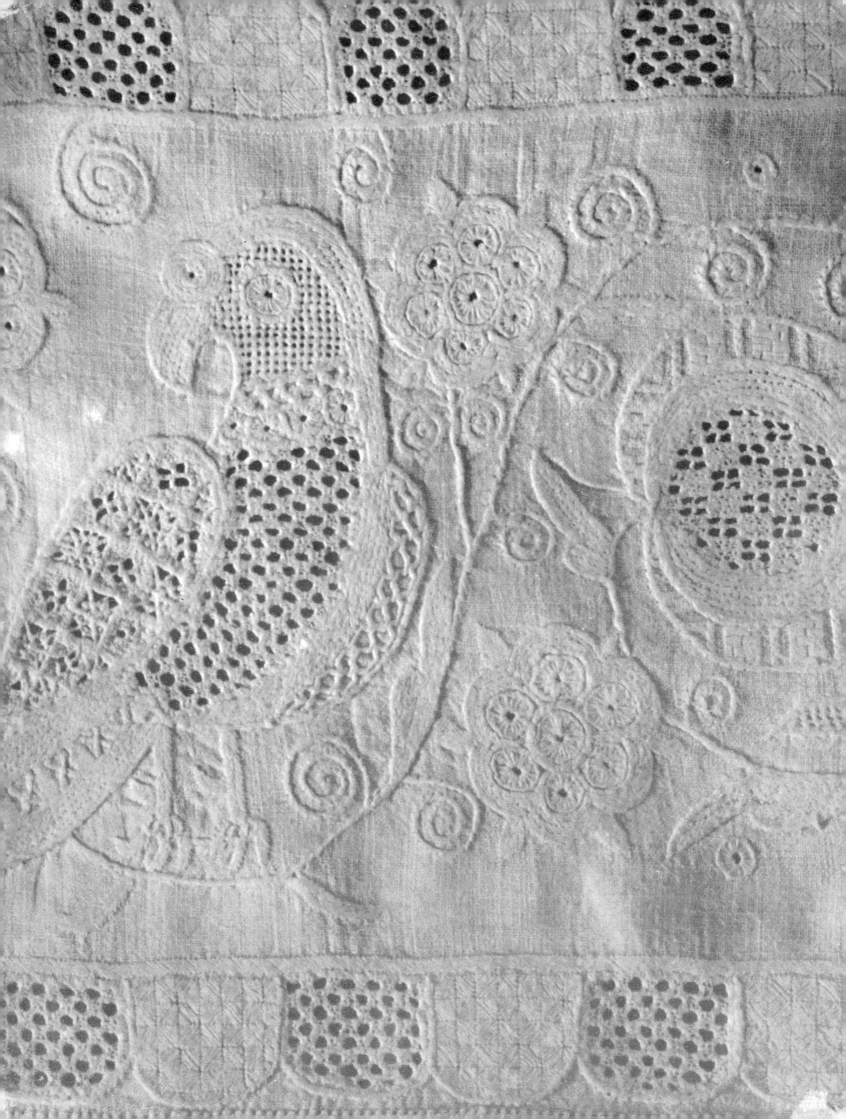